1407 BROADWAY

1407 BROADWAY is a sizzling passionate story of two unusual people. Joel Gross captures with astonishing accuracy the frenzy and incandescent sexuality of his characters: Jonathan, a good-looking, hard-driving sportwear manufacturer and Valerie, a beautiful, shimmering blonde and heiress to one of America's largest industrial fortunes.

Valerie is 'on the market' again, having divorced her husband, but none the less she is totally unprepared for the effect Jonathan has on her. Jonathan is also knocked out by Valerie. He has never met anyone like her before. And he also realises that using her name on a new line of clothes could mean the survival of his ailing company. Valerie is also determined that she must leave her own mark on any business venture – much to the horror and disgust of her parents who are singularly unimpressed by Jonathan.

**Also by the same author,
and available from NEL:**

The Books of Rachel
The Lives of Rachel
Home of the Brave
This Year in Jerusalem

About the Author
Joel Gross, now in his thirties, has been
writing since he was nineteen. Apart from
many novels, he has also written for *The New
Yorker* and television. His plays have been
performed off-Broadway. He lives in New
York City.

1407 BROADWAY

Joel Gross

NEW ENGLISH LIBRARY
Hodder and Stoughton

Always, for Linda
Copyright © 1978 by Joel Gross
First published in Great Britain in 1985 by
Judy Piatkus (Publishers) Ltd of London
NEL Paperback Edition 1987
British Library Cataloguing in Publication Data

Gross, Joel
   1407 Broadway.
   I. Title
   813'.54 [F]   PS3557.R58

   ISBN 0–450–40267–3

Printed and bound in Great Britain for
Hodder and Stoughton Paperbacks, a
division of Hodder and Stoughton Ltd.,
Mill Road, Dunton Green, Sevenoaks.
Kent (Editorial Office: 47 Bedford
Square, London WC1B 3DP) by
Richard Clay Ltd, Bungay, Suffolk

Always, for Linda

Love yields to business. If you seek a way out of love, be busy; you'll be safe then.

—OVID, *Remedia Amoris*, 143

Part One

New York

1

"Is this Valerie Holmes?"

"What time is it?"

"I'll answer your question after you answer mine." The voice on the other end of the line was confident, heavily inflected with a sense of mockery. Valerie raised her head from the pillow and tried to sit up against the hard, cold headboard.

"Who is this?" she said.

"Listen," said the voice. "We're not going to make any forward movement in this relationship if all you do is ask, ask, ask. I'm going to tell you what time it is, and then I'm going to tell you who this is, but I'd really appreciate it if you'd just come right out and tell me that I'm talking to Valerie Holmes before we go any further."

Valerie shivered against the cold of the room as her body continued to wake. A bright sun glowed through the heavy drawn curtains covering the shut-up east windows, and she suddenly threw her legs out of the bed and walked three shaky steps to the chaise longue where she'd dropped her flannel robe the night before. "Just a minute," she said, and as she tried to retain the telephone receiver between her shoulder and her ear, at the same time slipping awkwardly into her blessedly warm robe, the phone cord dragged the main body of the phone off the night table and onto the floor with a devastating crash. "Oh, damn," said Valerie, and she bent down to pick up the phone, and then she placed the receiver on its hook. If it was important, he'd call back. She pulled back the curtains and squinted out at the tiny ribbon of highway, its

9

background of tainted river—carrying a lone yacht, and a blurry flotilla of garbage barges, and the false romance of the bridges to Brooklyn—glittering in the sun. She got down on her knees and found her furry slippers far under the bed, and as she proceeded to flatten herself to the carpet and edge her way to her goal, the phone rang. It rang three more times before she'd gotten hold of the slippers, slid them out from under the bed, edged herself back out from her exploratory position, and stood up, out of breath.

"Just a minute, please," she said, not giving him a chance to reply, before placing the receiver gently on the floor. Slowly, luxuriously, she put on her furry slippers, she tightened the belt of the thick bathrobe, she drew up a massive wing chair to the sun-dashed window.

Valerie picked up the phone and walked with it to the chair. When she was good and comfortable, beginning to be warmed by the sun, she said: "This is Valerie Holmes."

"It's eight-thirty," he said, "and my name is Jonathan Singer, and I suppose I deserve that crash in my ear."

"Who gave you my number, Mr. Singer?"

"Do you remember last night?"

"I'm afraid I don't know what you're talking about."

"We met last night, very briefly."

"I don't remember meeting a Mr. Singer."

"We weren't introduced," he said. "You were wearing an entire collection of Hugh Robertson peasant clothes on your back—ruffles and lace and six or seven kerchiefs and scarves—It was too bad about the rain."

"None of this explains who you are, Mr. Singer," said Valerie. "If you're a reporter, I have nothing to report; if you're a charity-ball man, you're calling much too early in the morning; if you're a friend of my ex-husband's, tell him I said hello and to please mind his own business."

"You don't think I sound like a charity-ball man, do you, Valerie?"

He didn't use the first name like an insult, so she let him go on.

"All right, I'll tell," he said. "Last night, near Pronto's on Park Avenue, some guy in a tux with narrow lapels was trying to grab a cab in the rain. It was a little pathetic, and if I wasn't in such a rush, I might've given him a hand. You know the type—the rain is coming down in buckets, and he waves his hand from the sidewalk in the dark, hoping that some cabbie with X-ray vision is going to bother spotting him, with every doorman in the city blowing whistles from every corner."

"I don't believe it," said Valerie. She tried to remember a very tall man, with thick shoulders and a trench coat.

"Wait a minute, don't jump to conclusions. This isn't Andy Warhol."

Valerie had been with her brother Tom, walking back from a terrible dinner party, when the rain had started up. Tom had parked her under Pronto's awning and raced up the street to Park Avenue, where he proceeded to drench himself for all of ten minutes, until a cab finally had stopped to let someone out at the corner at which he'd been standing. Immediately, an enormous doorman with a giant black umbrella materialized with a complement of three young giggly women and a silent Andy Warhol, his dark glasses streaked with rain. Tom had turned around and yelled for Valerie to join him; and in that moment, the doorman had opened the cab's door for the Warhol group.

"I'm afraid that's my cab," said Tom to the doorman and to Warhol, whom he'd met several times before. Warhol said nothing, and continued to stand outside the periphery of the doorman's umbrella, letting the rain slide down his face and neck.

"Just get in, Mr. Warhol," said the doorman, ignoring Tom. Valerie had come up, breathless and soaked with rain.

"Let's take it," she said to her brother. "They've got the umbrella."

"It's Andy Warhol," said Tom.

"He doesn't remember us," said Valerie. "Come on."

11

At that moment she saw the tall man with the thick shoulders and the trench coat. He was standing on the other side of the cab, the driver's side, and he was knocking on the driver's window. A moment later she heard the cabbie shout something to the doorman, something indecipherable in the crash of rain. Incredibly, the tall man had gotten the cabbie to open the back door on his side of the cab, and a very short woman wearing a newspaper over her head jumped into this opening, followed a moment later by her companion.

"What the hell d'yuh think this is?" said the doorman.

Valerie couldn't hear the cabbie say, "It's taken." But the tall man had managed to lean over the woman, smile at the little mob of people—doorman, Warhol, his three associates, Tom, and Valerie—with perfect aplomb, and say, "Wow, Andy Warhol," and wrench the door from out of the doorman's grasp and slam it shut against the wild weather.

This was the man that Valerie tried now to remember, without much success. But the hard city voice fit what vague outlines—brutal and mocking and self-assured—she retained.

"You're the man who stole our cab," said Valerie.

"Listen, how about lunch today? I figured I'd call you early, give you lots of time to break any other appointments you might have been trapped into making."

"Mr. Singer, unless you tell me at once how you managed to get my phone number, I'm going to hang up."

"I've got a friend who used to work for *Women's Wear Daily.*"

"Who?"

"Like I said, he's a friend. Before you say another word—"

She interrupted him: "Who else at *Women's Wear* knows this number?"

"Oh, for Chrissake, who cares? Have you been getting hassled or something? Pull out your phone. First of all, my friend doesn't even work for the paper anymore. Second of all, it was like pulling teeth to get this number, because he's one of these little faggots who carries around a wad of useless society secrets like he's number one at the CIA. Third of all, he's not my friend, but I just don't happen to feel like screwing him because some little rich girl won't let me finish any of my sentences, because she's too pissed off at some member of the lower orders actually having penetrated one of her seventeen phone numbers at one of her sixty-five homes, chalets, mansions, beach houses— especially," he said, swallowing to get back his breath, a loud, uncomplicated sound that brought a smile to her lips on the other end of the wire, "especially when of all things, she should feel flattered that (a) she was recognized at all, and (b) that I took the trouble to track her down."

"And I thought you only recognized Andy," she said.

"I recognized the clothes, and later on I remembered why they seemed to belong to your face. I'm in the rag business."

"You're in the *what*?" She knew what the rag business was, of course. Her question was actually a statement: She didn't like the rough sound of the phrase.

"Rag business, rag business," said Jonathan Singer. "Clothes, you know."

"I see," said Valerie. "But I'm afraid I still have no idea why, as you say, you've taken the trouble to track me down."

"I've got a proposition, Valerie."

He said nothing for so long after this that Valerie could only assume he was attempting a pregnant pause. She crossed her legs, sighed into the phone, and finally he spoke: "Maybe I should wait until lunch; I'd hate to blow it all, just when we started to get to know each other."

"Mr. Singer," said Valerie. She sucked in a great breath of air and prepared for her explosion. "First you have the nerve to wake me up at half past eight in the morning, then you refuse to identify yourself, then when you have told me who you are, you won't even give me the courtesy

13

of knowing how you managed to get my phone number. Now, to top it all, you tell me that the purpose of your call is to make some sort of proposition to me, but you refuse to tell me what this proposition is." She had tried to sound angry, or, at the very least, exasperated, but had not really achieved anything more than the mildest annoyance until the last part of her speech.

"Oh, damn," she said. "Will you excuse me for a minute?" The house phone was buzzing, and she quickly made her way through bedroom and foyer, down the grand staircase, along the great hallway, through library, dining room, kitchen, and into the butler's pantry. Out of breath, she picked up the phone.

"Delivery," said the man who guarded the service entrance to the Beekman Place apartment in which the Holmes family had kept a duplex for more than thirty-five years.

"This is Miss Holmes speaking," said Valerie. "Weren't you told that no one's home? I'm the only one here."

"I'm sorry, Miss Holmes," said the voice. "I thought sure there'd be a maid. You want the flowers sent up?"

"What?"

"Flowers. There's a flower delivery for you, Miss Holmes. You want I should send it up?"

Valerie tipped the delivery boy a dollar and tore through the involved wrapping of the four dozen American Beauty roses until she'd extracted the card: "I hope we're having lunch. Best, Jonathan Singer."

"I'm still holding," he said, when she'd finally got back to the phone.

"You'd better have something awfully interesting to say over lunch, Mr. Singer."

"I do."

"Thanks for the flowers."

"Listen, Valerie," he said. "How about if we meet at twelve-thirty, on the street, right in front of the main entrance to 1407 Broadway?"

"On the street?"

14

"I mean if you don't mind. I'd like to eat around there anyway. I'd like to show you the area."

"You said '1407 Broadway,' right?"

"Yeah. Don't worry, I'll find you. I have a feeling you're going to stick out in that crowd."

2

One of the many things that Jonathan Singer liked about 1407 Broadway was that it rented space to two barber-shops, both of which had talkative barbers who liked to shave shut-eyed immobile faces. When he'd gotten off the phone with Valerie Holmes, it was still before nine o'clock, and he didn't feel like lying in wait for the eighteen employees of Lorelei Paris, Inc., as they straggled in to work. He threw on his leather sports jacket, walked through the empty showroom, and opened the heavy steel door to the hallway he shared with one other business, Kathy Originals, a sportswear house named for its owner's long-since dead French poodle, a house at least ten times the size of Lorelei Paris. When he got out of the elevator in the lobby, he quickly avoided being sighted by his slow-witted, sloe-eyed receptionist, by a Mr. Katz of Slutsky-Katz-Karbowitz Kreative Textiles, and by a two-sewing-machine manufacturer who used to sell jersey dresses, freshly pirated, to his mother's store on Union Turnpike in Queens. It was the nine o'clock rush, and if he lingered, he'd have a chance to say hello to the ten thousand familiar faces he'd learned to threaten and cajole, refuse and regret, during the ten years since he'd left college at nineteen to make it rich before he was thirty. He hurried to the barbershop.

If he wasn't yet rich, he was very close to it; and he still had six months before his thirtieth birthday. And lunch with Valerie Holmes.

"Well, Mr. Singer, you kill anybody lately?" Jonathan had already closed his eyes, and his lips began to relax into a smile. The barber removed the hot towel and began to scrub the lather into his thick stubble. "I'm only asking because they say the big buyers are starting to walk around here with bodyguards. I swear to God, that's what everyone's coming in and telling me. They're making so much goddam money, these buyers, that they need a guy walking next to them with a concealed bazooka. I mean that's what this city's coming to. A guy can't even take a bribe without some crook trying to mug him for it. I mean a bribe's earned money, just like anything else, am I right, or am I wrong?" The hot lather settled into every open pore as the barber held Jonathan's nose and paused to examine the lay of the land. Slowly, the barber's babble drifted into the background, along with the delicious scraping of the blade through his beard and the chattering from adjacent chairs. He was trying to remember Valerie Holmes.

First of all, she was a Holmes. Her grandfather—or maybe it was her great-grandfather—was Samuel Holmes. And Samuel Holmes—Well, even if Jonathan had never finished high school, he'd have known that name: Rich as Holmes. Who do you think you are, Samuel Holmes? It's very nice of you to be playing the Holmes with my money. I wouldn't trade places with him for all the money in Samuel Holmes's pockets.

Before high school, any mention of Samuel Holmes's name in history class was served with respect: He was an empire builder, a creator of railroads, an advocate of our Manifest Destiny, a founder of banks, a contributor to the American capitalist system, to the very fabric of the American dream.

In high school, his name was tarnished, but in a rather grand way: robber-baron. But at Jonathan's high school, nestled in a half acre of dead grass between two parkways in Queens, populated by the striving children of lower middle class workers, the term was hardly one of opprobrium. Happy in their new cars and large-screen TV sets, these workers taught their children neither to hate nor to

17

be in awe of a Holmes. Anything was possible in America. In the lists of the crimes of Samuel Holmes, there was an air of splendour, a romance of raw power that derived from nothing more evil than a sense of acquisition. The desire to acquire things through work, through purchase, through clever machinations, was never painted as a base desire, not in the borough of Queens. No matter what his history teacher told him, Jonathan could never remember being raised to any heights of indignation at the mention of Holmes's name. Perhaps he should mention this to Valerie Holmes.

"If I say something funny, try not to smile, at least not so suddenlike," said the barber. "We don't wanna screw up your face."

Jonathan couldn't for the life of him remember the name of Valerie's father. Her mother's name was Margaret, and it was obvious from the adoring pages in *Women's Wear* that she was trying to remain thirty years old for the rest of her natural life. Still, for an old broad, she wasn't bad-looking. What she did was wear a hell of a lot of clothes, and go to a hell of a lot of parties, so she had no particular claim on his memory. If he couldn't remember the father at all, it must've been because his name was something like Samuel Holmes III, or Samuel Holmes IV, with a stuffy job in the family bank created for him by the original Samuel a hundred years ago.

Other children? Jonathan wasn't sure. Maybe there was a brother. It wasn't a big family, that was certain. They probably didn't want to cut the inheritance up too much, otherwise each kid would end up with a lousy couple of hundred million instead of the billion that they each had coming.

What else did he know about her? There was a big spread about her marriage, very recent spreads about her divorce. She couldn't be much more than twenty-three or twenty-four, because he remembered reading about her coming-out party just after he'd had his first wedding anniversary. His party had cost two grand and wrecked a

18

good part of Lorelei Paris, Inc.'s first showroom. Her party was supposed to have cost a half million dollars, but he didn't really see how anyone, even a Holmes, could spend that much money in a single evening.

He didn't remember her husband, except that he was a born-richie too. When they went to parties or openings, there were pictures the next day in some of the columns, but he didn't always notice them, and when he did, he never spent much time examining husbands. After the divorce, there was a flurry of articles about her: "Who's Next for Valerie Holmes?" "The Ten Most Eligible Men in America and Valerie Holmes." "Wanted: An Heir for the Heiress."

If I wasn't married, he thought, they'd have to add my name to the list of candidates.

"Sorry!" said the barber. "Hey, I didn't nick you, did I?"

"My fault, Tony," said Jonathan. He tipped him two dollars, and walked out through the lobby and out the Broadway exit. A cab was letting out a buyer with a bad leg in front of the building, and Jonathan ran over to help her.

"Who're you?" she said.

"Just offering my assistance, ma'am."

She took his hand suspiciously, and he helped her maneuver herself out of the cab and onto the sidewalk curb. "You're a salesman, aren't you? A salesman from 1407?" She seemed determined to discover the reason for his having helped her out of the cab.

"Wait a second," said Jonathan to the driver. "You're taking me uptown."

"Let me have your card. If you're a salesman, you ought to be throwing it in my face. Don't act like you don't know me. You know *me*. I'm Mrs. Laurent."

"Are you with Bradlee's, ma'am?" said Jonathan.

"I'm not with Bradlee's, you know perfectly well I'm not with Bradlee's, you know who I'm with."

"I don't, ma'am," said Jonathan. "I'm with a small little

19

place, with a couple of hot runners. Bradlee's has been calling—I figure you were an important person. You've got that look. So I figured you might be Bradlee's."

"Bradlee's is calling you, eh?" she said. Jonathan had his card out. She took it. "I'll be there at nine-thirty tomorrow. And I want *you* to show me the line."

Jonathan got into the cab and said: "Bloomingdale's."

"You know that lady?" said the driver.

"No," said Jonathan.

"What a pain in the ass. She wouldn't let me go over twenty miles an hour." The driver lurched across Broadway, sideswiping a less fleet panel truck, and all the while looking into his rearview mirror, making sure he was in no way discomfiting his passenger.

"Hey, man," said Jonathan. "I drive a Porsche. You do whatever you feel like."

What he felt like seemed to be a mad careening along Thirty-eighth Street, weaving the junky car into every available opening in the phalanx of trucks and hand trucks, wrenching his wheel right and left, oblivious of the potholes that longed for a chance to crack his axles. They went uptown along Third Avenue, and Jonathan looked at his watch with pleasure: The minutes were indeed on their way to twelve-thirty. Narrowly avoiding another frustrated race-driver in a yellow Checker, the driver ran over a rut that bounced his passenger out of his seat, nearly cracking his head.

"Stop the car," said Jonathan.

"Hey, sorry, I didn't mean that," said the driver, turning around in his seat and continuing to drive uptown. "I mean you said I could nail it, so I did."

"I said stop the car," said Jonathan. The driver slowed down. "*Pull over.*"

The driver pulled over, still turning around to Jonathan to express his apologies, so that he missed the sight of the three hookers watching the traffic from where they leaned against the boarded-up storefront of a building slated for demolition. "Don't go away," said Jonathan.

"What?" The cabbie saw the hookers, and looked from them to his rider.

"Keep the meter running. We're still going uptown."

All three had white-blond hair, and the two uglier ones seemed to be friendly. Jonathan looked at the prettier hooker and said: "Anybody here a size nine?"

"Yeah, we're all size nine, honey. You want a size nine, you get a size nine," said one of the uglies, and then she turned to her friend and shook her head.

"I want a size nine," said Jonathan, still looking at the prettier hooker. "Is that your size?"

"You for real, man?"

"Yeah." Jonathan took out a fifty-dollar bill. "I want a size nine to come over to Bloomingdale's with me to try on some clothes."

The uglies stopped giggling and started staring.

"I'll bring you back in two hours."

"Fifty bucks for two hours ain't shit," said the other ugly.

"You ever been to Bloomie's?" said Jonathan.

"She's been there," said the first ugly.

"No, never, man," said the prettier one.

"You really a size nine?" said Jonathan, fingering the fifty.

"Sometimes I be a seven," she said. "But not usually."

The cabdriver blew his horn, and Jonathan turned around to him and held up his hand. Maybe the hooker was a size nine, he thought. He could just imagine the look on his mother's face as she bumped into the two of them going up the escalator. Maybe she's black, Mom, but you've gotta admit—blond hair.

"Come on," said Jonathan. "If you're a good girl, maybe I'll buy you a dress."

"You sure being dumb, girl," said the first ugly, arranging her bangs, but the prettiest hooker was already heading for the cab.

"What're you looking at?" said Jonathan to the cabdriver.

21

"Huh? We still going to Bloomingdale's?" he said.

"Just drive," said Jonathan.

The girl's name was Louella, and she'd been in New York all of three days. As far as she was concerned, Third Avenue and Fiftieth Street could have been the center of prostitution in the city—a very bad guess—and it had given her the mistaken impression that New York was a very quiet, reasonable place to make a living. The two uglies were her sisters—one of them, a half-sister. She had gotten her hair stripped and dyed in Atlanta, and she felt that the job done to her hair down south was far superior to that done to her sisters' hair in New York. Louella was sixteen, her sisters eighteen and nineteen; and all three lived in an apartment near 138th Street on Riverside Drive with the older sister's unemployed husband.

"Bloomingdale's," said the driver.

"I never been this far downtown," said Louella.

"We just went uptown," said Jonathan. He told the driver: "If you can be back here waiting for me at twelve o'clock, I'll give you three bucks over the meter."

"Sure," said the driver. "You know that Bloomingdale's is a department store, man? I mean it ain't no hotel."

Jonathan took her straight upstairs to the Paradox Shop. She didn't have any trouble with the way people stared at her, because she was too busy ogling Bloomingdale's. "Jesus," she said. "Jesus, this sure is nice."

"Don't you have places like this in Atlanta?"

"I never seen nothing like this nowhere. I feel like I died and went to heaven." A pair of white thigh-high boots displayed on an impossibly chic ebony wood mannequin prompted a sigh from the girl that disquieted the ring of blasé shoppers who'd paused to observe her. "Can you dig this?" she said.

"I don't handle accessories, honey, I'm strictly a junior sportswear line," he said, and he steered her into a little alcove of jungle-print pants suits, bias-cut corduroy

22

jackets, and alpaca cowl-neck sweaters. "This is what I want you to look at."

"What for, honey? You going to buy me something?"

"That all depends on your taste," said Jonathan. "Look, I just want you to browse around, and see what appeals to you."

"Hey, man, this stuff—" she said, picking up a price tag and letting out a high-pitched giggle. "Jesus," she said. "This is sick. This says—"

"I know what it says," said Jonathan. "Forget the price. I'm asking you to look around to see what you'd like to buy for yourself, if the price wasn't so crazy."

"But I always look at the price first thing," she said. Jonathan picked one of the size nine jungle-print pants suits off the rack and handed it to Louella.

"You go ahead and try this on," he said.

"You mean it?" She was looking at the suit with evident distaste.

"You don't like it, Louella?"

"It's just looking at you, man. I mean it sits there, and it's ugly," she said. Jonathan put it back on the rack. He handed her the bias-cut corduroy jacket, one of the alpaca cowl-neck sweaters, and a pair of flamboyantly belled corduroy slacks. She handed him back the slacks, shaking her head. "I want something I can stick into my boots," she said, and she found a pair of skinny straight-leg corduroy jeans and added it to her outfit.

"Can I help somebody here?" said a saleswoman, looking with perfect equanimity at the pile of clothes in the hooker's arms.

"Yeah," said Jonathan. "Show my friend where she can try these on."

When she came back out, Jonathan tried to black out the white boots and the blond hair, and see if he had an outfit worth pirating for his budget line. Louella had picked up the collar of the corduroy jacket and buttoned it up so that the long cowl of the sweater spilled freely over the tight front of the jacket. The girl took long steps

23

toward him on her five-inch platform soles, smiling furtively at the many mirrors along the way. "You like it?" said Jonathan.

"It's *bad*," she said, "real bad," and she swung around, a natural showroom model, to show him the back as a further sign of her approval. From behind his back, he heard a whoosh of disbelief; the saleswoman's professional dispassion with her unusual customer was not to be shared by every stray shopper in the store. Jonathan turned, and his eyes burned into the pair of jobless young wives, dressed to kill in French jeans, waving their jeweled fingers from the tips of their reconstructed noses to the tops of their empty heads.

In the next hour and a half, she selected a black mohair blouson jacket, a deep-blue chenille sweater with thick ribbing, a gold-on-gold lamé dress, a red silk Charmeuse cardigan, and a shocking-pink sleeveless angora blouson. But it was not from her taste that Jonathan felt he must protect her, but from the instant, incorrect assumptions of a hundred shoppers transfixed by her black face, blond hair, and whore's make-up. Still, there was only so much gratification he could find in stepping on toes, slamming into shoulders, coughing into faces, clearing his throat, and asking a fat matron or a trim ballerina or an elegant banker looking for something to purchase and finding this unlikely vision of Louella, "Just exactly what is it that you're looking at, madam [or sir]?" And if Louella didn't notice, or didn't deign to notice, the stares, that made it all the worse, as far as Jonathan was concerned. He wanted her to know that the starers were there, they existed, they were bad. He wanted her to know, too, that he was not one of them.

Since the articles that caught Louella's fancy were products of some of America's heftiest name designers—John Anthony, Calvin Klein, Hugh Robertson, Kasper, Milton Brommel—the fortunate saleswoman rang up purchases totaling over twenty-one hundred dollars. Jonathan gave her his charge card, and while she called the accounts office to check up on him, he found Louella lost in thought in front of the thigh-high boots on the black mannequin.

"I said I was going to buy you something," he said.

"Man, I just checked out the price," she said, shaking her head.

"What size shoe are you, Louella?"

"Never you mind," she said. "I just want to know if you're satisfied so far."

"Sure," said Jonathan, and then he remembered that he owed her fifty dollars. He took the bill out of his wallet and gave it to her. "I'm very satisfied."

"Yeah, and you must be crazy too. What's all that stuff for—you got a girl friend who's size nine?"

"Not exactly."

"I mean you ever want to do this trip again, man, just check me out."

"What size shoe are you, Louella?"

"I ain't telling. That's crazy spending three hundred bucks for boots, man. I don't care how rich you are, it just ain't right." Suddenly she looked up at him. "I got a kid home, mister," she said. "That's what I'd do with that money."

Jonathan didn't believe her about the kid, but he admired the way she was trying to turn a lucky break into a run of good luck. "You'd rather have the cash than the boots," he said.

"Yes, sir."

He started to explain that he could write off clothing purchases at Bloomingdale's for his business, but he'd have a hell of a time justifying a three-hundred-dollar cash payment to a hooker who'd been serving as a fashion consultant for two hours' time. She didn't seem to understand the drift of his explanation.

"What about two fifty?" she said. Louella had taken up a stance against a lingerie counter, and for a moment Jonathan had the idea that any chance passer-by would think the two of them were dickering over the girl's professional price. Their saleswoman rescued Jonathan, giving him his charge card and handing him two shopping bags filled with his purchases, maintaining the same unflappable, courteous look that had long since won his heart.

"Come again," she said to him, and grabbing hold of an astonished Louella, she told her her name and handed her her card. Coming down the escalator, Louella felt the shoppers' stares for the first time.

"I think I'm freaking everybody here, man," she said.

Jonathan looked at her. "I'd prefer you as a brunette."

"You don't know what goes down on the street, man. Blond is the shit, and that's it," she said. Louella was very clearly insulted, and she turned her head away from him as they rode down to the street level. He thought of what else he could have told her: not to use lip gloss for eye makeup, not to bleach her eyebrows orange when her hair was platinum, not to paint in red blotches against the natural contours of her lovely face. Jonathan doubted that she was a perfect size nine, not because the clothes she'd tried hadn't fit her—they had—but because an exact, perfect size nine, someone who could serve as a pattern maker's fitting model, was a rarity, enough of a rarity to be paid thirty dollars an hour.

"Hey," he said to her as they left the store, "I got an idea." She was still angry at him for his remark about her hair, but he was momentarily oblivious of anything but his sudden desire to take this girl under his wing, and do nothing less than change the course of her whole life.

"Are you going to take me back?"

"Wait, wait, there's our guy," said Jonathan, and he called to the cabdriver sitting impatiently in his car, pointing out his Off Duty signs to the noontime crush of taxi seekers.

"How'd you like Bloomingdale's?" said the driver, trying to make a joke out of it.

"You just drive," said Jonathan.

"You gonna tell me where?"

26

"Yeah, yeah," said Jonathan, looking at the girl, "1407 Broadway."

They turned round to go downtown on Lexington at Sixtieth at three minutes past twelve, and, try as he might, the cabdriver could get them to the west side of Broadway between Thirty-eighth and Thirty-ninth streets no earlier than twenty-five minutes to one. Jonathan had ample time to explain his idea to Louella.

"You mean you're not going to give me any more money?" she said.

"You turn out to be a perfect nine, and I'll give you a bonus. I'll give you two hundred bucks."

"The boots were three hundred, man."

"Listen, are you going to do what I told you? Go up to Lorelei Paris—What's the name of the place?"

"Lorelei Paris."

"What floor?"

"Twelve."

"And who do you ask for?"

"You just keep changing the subject, man. You don't want to give me my money, just tell me right out."

"You ask for Mr. Schwartz in the back. Tell him the boss sent you. And you're bringing him the new line for him to play with. And the boss said for him to check you out as a fitting model," said Jonathan. "You got all that? You sure you got all that? I can't go up with you."

"I be very smart. How much are you going to give me?"

"I'm trusting you with all that merchandise, aren't I? You know, for a black chic with blond hair, you're acting very Jewish."

The cabdriver blew his trumpet note through his shut-up fist. "This is the place," he said. "At last." Jonathan paid him, adding five dollars to the promised three-dollar tip. Louella got out of the cab, clutching the Blooming-dale's bags in one hand, shaking her blond hair in the bright light. She left her free hand open for Jonathan to slap in four more bills—fifties—and then she nodded with satisfaction and headed towards 1407. Jonathan watched the way the unnatural hair, combined with the absurd hot pants, cripplingly high boots, and hideous makeup, drew the stares of yet another crowd. But he had no time to dwell upon the mysterious relationship between clothes and makeup, and the factitious personality they united to create. A very young woman with natural blond hair, a touch of mascara, a black silk shirt, and a pair of artistically faded jeans was standing at his elbow. She seemed so short, and so young, that before he could bring himself to speak to her, he looked down at her feet: Valerie Holmes wore white tennis sneakers.

"Sorry I'm late," he said. "I'm Jonathan Singer, call me Johnny."

"Don't you think it would be more discreet," she said, but without a trace of unpleasantness, "to pay your girl *inside* the taxi?"

3

Valerie Holmes displeased her parents in three major interconnected ways: She insisted on going to college at Barnard, in the dread city of New York; she insisted on supporting an unfashionable charity; and she insisted on marrying Phillip S. Raymond III. Her parents supposed that her infatuation with New York and Barnard was a direct result of her infatuation with the unlikely lover, Phillip S., and that both infatuations—studying Shakespeare at Barnard, and Shakespeare with Phillip across the street at Columbia—led to their mutual vociferous support of the New York Authentic Shakespeare Company, a sorry troupe if ever there was one.

Phillip was a scholar barely one year older than Valerie. He was neither handsome nor athletic; he was merely pale, and with the added cachet of a high forehead. Unlike most preppies, he didn't sport jeans and track shoes under his Brooks Brothers blazer, but wore baggy pants, solid walking shoes, and carried extra pens in his shirt pocket. He spoke in a clear, determined whisper, and when he told Valerie he loved her, less than a year after her spectacular half-million-dollar coming-out party at her parents' California estate, she relished every word. At eighteen, Valerie had lost interest in her brother's uninteresting friends, in her mother's weary attentions to the thousand details that made up a successful benefit ball, in her friends' urgent desires to prove themselves—rich though they might be—decadent, debased, and destitute.

In their place, she fell in love with Phillip. She could

have met Phillip because of the proximity of his parents' estate to that of the Holmses; but perhaps proximity was less important than a relative similarity in size—the Raymond's estate was only a little less grand than the Holmses', and Phillip and his entire family had been invited to Valerie's fabulous coming-out party.

"I wasn't there," he told her, when he'd taken her into a corner on the back patio of a house in Laurel Canyon four months after the event. "I understand it was one of the most vulgar events of the century."

The house in Laurel Canyon belonged to a nineteen-year-old reprobate socialite, a swift dropout from Columbia University, where he'd met both Phillip (his most "intellectual friend") and Valerie's date that evening, an Orange County sun-worshiper with a father who owned "lots of ships." Everyone else had been enjoying the plentiful dope, which amplified the sounds of the crickets and the big-engined little cars screaming around the hairpin turn in front of the house, ten minutes from Sunset Boulevard.

It was a brave thing for Phillip to have said to Valerie. She was pretty, a famous deb, shielded in some powerful, intimidating perfume. And her date was six feet three inches, and bored enough to enjoy the chance of bouncing the A-student's high forehead off the brick walls of the dope-scented living room. But she didn't take offense. It *was* a vulgar party, she admitted. She didn't enjoy smoking dope. Her date was just a casual acquaintance. She didn't know what she wanted to study. No, she hadn't read Shelley—nor Nietzsche—not even Shakespeare. "You have a very intelligent face," she told him.

He wrote her a poem after their first meeting; and because she didn't laugh at its contents—vague nineteenth-century yearnings for truth, beauty, and peace—he pursued her on a hundred fronts simultaneously. Valerie was given reading lists, urged to learn Italian besides her very good French, taken to the theater in distant Los Angeles, lectured on the necessity of culture in a world where everything else is sordid and shallow. Since Phillip's father was one of the cousins who inherited the Raymond oil fortune, the remote possibility of his having been a fortune hunter had to be scratched by the Holmes family.

Phillip was beginning his second year at Columbia and spoke with perfect rapture of the cultural joys of New York; Valerie insisted on attending Barnard instead of the small bucolic private college in southern California her mother had had her heart set on for her only daughter. There was no question, however, of Valerie Holmes staying in a dormitory in upper Manhattan. The Holmses didn't feel themselves to be paranoid about the possibility of kidnapping; they thought of themselves as being unfortunately realistic. The heiress to one of America's great fortunes could not be allowed to wander around at any hour of the day or night with only Phillip S. Raymond III for protection. Mrs. Holmes was often in New York anyway; she would simply make the grand sacrifice of selecting additional servants to fill out the skeleton staff at their cavernous Beekman Place apartment. And she would remain with Valerie in New York—whenever convenient.

Valerie allowed this arrangement for more than a year. They had the use of a Holmes chauffeured limousine, and the chauffeur was far too polite to notice their fumbling embraces in the dark passenger compartment after an evening of library study, Viennese food from the student restaurant on Amsterdam Avenue, an Antonioni movie at a West Side art theater, or a student production of *Macbeth* (with merciless "contemporary relevance").

"Are you on the pill?" her mother asked her one morning at breakfast. Valerie had been surprised to see her back from the Costa Smeralda in Sardinia a week before she was due; she'd been astonished to find her at the eight o'clock breakfast table.

"No," said Valerie. "Not that it's your affair, Mother."

Her mother weighed this comment while Valerie wondered what on earth had prompted the question. She'd be damned if she'd volunteer the information that she was still a virgin—and that, for all she knew, so was Phillip.

"Maybe not," said her mother. "But here's a prescription for you." And then Mrs. Holmes stood up, placed an envelope in front of her daughter's cereal bowl, patted her head, and left the breakfast room. A week later Valerie bought her first supply of birth control pills and started counting the days till she'd be able to safely seduce Phillip. It was less a question of her lusting for his scholar's body than a powerful curiosity about this great secret of adulthood. She'd gained ten pounds and waited two and a half months before coaxing Phillip into her bedroom in the Beekman Place apartment. Once again Mrs. Holmes was away, and either of the lovers could have shouted for help without getting a response from the sleeping downstairs servants.

"Is it safe?" Phillip whispered, and Valerie said that it was, without detailing an explanation. They stripped off each other's clothes, they kissed each other passionately on top of the bed sheets, they panted as quietly as they could. It was clumsy, it was quick, and it hurt Valerie a lot more than it hurt Phillip. Still, each felt that the experience was sure to improve with repetition. For Valerie, the major improvement was getting between the bed sheets rather than on top of them. She enjoyed falling asleep in the crook of Phillip's arm, and enjoyed knowing that she was no longer a virgin, no longer excluded from the experience of having had sex. But she didn't enjoy the act as much as its aftermath—falling asleep with her lover, waking up beside him, the sinful aroma of his semen and her perfume. Phillip enjoyed the act more than she did, but was perfectly content to skip it altogether: He hated sleeping with her in her parents' apartment.

Not out of fear of discovery, he explained. But simply because it wasn't "right." He wanted to marry her, had wanted to marry her for a long time, and, finally, on the evening after a half-hour telephone lecture from her mother in Sardinia about the evils of staying out late in New York City, even when accompanied by an armed chauffeur, she agreed.

They rode their burst of enthusiasm to a Connecticut justice of the peace and were married with much interior (Freedom, Autonomy, Adulthood) fanfare. She was not quite twenty. By the time Mrs. Holmes had returned from Sardinia, the pair had set up housekeeping in a one-bedroom apartment on West Eighty-sixth Street, perhaps the closest to hardship either of them had ever come. (The rent was two hundred and eighty dollars a month, and Valerie assumed that such a sum would insure a daily supply of hot water, adequate heating, and sanitary hallway facilities. But then she had always led a life apart from reality.) A proper church wedding was arranged by Mr. and Mrs. Roger Holmes for their daughter and son-in-law six months later, followed by an immense wedding breakfast at the California estate. By the time of this second wedding, Valerie had already begun to weary of her new husband but, like most disenchanted newly-weds, stoically decided that the fault lay not with her spouse, but with her own confused feelings.

Valerie was bored.

"But how on earth can you be bored, darling?" Phillip would say. "There's a thousand books that must absolutely be read before we die that we'll never have the time to open. A hundred perfect languages to relish that we'll never have the faintest inkling of. A hundred instruments we won't find the time to learn to play, each more beautiful than anything we could imagine. And how can you be bored when you haven't seen every Rembrandt hanging in New York? When you haven't seen all of Shakespeare's plays staged the way he would've wanted them? There's so much to do, so many things to be that are beautiful, it's impossible to be bored."

Valerie tried to do what Phillip urged her. She studied diligently, shocking her family with her string of A grades. She dutifully attended concerts, plays, poetry readings.

33

She beleaguered her ever-beleaguered family with requests for financial assistance for the Authentic Shakespeare Company. But all this noble self-improvement, all this searching for truth and beauty, only served to intensify her ennui, heighten her sense of uselessness. It was as if she were in training for some great task—with no great task existing. Valerie's disenchantment with her husband grew as she felt herself more and more to be the stupidly enthusiastic pawn in a world he had created, and in which she now refused to believe.

Severing their relationship proved difficult. Phillip felt that Valerie was going through some period of emotional maladjustment, and, rather than listening to what she told him, he continued to tell her that she was *not* bored, that she *did* love him, and that she *was* precisely the same as she had always been—except for this passing phase. He insisted that she see a psychotherapist, who would be able to explain to her precisely why her husband was correct and she was incorrect. Valerie left Phillip after a protracted period of mutual one-way dialogues and moved back to Beekman Place. The legal separation was difficult in coming, because Phillip kept on insisting that they weren't separated, that Valerie had a home with him, and that she was simply visiting her parents. Eventually, separation and divorce were effected, and Valerie went off to the little college in southern California where her mother had wished to send her to begin with. Here, her Barnard training made her an impossible student. She wanted much more than her junior league professors could provide, and, for the first time in years, a society girl was hustled through the graduation process by a faculty overgenerous with credits.

The night she was spotted by Jonathan Singer was her sixth night back in New York, after more than two years in California. More than the garment manufacturer could possibly know, Valerie Holmes was ready for a proposition. At twenty-three, she had arrived in New York precisely for that reason—to discover a proposition so

34

intriguing that it would take hold of her wasted energy and talents, and drive her to some all encompassing goal, a goal of her own creation.

"Come on up here a second," said Jonathan, gesturing to one of two high chairs set up by a shoeshine man at the corner of Broadway and Thirty-ninth Street.

"I'm wearing sneakers, Mr. Singer. I don't need my sneakers shined."

Jonathan climbed up and sat down on one of the chairs, and smiled at the shoeshine man. "How're you doing there, Sammie?"

"Real good, sir, real good, sir." Very slowly, he opened a can of brown polish and began to dab Jonathan's glossy boot-shoes with an ancient rag.

"Get up here," said Jonathan. "I want to show you the sights. Sammie, go on and tell that girl to get up here."

"Go on," said Sammie.

Valerie climbed up and sat down next to Jonathan. The fact that she'd broken a lunch date with Barbara Nicholas, her old Barnard friend, brought a smile to her lips. "Something very important's come up," she'd told her, leaving her friend very much in doubt as to what could possibly be important in the life of Valerie Holmes. Barbara had worked with Valerie and Phillip on their fund-raising drives for the Authentic Shakespeare Company, and, by the sound of her husky breathing, Barbara was prepared to welcome Valerie back to New York with a request for family funds for the downtrodden Shakespeareans. "It's a business thing," Valerie had said. "I'll tell you about it when I see you."

"Business?" Barbara had said with some alarm. "What kind of business? I hope you're not investing your money in something that Tom or your parents don't know about."

"I'm saving all my money for the Authentic Shakespeare Company," Valerie had said. "Don't worry about a thing. As of this moment, I am still uninvested, unemployed, and perfectly useless."

"I'm glad you like it up here," said Jonathan, misinterpreting her smile. He had blue eyes and black hair, and all the lines of his face were rough and healthy and handsome; his features marked him as quick rather than intelligent, open rather than subtle, physical rather than intellectual. She imagined him a high school basketball star, the vice-president of the student body, the loudest voice in the boys' locker room. "Hey," he said. "Your last name is still Holmes, right? I mean, you don't have your ex-husband's name?"

"I never took his name, Mr. Singer."

"Oh, great," he said, exhibiting a pleased face, though his pleasure at the commercial availability of the Holmes name was considerably diluted by the fact of her reluctance to accept her husband's name: Jonathan had a sentimental appreciation for most of the artifacts of married life, particularly in the women he met who were or had been married. "Because the name is very important to this whole thing."

"Yes, your proposition."

"By the way, I've already asked you, call me Johnny."

"Johnny," she said, as if she were holding up a dirty bit of linen to exhibit to her maid. "For Jonathan."

"Look, I want to explain something to you, because I have a feeling that this entire meeting is off to a bad start, Valerie."

"Not at all."

"I'm talking about that girl you saw getting out of the cab with me."

"Believe me, Mr. Singer, no explanation of that girl is necessary."

"She's a hooker I saw working Third Avenue. I was in a cab going to Bloomingdale's, and I picked her up on the way."

"I see," said Valerie, enjoying his confusion. She could hardly believe it when five minutes after arriving in front of 1407 Broadway, looking about dazedly in the great crush of people for someone she wasn't at all sure she'd recognize, she saw him with the blond-haired black prostitute, paying her off in front of their cabdriver and about ten thousand other people. When he had gotten rid of the girl, and Valerie had joined him, letting him know at once that she'd seen everything, she'd allowed him to steer her toward the shoeshine stand on the corner, if only to return to the big man some semblance of control. "The prostitute was hitchhiking—"

"Are you listening to me?" said Jonathan, obviously very angry.

"I beg your pardon."

"Oh, Christ—'I beg your pardon'—listen to me, I'm telling you something, and you're not paying attention. Whores don't hitchhike."

"Yes," said Valerie. "I'd often thought that to be the case."

"I picked her up and offered to pay her for two hours of her time in Bloomingdale's," said Jonathan, and when Valerie Holmes began to laugh, he grew so suddenly angry that Sammie stepped back from the second shined shoe and cleared his throat to signify that his job was over.

"All right, sir?" said Sammie.

"What? Yeah, that's great," said Jonathan.

"I'm sorry," said Valerie, still laughing. "But what you said—it's very funny to think of you and your friend in Bloomingdale's."

"Can we sit here for a minute?" said Jonathan, giving the shoeshine man a five-dollar bill.

"Sure," said Sammie, taking the bill. "As a matter of fact, you can sit there as long as you want. I'm going to lunch."

"Yes, lunch," said Valerie. "I was under the impression that you were taking me out, Mr. Singer."

"Is that why you wore white sneakers?"

"You didn't say it would be a formal occasion."

Jonathan watched Sammie join the throngs headed downtown, and for a moment he wondered where the shoeshine man took his lunch. He wondered if, in all his years in the garment center, Sammie had ever eaten in Dubrow's and decided at once that he would take him there.

"Look, about the girl," said Jonathan, a bit wearily: "I'm going to tell you once, and then we'll forget it." Valerie turned from him and looked down at the crowds in the street. She had never seen such a pedestrian-jammed section of the city. Everyone seemed to be shoving and talking and hurrying at a mad pace. Cabs and trucks drove at full speed toward recklessly crossing walkers, oblivious to all horns, threats, execrations. Jonathan's explanation ran on—some bizarrely incomprehensible story about asking the prostitute to try on clothes for him, and about how sad it was for her, being that she was only sixteen—and Valerie nodded at him pleasantly, letting him get it off his chest. It was the first time she'd be having lunch with a man who'd just spent the morning with a prostitute. At least, she thought, he'd have worked up a good appetite. "So as a matter of fact," he said, "you'll probably be meeting her later on today."

"Yes," said Valerie. "Wouldn't that be nice?" She had missed the major part of his explanation, but she knew enough to get out of her chair when he got out of his, and to follow him into the crowd.

"That's 1407," he said. "I'm on the twelfth floor."

"You are?" she said. "You mean, that's where your place of business is?"

"I just finished telling you that," he said. She could see he had a very Mediterranean sort of temper, ready to explode at the slightest provocation.

"I'm sorry, it's so noisy here," she said.

"Well, you'll have to get used to it, if you ever want to enjoy this part of the city."

"I suppose so, Mr. Singer." He took hold of her elbow with his powerful hand, to prevent her from being lost in the surging crowd. As they stepped into the gutter to cross Thirty-eighth Street, she shook off his grip and strode and sidled and dodged her way back onto the sidewalk. A siren started up from somewhere uptown and began to scream its plaint closer and closer to where they walked. He asked her if she'd ever eaten in a dairy restaurant, and she explained that she'd been born and spent much of her life in California, the hotbed of vegetarianism.

"Yeah," he said. "So you never ate in a dairy restaurant." She didn't understand what he meant by that, and, as she turned to the passing ambulance, its siren was joined by another—that of a police car running east on Thirty-eighth Street—and the noise was so loud, so disorientingly mad, that Valerie turned to look at Jonathan and laugh at the cacophony about them.

"Jesus Christ," he said, grabbing her again with his fierce hand and pulling her instantly out of the path of a speeding hand truck, propelled by two sweating thugs screaming, "No brakes, no brakes!" as they kept to their straight-line path, trying only to pick up speed.

"Thank you," she said, stopping in her tracks to look after the hand truck, realizing that she had been spared from being run over by the four-wheeled cart, bearing a rack of fifty plastic-covered dresses, by a split second.

"What?" said Jonathan. She realized that he couldn't possibly hear her over the sirens of the police car and the ambulance, and as she yelled "Thanks," nodding her head for emphasis, a fire truck coming west on Thirty-ninth Street turned into Broadway to join the madness.

"Just keep moving," said Jonathan, impervious to the crowds, the hand trucks, the noise. This time she took his arm, as was proper, and walked quickly with him to the dairy restaurant on West Thirty-seventh Street where he was to make the proposition to her that would change both their lives.

4

Both parents of Eddy Singer (née Schwartz) had expected
their first child to be a big, strapping boy named Edward,
who would grow up into a professor of zoology like Mr.
Schwartz's brother, Professor Jeremy Black (née
Schwartz) of Cornell. In this wished-for paragon's place,
Edwina Schwartz, small and frail and two months premature, was born. She grew up an only child in a small house
in Bayside, Queens, with lots of dresses—her dad was a
factory man in the garment center.

Willy Schwartz was a cutter and a pattern maker and a
stylist, and if he had had peace of mind, and enough pats
on the back to give him a fillip of self-confidence, he could
have been quite a fine designer. But the garment center's
endless destruction of small businesses, and endless creations of new ones formed from the wrecks of the old, left
him with little confidence, security, or cash in the bank.
He was forever picking the wrong people with whom to go
into partnership. His peculiar knack was to ferret out the
most charming beggars, incompetents, and frauds beating
the sidewalks along Broadway and Seventh Avenue and
discover in them something worthy of trust. Five times
he'd been a partner in garment-center manufacturing
companies, and five times he'd been swindled and left to
go off and find a job. After the fifth failure, the only job
he could find where he'd still be in charge of a "factory"
room was with a one-year-old hotshot firm, Lorelei Paris,
run by a loud-mouthed kid of twenty-three who got his
start by pirating one of the fresh Paris copies being
hawked at Saks Fifth Avenue and turning it into a hot

runner in acrylic. But Willy Schwartz needed the job very badly, if only to send his daughter to the Art Students League, and pay for her fourth-floor walk-up in a dilapidated building on Charles Street in Greenwich Village.

Willy Schwartz's employer, Jonathan Singer, didn't care for Eddy's choice of living quarters at all. He had taken her out on the strength of her high school graduation photo, hanging on the wall in the back room of Lorelei Paris, not far from where an unsmiling Willy liked to perch on a high stool.

"She's got a lot of boyfriends, Mr. Singer; I don't really see what's the point of me giving you her number."

"Willy, I'm a nice Jewish boy—"

"Jewish you might be," he admitted.

"Just because I fool around with a couple of showroom girls, doesn't mean that every time I go out I turn into an animal, Willy."

"It's not her I'm worried about, Mr. Singer," said Willy finally. He said it with enough of a sigh to convince Jonathan that the girl would be well worth getting to know. When he'd finally gotten her phone number, it took him two weeks to get her to be in long enough to answer the phone, and then it was another month before he could arrange a date with her.

"So you're my dad's boss," she said when he'd walked through her door. He looked from her to where a draped canvas perched on an easel, and then he took in the remainder of the sleazy studio. It didn't take long. She hadn't even bothered to make the studio bed.

"Can I see the painting?"

"No," she said.

She was dressed in a paint-splattered work shirt and jeans, and he began self-consciously to loosen his silk tie. "Are you hungry?"

"No."

"You ever been to the Penguin before?" he said, sitting down on a cracked-leather Mexican ottoman.

"No."

41

"You see, it's a little bit dressy."

"Listen, man," said Eddy Schwartz, "I'm not changing, OK? With this I can get in anywhere. I tell them it's a Dior original."

"Dior's dead."

"Look," she said, "I don't want to talk the garment center, if that's OK with you. I get enough of that when I go home."

"OK," he said, putting up his hands. "The Penguin's nice, if you like steak. Anyway, that's where I made the reservation."

"Anywhere's OK." Suddenly, she sat down on a second ottoman, and she pulled it very close to where he sat. "Hey, I'm sorry."

"What?"

"You just came in at a bad moment. I'm feeling rotten and I took it out on you, just because you happened to walk through the door."

"Forget it," he said. "If you want, punch me one in the gut. I do sit-ups."

"You want to do some dope?"

"Sure."

If she was beautiful before, the dope sent her the rest of the way to the hall of angels. She showed him her unfinished canvas—the source of all her initial moodiness—and he nodded his head sagely before it. "I really think it's no good," he told her, and she told him that was fine to say, if that was the way he saw it. They walked in a light drizzle to the Penguin, on West Ninth Street, and his hunger, and the street lamps spraying their light through the wet, and the music of her booted feet scratching at the lines in the sidewalk—all this raised him to a dizzying height, a height of grand expectations that was met during the course of the evening. Jonathan enjoyed the food he devoured in front of her more than any food he'd ever had. Jonathan enjoyed the way she pulled her long hair back from where it fell over her face to a neat position behind her ears. Jonathan enjoyed the way the waiter clattered the dishes, the way the dessert slid down his throat in two bites, the way her knee rubbed his with determination.

"I've never been this stoned in my life," he told her.

"You ought to do it more often," she said.

"I like it here," he said, meaning the restaurant, meaning in her presence. They went back to her terrible little studio, and they smoked some more Acapulco Gold, and they made love, and then they fell asleep. She woke him up at a little past four in the morning.

"Hey," she said, "do you think you could go back to your place? It's late, and I've got an early class."

"Are you serious?" he said. Neither of them was stoned, and it was too late and too dark and too fast for him to remember his infatuation. He washed his face in her bathroom, and recoiled a bit at the stench of roach killer and the pile of old laundry under the sink. The next morning at Lorelei Paris, Willy Schwartz asked him if he'd had a good time. "Sure," he'd said.

"Listen," said Willy. "You got a good head on your shoulders. Maybe she'll straighten out one day. But don't get it into your head that you're going to do it."

"Hey, listen, I had a very nice time. Your daughter doesn't need any straightening out." Willy Schwartz looked at him sympathetically, nodding his head. That same nod, that same look, was to be repeated many times, an endless procession of sympathetic moments offered from father to suitor—from father to son-in-law.

Willy tried to twist that look into the semblance of a smile when his son-in-law entered the factory of Lorelei Paris, chattering with a familiar urgency to a very young *shicksa*—probably a buyer right out of college. "Hey, Johnny," he said, "when you got a minute."

"I got a minute right now, Willy," said Jonathan. He was thrusting the young blonde forward, and Willy could see that the girl was not used to rough treatment. "Valerie, I'd like you to meet Willy Schwartz, the best factory man in New York."

43

"If I was so good, what the hell would I be doing with a schlock house like this, eh?"

"That's very funny, Willy," said Jonathan. "Willy's also my father-in-law."

"Yes," said Willy, and the smile flickered bravely before vanishing altogether. Valerie had already heard about Jonathan's wife, heard enough to know that her name—Eddy!—was being invoked as a kind of credential; Jonathan was letting her know that all his showmanship, all his wit, all his tough-guy rapport with waiters, truck-drivers, salesmen, all his good looks, all his calculated grasping of her elbow, hand, the small of her back, all these were simply part of the everyday, merely friendly Jonathan Singer. Johnny was not trying to be too nice, because Johnny was married—and he would tell her this again and again, till they would both have it absolutely by heart.

"Willy," said Jonathan, his voice rising slightly, but enough to let the older man know that something important was taking place, something to which he must pay full attention, "Willy, this is Valerie Holmes."

"Very nice to meet you, Miss Holmes."

"Willy," said Jonathan, "Valerie Holmes. *Holmes.*"

"Yeah," said Willy. "I said hello, didn't I?"

"You never heard of Holmes—the name Holmes doesn't mean something to you?"

"Johnny," said Valerie.

"You mean Holmes, like in Rockefeller?"

"Yeah," said Jonathan.

"You got a Holmes in here? I just shook hands with a Holmes?" The older man was smiling at Valerie now, smiling like a small child who's just been told that the man he's shaken hands with is nothing less than a police detective.

"You did, Willy," said Jonathan.

"Sure," said Willy. "I recognize you. You're in the papers."

"No, I'm never in the papers," said Valerie.

"She's in the papers all right, Willy," said Jonathan.

"You mind if I ask—?" began Willy. Then he let the question drift, turning his palms toward the ceiling.

"Listen," said Jonathan. "Valerie here is just taking a look at our operation. Just a very quick once-over, you know, to check out our line. We've got a little business proposition in the air."

"In the air?" said Willy.

"I'm going to show her the line, Willy," said Jonathan, and he clapped his father-in-law on the back, so that the man returned to his high stool, and to the examination of one of the garments purchased that morning at Bloomingdale's.

"What's a factory man?" said Valerie, when Jonathan had finished steering her through a line of silent Cuban seamstresses, had introduced her to a very old Italian cutter wearing glasses with the thickest lenses she'd ever seen, had waved a hand at the racks of finished garments waiting to be shipped, and had introduced her to one of several shipping clerks—the only white boy, a neighbor of Jonathan's mother in Queens.

"That sounds funny," said Jonathan. "Coming out of your lips."

"What do you mean?"

" 'Factory man.' That's rough for your mouth, kid."

"You'd be surprised what's passed through this mouth," she said. "He seems very nice, your father-in-law."

"He is."

"It must be a difficult situation sometimes," she said.

"Something that would never happen in your family."

"No," she said. "I don't think Daddy would have taken a job working for Phillip." She smiled at the idea. "Even if he had, you can be sure Daddy would have taken over the running of the show in any case." They'd come out of the back, returning to the gleaming, overlit mirrored showroom. It was so bright that Valerie found herself squinting, just as she had when he'd brought her up to see

45

"the operation" after they'd finished lunch. The long row of bright dresses arranged along a storeroom rack on plastic hangers—Jonathan's junior sportswear line for the coming spring—was so horrible that she'd simply nodded as cheerily as she could, and turned her head to examine the rest of the place. Now she turned her eyes away from the dresses again, only to find their hideous images across the room in the terribly unflattering mirrored wall, against which were arranged little white tables, with little white telephones. Here, Jonathan had explained, his salesmen made his pitch to the buyers from the big and small retail establishments that bought his budget line.

"Are you coming?" Jonathan said, standing in the doorway to his office at the back of the showroom. It seemed that the girl was forever going off on a tangent, thinking of something else—a real dreamer, he decided; the best kind of silent partner. Now she was staring at the track lights in the ceiling. What *they* could possibly have to do with his proposal he didn't know.

"It's these lights," she said.

"What?" said Jonathan, going up to her. Very well, if she wanted to be dragged into the office, he'd take hold of her arm and drag her.

"Wait a minute," she said. "I just want to make a suggestion, if you don't mind a little constructive criticism."

"I don't want any criticism at all. I just want you to come into my office and tell me what you think."

"These lights are too bright," she said.

"What?"

"You should tone down the wattage by about half," she said.

"The way you've got it now, the bright lights, the mirrors, those bright colors on the dresses—you could go blind in here.

"No one's ever complained before," he said. But he was listening.

"If I were a buyer, I wouldn't feel very comfortable in

46

here unless I was wearing sunglasses. You don't feel like lingering in a place where you've got to squint all the time."

"I don't squint in here," Jonathan said. He looked up at the ceiling lights, suddenly very cross. He walked across the room and into his office, and from where she stood, Valerie heard the buzzing of an intercom. "Angela, get your ass in here, will you please?" she heard him say, and a moment later, the very pretty, very erect, and black-eyed receptionist entered the showroom from her little cubicle at the front.

"Did you want something, Mr. Singer?" she said, standing at attention in the center of the showroom.

"Just look over there, Angela. Just look over at Miss Holmes."

"Is this Miss Holmes?" she said, looking at Valerie.

"Is she squinting?" said Jonathan angrily.

"Yes," said Valerie. "She is."

Angela remained where she was, guilty of squinting, prepared to take whatever punishment her crime called for. Jonathan walked over to Angela and looked at her closely. "Shit, you're right. How the hell didn't I ever notice that?"

"You don't always notice things that you're used to living with," said Valerie.

"That's really funny," he said. "I spend all this time trying to show you how much I got on the ball, and you're not here ten minutes before you start making suggestions."

"That's just the type of girl I am."

"I mean here I am, sitting on top of this little operation, and I've got this terrific idea, and the only way it's going to be terrific is if I can sell you on the fact that even though we're small here, we're fast, we're smart—and you probably figure me for a dope."

"Come on," she said. "It's not that important."

"Angela, would you get out of here, please?"

"Yes, sir, Mr. Singer," she said.

47

"And what do you mean, it's not important," said Jonathan, turning back to Valerie. "You know damn well it's important. This is where we do it, this is the place where they make us or break us. I mean, how the hell couldn't I have seen that those poor bastards have to come in here and squint, because some idiot's put in too much light? Jesus Christ."

If it was an act, he played his part very well, she thought, as she followed him into his little office. Over lunch, he had first praised her—for "her image"—then went on to praise himself—for what he'd built up "from nothing." He was involved with a certain segment of the "rag business," he said, which involved quick thinking, fast turnover, and a certain amount of friendly stealing. "Only we don't call it stealing," he'd told her, completely in earnest. "In the rag business, if you borrow someone else's design, that's a copy, that's an adaptation, that's a pirate, that's a translation—you don't say 'steal.' " The meal had fascinated her, not just because she'd never lunched in a dairy restaurant, whose raison d'être was less to satisfy the cries of animal lovers than to present an array of mock-meat products whose absence of any and all parts of beef precluded the possibility of the establishment's breaking any of the Jewish dietary laws, but because she'd never come up against anyone so hungry in all her life. Jonathan hadn't only been hungry for her agreeing to the terms of his proposition. He'd been hungry for the lunch he ordered: mock chopped liver, made from some sort of soybean base; a course of some sort of greasy potato pancake, served with sour cream; a steaming vegetable soup without a beef stock; a huge plate of mock steak—some kind of flat construct of eggs, vegetables, more soybeans, smothered in onions and ketchup; a dessert of pie *and* ice cream. And when it was all over, he wasn't even flushed. She'd managed a bit of soup and a half slice of black bread; he'd managed to wolf down his meal and talk at the same time—talk out his proposition, and talk out his life.

48

"Now sit down," he said. Valerie sat in the chair across the desk from where she assumed he would sit, quietly taking in the pile of account books, the scarred metal filing cabinets, the black-and-white photograph of a young woman in a work shirt with a paintbrush clenched in her teeth, a face contorted in a smirk at the camera. Instead of sitting in his swivel desk chair, he continued to pace behind her back. "Well, OK," he said. "I'm sorry if I lost my train of thought."

"You lost your good temper," she said.

"All right, my temper!" he said. And now he sat down on top of the desk, his knees dangerously close to her face. Looking down at her, he said: "Would you please tell me what you think?"

"I think it's interesting."

"Oh, Christ."

"And I'd like to think about it."

"You'd like to think about it?" he said, getting off the desk. "OK, that's good, that's pretty good. If she wants to think about it, that means she thinks maybe it's not such a bad idea, it might be something of a kick, and maybe, just maybe, Johnny Singer's going to get out of this garbage and into some better-priced line, unless, of course, you ask anyone but yourself for their opinion."

"You certainly have a way about you, Mr. Singer."

"Are we going backwards? Aren't we still Johnny?"

"Johnny," she said. "I know what you want. It's something I can let you have very easily. It may not thrill my family, but if it's something I wanted to do, I'd do it anyway."

"OK, OK—" he said. "There's a 'but' in there. What's the 'but'?"

She was looking again at the picture of his wife. He wondered if she could possibly catch a glimmering of what beauty she possessed from the little jokey shot. Jonathan thought that if his wife were to walk into the office at that moment, it would somehow knock Valerie off balance; for all her money, all her snooty family's blood, the presence

49

of such beauty would stick a pin in her balloon of universal contempt. She would be in the presence of something she didn't have, something she couldn't be.

"All you want from me is really an endorsement."

"Sort of—"

"Let me finish, please," said Valerie, and he found himself once again growing angry at the accent she affected. He didn't know if it was Audrey Hepburn trying to sound like she'd spent the last few years in Beverly Hills, or some breathy Hollywood starlet trying to sound like she'd spent the early part of her life with the queen at Buckingham Palace. "You want me to represent a new line of sportswear, appearing under your label, for your company, but bearing my name. 'Valerie Holmes for Lorelei Paris.' That sort of thing. I've seen it before, and so have you. It's hardly original. You have the idea that my name, and my picture, may actually help sell a new line, built around a class approach. I suppose that's because you think the Holmeses are so classic."

"Yes, I do," he said seriously.

She ignored the interruption. "But even assuming that my face and my name will help sell a new line of medium-priced sportswear that your company will design, you have to ask yourself: Why should I go ahead and agree to give you my permission to use my face and my name? What do I have to gain from this whole exciting venture, Mr. Singer?"

"Johnny."

"Yes, Johnny. What? Tell me? How on earth did you propose to induce me to sign up for this idea of yours? Did you think the money would encourage me?"

"I could go a little higher."

"I'm sure you could go a lot higher, but that's not the point. You don't think I'm in need of money, do you?"

"Everyone could use a little more."

"Maybe, Mr. Singer," said Valerie Holmes. "But I'm afraid that I'm one of those rare individuals who need some other incentive than the mere possibility of making more money."

"What the hell else can I give you, kid?" he said. If he understood what this bird was telling him, it didn't make any sense. There she was, her blond face just as fresh and clean as when he first saw her, her legs neatly crossed, her posture perfect, still listening, still talking; so she must be interested in going along with his idea in some form. And it didn't seem possible that she'd be holding him up for some more money. "Tell me what you want."

"What's a factory man?" she said.

"*What?*"

"I'd like to know what a factory man is. Could you tell me?"

"Jesus," he said. Then he sat down behind his desk, played his fingers along the armrest, and took a deep breath. "You wanna know what a factory man is. OK, I'll tell you what a factory man is. A factory man is a guy who works in the factory." He smiled and shrugged his shoulders. "What else do you want to know before you give me a straight answer?"

"Mr. Singer, I'm afraid we're not getting through to each other very well."

"A factory man is a guy who works in the factory. The factory is back there. Wait. OK. We call the factory man the guy that runs the whole factory. All right? What that means is he's in charge of styling, he's in charge of designing—that's if there is any designing—he's in charge of the cutters, he supervises everything. If there's sewing, he'll supervise that. What we give out to the contractors, he'll supervise that. I mean let's face it, if you don't have a good factory man, you're dead in this business. I don't know if that answers your question at all. Does it?"

"It's a beginning," she said. "You're very stingy with your explanations. I have no idea what a contractor is. I'm not sure what you mean when you say 'styling.' I don't know if that's another word for stealing styles."

"I already told you that we don't use the word 'stealing' at all."

Willy Schwartz chose that moment to burst into the office. "I'm sorry, Johnny, but I forgot all about it before."

"Forgot all about what?"

"The black girl."

"What black girl?"

"Jesus, I'm talking about that crazy hooker you sent up here, Johnny. Do you really want to give her a job?"

Valerie Holmes was prepared to enjoy the exchange, but Jonathan didn't seem the slightest bit embarrassed. "You mean Louella?" he said. "How does she fit out?"

"She fits our nines."

"No shit," said Jonathan.

"But, Johnny," said Willy Schwartz, "you don't want to have a hooker around the showroom."

"If she's a perfect nine, she won't be a hooker much longer, she'll be a fitting model, right?"

"Same difference," said Willy, but he conceded his son-in-law's point. "But the fact is, she can't come in the way she looks. We can't let her walk around the back like that."

"How'd you like what she brought up?"

"Good styles, I liked everything."

"The hooker picked it all out, Willy," said Jonathan. "You get her a wardrobe from out of the back—a little of this and a little of that—and tell her what a pattern model is and what a pattern model makes."

"You're the boss."

"And her name's Louella, you got that? Louella."

Willy lingered at the door, but Jonathan didn't hurry him out. He'd lost his train of thought anyway. "Johnny— I'm going right now—I just wanted to know if she called or anything?"

"No, Willy. She didn't."

Willy gave Jonathan his sympathetic look and sidled out of his office.

"You got any more questions?" said Jonathan.

"What's a fitting model?"

"A girl who's a perfect size," he said. "Whatever size we use to set up our styles—I mean the first pattern. We're a junior house, so we need a size nine. Perfect means just that. The girl's got to be the right shape everywhere, with no variation, because the pattern maker plays with her after he's got his garment. She tries it on, and he sees where it's wrong, and she tells him too. If a pattern model feels it's tight in the armpit, it's tight in the armpit and we got to change the pattern. What else do you want to know?"

"That's very nice of you," said Valerie. "I mean, if I understand it correctly, what you're doing for that girl."

"Yeah, well, I'm nice. I'll be real nice if you say yes and make me a happy man."

"I've already told you that I need another incentive."

"Name it. I don't know what I've got that I can give Valerie Holmes, but try me."

"I want a job."

"That's what I'm offering you."

"No, I mean a real job," said Valerie. "I don't want to put my name on something that I didn't take part in. You want a classic line, let me help put it together."

"Do you know what you're talking about?"

"A little bit. You may not believe this, Mr. Singer, but I actually know how to sew on a machine."

"What's with the Mr. Singer? And who the hell taught you how to sew—your maid?"

"Yes, it was my maid. But what's the difference? I can still sew." Valerie got up from the chair and allowed herself to get a little excited. "I think I know what you want. You want classic sportswear, at not very expensive prices, and you want it all put together—one look—one look with my name. What would be more logical than letting me put it together, letting me steal my own ideas?"

"Because how are you going to know what the public wants? What if your ideas aren't just what the public's been holding their breaths for? This isn't a design house, this is a styling house. We take from the best, and we change a little here, a little there, and then we have a little mileage behind us. If it's been picked up by Saks and Bloomie's and Bergdorf's, we know how to change it over so that Korvettes is going to dig it too. You don't have any experience. How the hell can you expect me to let you try and design something from scratch when you don't know the first thing about the business?"

Valerie sat down again. As far as she was concerned, the argument was over. It was just a question of explaining something to him that hadn't quite penetrated. "Johnny," she said, "I didn't say anything about designing. I just want to put together the look that's going to be called Valerie Holmes."

"And just exactly where are you going to get this look from?"

"The same place you do."

"Wait a minute," he said, beginning to catch on, and liking it very much. She was smiling now, and he liked her smile, and he had an inkling of how fast she must be traveling. The hardest part of the journey was the first step, and that had been long since accomplished over the telephone that morning. Her smile was a response, not just to the proposition, but to the stimulus of thinking for herself, thinking fast on her feet, snapping out a decision that would be as sharp and witty as it would be wise. He was glad he'd pushed her, forcing the lunch date, taking her up to the office, not allowing time for slackening of their common interior rhythm. "Wait a minute," he repeated. "You don't mean that *you* want to do the stealing from stores?"

"Johnny," she said, "nobody *steals* in the rag business. I just want to be the one who pirates the styles."

5

"The most important point for you to keep in mind," said Thomas Holmes, fixing his blue eyes on his flighty mother, "is never to contradict me in anything I say about this entire matter. I hope—I repeat, I hope—that that is absolutely clear."

"How was Cannes?" said Mrs. Holmes, pressing the button for the maid.

"How would I know how Cannes was? You're the one who was in Cannes," said Thomas. "Father seems to have taken up residence at the Del Monte Lodge, and you seem just as eager as he to stay at least three thousand miles away from wherever there's any hint of trouble with your daughter."

"I've come back, haven't I?"

"Of course you've come back. You wouldn't miss the Winston's ball."

"I still haven't been asked a single solicitous question by my own son since he's entered this room. Go ahead, Thomas. Ask me how Cannes was."

"All right, Mother. How was Cannes?"

"Oh, you know Cannes!" she said slyly.

Thomas knotted his elegant hands and squeezed as hard as he could. If only he'd been born into a different generation of Holmeses. Not the first—he'd allow Samuel Holmes his blood-and-guts beginnings—but perhaps the second. He would've liked the challenge of creating order from a chaotic start, a financial empire with carefully articulated hierarchies, with safeguards and checks and balances, to protect against the certain fallibility of future flaccid generations. Perhaps it wasn't entirely fair to think of his father as a watered-down descendant of the original fiery Holmes. Father did, with the faithful help of extra-family experts, manage to keep a wary eye on the state of the bank; the extensive real estate holdings in California, western Canada, and Venezuela; and the extremely complex interwoven interests in various multinational oil companies. But keeping an eye on what were, in a fundamental sense, political as well as economic holdings was not the same thing as using those holdings to advance both the family and the family's interests. Father's politics were largely confined to attending Republican party banquets and making sizable contributions to the election funds of those political candidates with whom he'd attended school. He liked to listen to Thomas's talk about the dangers of the Third World, but he didn't take his son's worries very seriously; Armageddon wouldn't arrive for many generations. Thomas's uncle—his father's younger brother—had developed far greater political acuity than Thomas's father, but, unfortunately, that acuity was largely directed at channeling as much money as possible from the Holmes Foundation into the coffers of too many Third World dictators posing as saviors for hungry people. Thomas's own role in the bank was certainly important, particularly so for a man of thirty, but it was not of such supreme importance that the possibility of it being part window-dressing, part sinecure, could be discounted; and it certainly allowed him no powers of a political nature. He did not, like his father, have access to presidents, and it vexed him that his father used his access not at all.

Now, at the beginning of a very small problem, he was sure that he alone of all his family could see how the problem could grow into something large and embarrassing, something for the mob to point to as another absurdity of the rich.

His mother was laughing like a schoolgirl, all her teeth bared, and her lineless face thrown up to catch the sun

56

through the conservatory skylight. He wondered if she knew how much he hated this room crammed with healthy plants, and if that was why she'd received him here rather than in any other room in the vast apartment. "Well, you know," she continued, "the tourists have gone back to Lyons and Philadelphia and Manchester and Düsseldorf, or whatever other terrible places they have to go to earn their money, and they've left the rest of us in peace. Now it's just a few good friends, a few good boats, a few good dinners, and all the while the weather's cooling off just perfectly, just like we ordered it. And now that Luciana's husband's gone back to London, she's begun to throw parties every night on the yacht, just as a diversion, mind you. Just so nobody can say she was all alone with that obnoxious little Italian she's so crazy about, even though he doesn't seem to care too much what anyone thinks. He just goes right ahead and grabs in public. He probably thinks he's being romantic. His name is Rolando, can you imagine?"

"Mother," he said, "I'm glad you enjoyed your latest vacation." Before he could return to his main subject of the day, Mrs. Sharon, the antique Irishwoman who'd been dogging his mother's steps with cynical devotion for more than twenty years, knocked once on the open door and advanced with a heavy step.

"Perhaps you'd be wanting something, Mrs. Holmes?" she said, smiling at some private joke.

"That's a very good guess, Mrs. Sharon. I'd love some breakfast tea. What about you, Thomas? Some tea to calm you down? Nothing like tannic acid at this hour of the morning."

"Thank you, Mother, but I had my breakfast two hours ago."

"Gets up early for a Holmes," said Mrs. Sharon sharply, but as Thomas turned to face her, all he could see was her jocular smile, smooth and ruddy and practiced—nothing on which to pin an attack.

"And, Mrs. Sharon, please," said Mrs. Holmes, "don't

bring up any rolls or scones or muffins—just tea."

"There's some croissants, still warm from the bakery," said the maid.

"Really? Who ordered them?"

"I did, of course," said Mrs. Sharon, a bit annoyed with her employer's characteristic morning obtuseness. "And you'd be missing something if you didn't have a good old New York croissant now that you're finally back from France."

Mrs. Sharon dropped that country's name as if it were something vile on her tongue, and after a moment, Mrs. Holmes gave in. "Oh, bring me up whatever you want," she said.

"Nothing for you, Mr. Holmes?" said Mrs. Sharon.

"No," said Thomas, with a rudeness that didn't have time to register, for Mrs. Sharon had turned around and taken one step into a very excited young woman.

"And while you're at it," said Valerie, hugging the maid in the doorway, "you can make me some buckwheat pancakes—that is, if you approve."

Mrs. Sharon approved, and was soon whistling away downstairs. Thomas edged slowly back from where his sister was entering the room. "Hello, beautiful," said Valerie to her mother.

"Hello, darling," said her mother, and as soon as mother and daughter were embracing, Thomas felt himself closed out, an intruder whose language would be incomprehensible to them as Swahili.

"Now what is all this terrible nonsense that Thomas has been filling me up with all morning? I want you to sit down at once, and we must both be very serious, so that your terrible brother doesn't find us lacking in decorum or gravity."

"Mother, you didn't come back from Cannes just for me?"

"Of course just for you—aren't you my best reason?"

Thomas said, "Mother's come back for the Winston's ball, Valerie. I've only been here a few minutes, and

58

we've been too busy discussing the weather in Cannes to get around to your problem."

"Oh, it's no problem," said Valerie. And she walked right up to where he was slouching against the wall and gave him a bright little kiss and squeezed his cold right hand.

"Actually," said her mother, "Thomas has begun to tell me a bit, but I'm probably still a bit unresponsive after my trip. You know how I loathe flying."

"How was Cannes, Mother?"

"Oh, for Chrissake," said Thomas.

His mother went into her girlish routine: "Oh, you know Cannes!" she said, and he could see that she'd already forgotten everything but the latest gossip. He went over to her gravely, as she was halfway through her story about Luciana and her Italian, and rather than throttle her, he put his arms about her from behind her back, very gently, and placed his chin at the top of her head, and from this position, faced his sister.

"I have to get back to the bank, Mother. I'd like to have my say, and I'd like to hear your opinion on the matter, and then I'll leave the two of you alone for as much gossip as you can bear."

"Thomas, your chin is hurting me."

"Sorry, Mother." Quickly, he raised his head and took his arms off his mother. Valerie was beginning to laugh now, whether at his hasty retreat from his mother or at some other point of ridicule, he couldn't say.

"All right," said Mrs. Holmes. "Where do we begin?"

"At the risk of repeating myself to the two people in the whole world who make it their business to listen to what I say as little as possible—" he began, but they both drowned him out at once.

"Come on, Tom," said Valerie.

"Now, Thomas," said his mother. "You know we always listen to you. You're our rock."

"But I wouldn't go so far as redeemer," said Valerie. "Sit down, Tom—please stop fidgeting, I'll make it all very easy for you. I'll make a clean breast of it to Margaret."

"Please don't call Mother 'Margaret.' "

"It's all right, Thomas. I think it's nice and modern," said Mrs. Holmes.

"Mother," said Valerie, "here's the problem. I've gone into business."

"Why, how exciting!"

"Mother!" said Thomas. "Would you please listen and say nothing until you understand what we're talking about here?"

"Yes," said Valerie. "As I said, I've gone into business with a small little clothing manufacturer, and I'm styling my own line of clothing, a whole coordinated line of sportswear for next summer. I haven't been this excited or happy in years!"

Not since she married Phillip S. Raymond III, thought Thomas. He said: "May I, Valerie?"

"Go ahead," she said.

At once he got up and began to pace the room, his hands, advocate-style, clasped behind his narrow back. Watching him, Valerie remembered Jonathan Singer's overzealous description of her escort on the night he stole their taxicab; he'd been quite quick to take it all back when he discovered that the escort in question was her brother. She loved her brother, and she realized that her love prevented her from examining the essential facts of his character: No matter what he said, no matter how he acted, it all came back to that fact that he was Tommy, her big brother, her only companion during the long expanse of childhood who was both a Holmes and a child. She supposed that others would find him a bit dull, but then they weren't privy to the secret of his long hours at the bank, assuming that all Holmeses spent the majority of their time flat on their backs, devouring seedless grapes, in the style of old Rome. He was actually a good athlete— No, that was the sister talking—he was a good tennis player, and a terrible athlete. Tennis was something that had been drilled into him as a very young child, perhaps as early as four years old. He hadn't had enough mileage yet to be contemptuous of the game, and those early fluid moves remained with him: a good straightforward serve that was practised enough to be almost as fast on the second serve as it was on the first; a terrific command of the back court, with an ability to finesse shots in any corner unless they'd been slammed; an easy, unerring lob for anyone who dared rush the net. His liabilities were a poor net game and an uneven temper. She wondered if Jonathan played tennis. If he did, he must be a very strong server, but be otherwise clumsy, forever hitting balls over the line, over the fence and into the woods.

"Your daughter and my sister is twenty-three years old," Tom was saying, "with an undistinguished degree in English and American literature. If her last name were anything other than Holmes, we would all have to be asking; 'How in the world has this totally inexperienced child been given such a magnificent job in an area in which she knows precisely nothing?' But because her name is Holmes, we don't even have to ask that question, do we?" He drew himself up very erect now and stared not at her, but at her mother. The hard lines on his face reminded her again of the photograph she'd taken of him right after his graduation from Harvard. There'd been some sort of protest going on—she'd been fourteen and automatically on the side of any protest, but didn't understand what was happening when a good fifty students, some with great beards under their mortarboards, got up in the middle of an old man's speech and left the assemblage without a word. When she and her parents had caught up with Tom after it was all over, he was still raging over the incident. She tried to get him to smile, and quickly, because she wanted a shot of him with the mortarboard in place. Tom smiled, and she snapped the shot, and the result was something so characteristic, so much the picture of Thomas Holmes, that she always laughed when she looked at it; because the laughter allowed her not to think what the

61

hard, determined lines meant. Not to laugh would mean that she saw in his face the capacity to punish, to pursue, to avenge. She didn't want to know anything mean about her brother, and so she'd cultivated a habit of laughing off his politics, laughing off his twisted sense of social justice. But she knew that laughter might get her nowhere today. She might actually have to talk to her brother, and give no allowances for the fact of their relationship.

"As is usually the case in these matters," said Thomas Holmes, pausing to extract a folded bit of paper from the inside pocket of his navy-blue suit, "Valerie has gotten herself mixed up with a fly-by-night company, run by a hand-to-mouth businessman, whose source of income and general business dealings remain hazy even after a week of investigation." Tom looked at her now, waiting for an indignant outburst.

"No, no, go on," said Valerie, "maybe I'll learn something."

"Valerie was approached by a company calling itself Lorelei Paris, Inc., a very small manufacturing concern that specializes in cheap women's sportswear for the least expensive department stores in the country. Somehow, the president of this company, a Mr. Singer, has gotten it into his head to create a line of clothing called Valerie Holmes."

Her mother was starting to look alert for the first time, sitting in her chair with a hungry expression—whether for breakfast or for more news was unclear. "It's not 'Valerie Holmes.' It's 'Valerie Holmes for Lorelei Paris,' " Valerie said.

"It's got your name in it in any case," said Thomas. "Our name. And from what you've already told me, they're not satisfied with just the name. They plan to use her picture, put it in magazines, department stores, wherever this cheap stuff is sold. That's where we'll be—pushing some Jewish gentleman's inferior merchandise to the very people who associate our name with the highest stratum of American society."

"First of all," said Valerie, "let's go back to that Jewish crack."

"There's nothing to go back to, Valerie. I haven't called anybody any names. I'm simply explaining to Mother the nature of your business, and the sort of person you're doing business with."

"The fact that he's Jewish has got nothing to do with it."

"All right," said Thomas. "Let's pretend he's an Anglican bishop. It really makes no difference. Because I want to tell you about him." Thomas unfolded the paper in his hand. "We're talking about a gentleman who would never be able to get a loan from our bank even though his reported personal income last year was in excess of eighty thousand dollars."

"That sounds pretty responsible," said Valerie. "When you consider what he started with."

"His reported income the year before that was a much less remarkable thirty-nine thousand dollars. The year before that was about the same, and the year before that was only twenty-two thousand, and the year before that— that's nice for him—was fifty-eight thousand dollars. Somewhere along the line he's obviously changed accountants."

"Where do you get all this information anyway?" said Valerie. "You're not the Internal Revenue Service."

"And I'm also not your Mr. Singer. I'm Thomas Holmes, remember? If you'd have a little more respect for yourself, Valerie, and for the rest of us, you'd realize that we can do a lot more for you than just get a few reports from a friend at the IRS."

"Who wanted buckwheat pancakes?" said Mrs. Sharon, walking with her great tray through the open door. She served Mrs. Holmes first, noting the silence that greeted her arrival, and went about her business with speed. She'd been cheated of Valerie's presence in the apartment while she was away in Cannes with Mrs. Holmes. And fully a week before they'd returned, Valerie had taken pains to move out to some tiny place in the East Eighties; she expected to be visiting it before Mrs. Holmes.

"Thanks, Mrs. Sharon," said Valerie, but the woman could see that even Valerie was distracted, eager to get back to some private affair. She picked up her tray and fled, with one last look of amused contempt aimed at Thomas's back; she'd left him a pot of black coffee.

"I won't go into the question of how he manages to get away with paying a ridiculously small percentage of this reported income in taxes," continued Thomas, not realizing that he was heading for the source of the rich smell of coffee among the potted plants and trees.

"That's a good idea," said Valerie. "I understand that Daddy's been on that fun list too—'Ten Millionaires Who Don't Pay Taxes.' I think that's the name."

"I hardly think that our family's financial background, especially when you keep in mind the enormous support that the Holmes Foundation gives to every conceivable charity, has to be compared to anyone's."

"OK, let's drop that," said Valerie. "Let's go back to Jonathan."

"*Jonathan*?" It was her mother speaking, holding on to the teacup with two hands. Thomas allowed himself a tiny breath of a smile.

Valerie made it worse: "Jonathan Singer, Margaret. The gentleman in question. Also known as Johnny." Her mother simply looked at her, not wanting to fall victim to such obvious bait.

"I was saying," said Thomas. "This Mr. Singer has an apartment on East Sixty-Fifth Street which rents for eight hundred and fifty dollars a month. He owns two cars, one in his wife's name—one a brand-new Porsche, the other a three-year-old Corvette. Both are garaged at a cost of over two hundred dollars a month. All this would be well within his income, except for the fact that he purchased a summer home early this year, in Amagansett, Long Island, for a reported sixty-five thousand dollars. Similar houses in the area are being sold for as much as one hundred thousand dollars, and we have a fairly good idea that Mr. Singer paid for a good deal of his home in cash."

"So what?" said Valerie. "None of this has got anything to do with me."

"It's got everything to do with you," said Thomas. "I'm talking about the man you're working for, the man who's going to promote himself by exploiting your name, by taking advantage of you."

"That's all in your mind, not in mine."

"Valerie, a man who puts out such large sums of cash, when all his reported income is spoken for by his ordinary costs of living, and whose bank accounts clearly can't account for any such expenditures, can only be a man who's running a crooked business."

"I wish you'd just come right out and tell me and Mother exactly why you insist on my giving up my association with Mr. Singer, and then I shall simply tell you that I refuse to do that, and then we can all kiss and make up, and you can go back to the bank, and Mother and I can have a good talk—"

"Valerie," said her mother, "please give your brother a chance to finish. He's obviously gone to a great deal of trouble to help you out. The least you can do is listen to what he's got to say."

Now her mother had committed herself. Valerie sat back carefully, shut her eyes, and listened to the list of Jonathan's crimes. Of the eighteen people who seemed to be working for Lorelei Paris, only fourteen were "on the books." Thomas supposed this to mean that the other four were illegal aliens. Jonathan's competitors had nasty things to say about his moral caliber; according to them, he was a vociferous briber of buyers and a procurer with a stable of girls waiting for the buyer who would purchase his merchandise. The rumor that Lorelei Paris's latest fitting model was, in point of fact, a prostitute was aired by Thomas in level tones, as he looked loftily over the head of his mother. The story of Jonathan Singer's home life was begun. His wife, Edwina, was absent from the home for weeks at a time, and Jonathan took advantage of the absence by going to bed with as many buyers as he could cram into his crowded schedule. Moreover, Edwina had several scrapes with the law for possession of small quantities of marijuana, and there was the distinct possibility that she was buying and selling drugs during her frequent trips to the West Coast. The neighbors spoke of violent fights when husband and wife were together, and suggested that one or both of them might be insane.

"How much did this all cost?" said Valerie suddenly. "I mean just exactly how much did you have to spend to drag all this nonsense out of the mud?"

"I'm sorry that you think it's nonsense," said Thomas. He poured himself a cup of coffee. His mother looked like she was on the point of a decision. Everything had been prearranged without her, but Thomas knew that she could create a lot of trouble if she felt that father and son had been unfair. "But I'd still like to know how you feel about working for that man given this information."

"Even without this information, you were against this whole idea," said Valerie.

"Because you have no business selling our name so cheaply," said Thomas. "Even with a reputable company it would've been a terrible idea."

"I'm not just selling our name," said Valerie, but then she stopped short of further explanation. She'd been working with Lorelei for a month now, and what she'd been doing there was so far out of the experience of her mother and brother, so far from any experience that they—her family—had ever allowed her, that she had no wish to share with them what they were predisposed to despise. She loved the frenzied shopping in a dozen stores, looking for bits and pieces of outfits that she'd match and blend into an idea to be copied for her line. She loved working elbow to elbow with Willy Shwartz, plaguing him with a hundred questions about fabric quality, production costs, the appointment of labor. Valerie had met at least eight fabric salesmen who had charmed her, charmed her into a non-wary stupefaction, into a perfect willingness to buy up whatever it was they wanted to sell her. She loved to watch Johnny work the buyers, she loved the language of the sell, she loved the brisk decisions and dares and compromises and chances and bluffs that made a deal. There was nothing she could tell her mother about a "runner"—a hot seller that everyone longed to create, or imitate, or at least get a piece of; there was nothing she could tell her mother about the way the blood was running through her body now, the hot blood of Samuel Holmes's descendant that had been lying stagnant, useless.

"All right, Valerie," said her mother. "You know what I think, don't you?"

But Valerie had no wish to hear what her mother thought. The task of translating the pure quality of her joy to be working for some constructive end into a simple line of defense, into an easily understandable purpose, exasperated her. "I don't care what you think," said Valerie. "You don't understand what I'm trying to do; neither of you do, neither of you ever will!"

Her mother looked at her sympathetically, as if she were the unfortunate victim of some passing malady.

"You don't see why I should work at all," said Valerie to her mother. "And you, you," she said to Thomas. "You think I should jump into something proper at the Foundation, something with a silly title and no work, no responsibility!"

"I suppose I should include the fact, Mother," said Thomas, "that this Mr. Singer, as I've already hinted, is something of a ladies' man."

"Oh, for Chrissake," said Valerie.

"That makes sense," said Mrs. Holmes. "A whole lot of sense."

"It's completely irrelevant to this discussion, Margaret," said Valerie. "There's no romantic interest, either from his part or my part. He's simply the nice young hotshot businessman who's showing me the ropes of an

67

industry that I happen to find fascinating, and who's given me an opportunity that I think is much too wonderful to give up, and even if the first attraction had to do with the fact that my name is Valerie Holmes, I think Mr. Singer has learned by now to be very impressed with me, very excited about what I can do for his company and what we can do for each other." It was all in a rush, and when she was finished, she sat down, feeling that the suspicions of mother and brother were probably confirmed by her outburst.

"Are you quite all right, Valerie?" said Mrs. Holmes.

"I am not at all in love with this man, can't you understand that?" She was up again, crossing the room, pausing to tear a dead leaf off the body of a rubber plant. "What I'm in love with is the idea of doing business. I like it. I love it. That's what I love, and that's nothing at all for you to be afraid of."

Mrs. Holmes cleared her throat and then said nothing for a good half minute. Valerie's examination of the rubber plant revealed no other signs of ill health. Her mother looked at Thomas. "Have you spoken about this to your father, Thomas?" she said finally. The pause had given the question the weight of a decree.

"Yes, Mother," he said.

"And?"

"Well," said Thomas. He turned his pale face to where his sister stood, waiting for the sword to fall. "Father has left it up to me. Or rather, he's agreed to implement what I've already suggested, in the event that you won't leave this venture immediately."

"I won't," she said.

Thomas ignored her, going on to finish his thought, as he always did: "Of course, since you've been working with this company for a month already, your Mr. Singer may want to cause some difficulties when you decide to leave. Father has also told me to see that those difficulties are taken care of with as little fuss as possible."

"Valerie," said her mother, "why don't you take the

day off, come have lunch with me, or maybe you'd like to take a drive somewhere—?"

"No."

"Just to give yourself time to think it over."

"I haven't got the time to throw around like that," said Valerie. "I've got a line to put together. It won't get done by itself."

Thomas still hadn't delivered his threat, even though all three knew precisely what it was. Carefully, he explained once again that it was all for her own good, for her benefit, and was merely a temporary gesture to help return her to her senses. Until such time as she should cease working for Lorelei Paris, Inc., Valerie Holmes, heiress to one of the world's great fortunes, would be left without an allowance, without any source of family funds, family security. The idea, easy to put into words, impossible to imagine, flew through her, lighting up all her features with what mother and brother assumed to be defiance.

"OK," she said, in a very little voice that was anything but defiant. She was brave, but she didn't have to waste her energy on blowing up her tone of voice. For the first time in her life, she thought, she would be on her own. It was all she could do to maintain her fake equanimity while her entire frame shook with the delicious promise of freedom.

6

Jonathan Singer drove up Madison Avenue, feeling very much the center of an irresistible force—a force of ambition and romance. It was late at night, a Tuesday, and the few pedestrians about walked with determined steps, to exhibit to hidden muggers their seriousness of purpose, their fierce intention to beat off any attempted interruptions. Still, they turned their heads when Jonathan, his hair whipping back in the late October wind, kicked the top-down Porsche up ten thousand revs for a fast down-shift to second gear and a flat-out twisting of the terrible machine through light traffic. Each gear had a different sound as he wound it up to the engine's limit. Jonathan liked the sound of redlining it in second best: It was loud, it was deep, and it suggested an enormous lusting reserve of speed, reined in only by the powerful low gear. Stopped at a light, Jonathan exhanged glances with a young woman in the back seat of a cab, her oblivious date lost in shadow. Slowly, he let a smile grow on his face, remembering the rainy night he'd seen Valerie Holmes for the first time, as she waited impatiently for someone to make up his mind about that famous taxi. A month later, she was practically his best friend.

No, that wasn't it exactly. There was too much he was keeping from her to call her his best friend. Primarily the fact that he was getting exceedingly anxious to creep into her bed one night and turn that teasing little smile into an open-mouthed scream of uncontrollable ecstasy. He didn't like having that much desire beating under his skin. It made the office too hot. When she showed him her latest finds for the line, he spent more time looking at her fingers, with their little under-developed nails, than the garments they pointed to. For a short girl, she had long legs. He liked the nape of her neck, the frazzled ends of her blond hair, the way she had of narrowing her eyes to listen to anything of importance. When she spoke words like "shrinking the marker," or "it's going to be a Ford," her finishing school accent made them absurd and endearing. He had the idea that he was in the process of changing her over, turning her from a spoiled child into a woman. Still, if she was his creation, he didn't know why he wasn't sure of her feelings for him.

The taxi surged forward, jerking the young woman's head. Easily, Jonathan followed the cab's rear, then swept through an opening on the cab's right, forgetting even to smile again at the young woman's open face. He let the momentary sense of disquiet pass; he would know very soon if Valerie Holmes wanted to do more with him than pore over fabric.

He turned right on Sixty-fifth Street and pulled into the line of traffic waiting to pass a parked limousine. It was close to two o'clock in the morning, and his own block had to have another traffic jam. He gripped the steering wheel and tried to think of something else, something to disarm his growing anger. The buyer he'd taken to dinner was from Cincinnati, with two kids and a husband who worked for Procter & Gamble. She'd met Valerie in the showroom, then spent most of dinner talking society gossip, all the while trying to get some dope on what exactly Valerie Holmes was doing with *him*. He'd mention it to Valerie in the morning—something to laugh about, and a good point of departure for his hand to take hold of hers, and to pull her against him with one great tug.

The line moved up a car length, and from behind him the cabs were beginning to lean on their horns. After dinner, the buyer had asked him if he liked dancing, and so he had to continue the evening into the night. After she made the obligatory call to Cincinnati and repowdered her

71

shiny nose, he took her to Studio 54 and let her gawk at the shiny people, with their clean well-cut hair. She danced a version of the twist, remembered from college sorority days, and it was so crowded there, and so thick with perfume and smoke, that he almost began to enjoy the way she danced her backside up against him at every possible opportunity.

That was the trick. Don't try and seduce the buyers. Let the buyers think that you're dying for them, but don't think you have a prayer. Cincinnati had spent the night trying to hint that he was indeed worthy of her, but he'd managed to miss the point, mercifully. He'd already been to the St. Regis, and that was about the only interesting thing that sleeping with her seemed to promise. But she'd gotten off on the dancing. When they said good night in the taxi, she stuck her thick tongue deep in his mouth to taste every last crevice. That usually meant a good order, and Cincinnati was a great town for Lorelei Paris.

"Shut the fuck up!" said Jonathan suddenly, turning his head to the lineup of honking cabs behind him, their headlights reaching for his eyes. He stepped on the clutch, threw the car in reverse, and back up on an angle to the curb, which further infuriated the stalled drivers; they weren't honking for *him* to move—they were honking for the limousine to clear out and let everyone pass.

As he turned the wheel sharply to the right, throwing in first, he carefully rode up onto the curb, and onto the sidewalk, and drove quickly the ten yards to where his own doorman stood shakily against the big glass door to his building.

"Hey, Tony," said Jonathan. "How ya doing?" And the doorman had no time to do anything but gawk as his own Mr. Singer drove past the limousine and back into the street, where he continued on for another ten yards, and turned right into the entrance to the garage that took up two subterranean floors in the thirty-six-story building in which he lived. Jonathan drove the last few yards of snaking ramp in first gear, gassing the car mightily, because he knew what the parking attendants expected from a Porsche.

"Hey," said one, raising his fist as Jonathan jerked to a halt in front of his chair. "How's my man?"

"Good, good," said Jonathan. Then he saw the look in the attendant's face—part sympathy, part contempt.

"What time tomorrow, Mr. Singer?" said the attendant.

"Nine o'clock good with you?"

"It's good with me, man, if it's good with you." Jonathan was out of the car, and the attendant took his seat behind the wheel, already gassing the engine, getting ready for the screeching flight to the lower level. "Hey," he added, "the 'Vette's back. I guess you knew that, man."

"Sure," said Jonathan. "Go ahead. See if you can park it on two wheels." He listened to the howling rubber as he walked to the elevator. When it came, he pressed the button for the thirty-sixth floor and examined himself in the tiny elevator mirror. Slowly, he cleared his mind of the evening with the buyer, of his hopes for the new Valerie Holmes line that would lift him from his budget range to a class that would land his image and name in *Vogue* and *Bazaar* and *Nouvelles* and *Town & Country* and *W*. He walked the long corridor from the elevator to his door and slowly, very slowly, took out his key and let himself in with a minimum of noise.

"Hello, darling," she said, before he was fully through the door.

"I wish you would've called, Eddy," he said, but stopped short of sounding angry. A fight was the last thing he wanted at this hour of the night.

"I did call, darling. I spoke to Daddy, and he told me you were out with a buyer. Don't I get a kiss?"

Her eyes were burning in a face luminous with clarity. When he held her, she pulled him tight with a brief surge of strength, then suddenly went limp in his arms. "I waited for you to come home," she said.

"You should've slept." He helped her onto the sofa, and she held his hand.

"Please," she said. "I'm cold." He sat with her and held her in his arms.

"Coke?" he asked.

"No," she said. "Something else. I needed it for the drive. I wanted to get home fast."

"What was the hurry?"

"I missed you."

"You didn't seem to miss me much when you left," he said, but she wasn't aware of anything bitter in his tone, and when she shivered, he held her more closely, feeling again what he always felt for her after an absence—an overwhelming desire to fix her spirit to one perfect role—this one, perhaps. He wanted only to have her consistent, to remain in love with him, in need of him, and not to be always changing her mood with any shift in the wind.

"I left," she said, "because I had to go to San Francisco."

"Because you wanted to."

"Yes, Jonathan," she said. "I wanted to go, because I had to show my paintings, and I had to see what they'd done, and hear what they had to say about what I'd done."

"And what did they say?" said Jonathan, caring not at all what her self-congratulatory Art Students League cronies, living off state, federal, and parental doles, thought of his wife's latest canvases.

"Jonathan," she said, suddenly turning to face him, placing cold fingertips on his rough jaw, "Jonathan, I'm not taking any more dope."

"You're flying right now, Eddy."

"No, no, no," she said, shaking her head from side to side, discounting the evidence of her eyes, her quivering body. "That was for the drive. Two days, two meals, maybe four hours of sleep. All the way from San Francisco."

"By yourself?"

"I listened to language tapes, French and Italian. *Je suis très fatiguée.* But now everything's *buono, molto buono.* I love you," she said.

She wasn't usually so extravagant with statements of emotion. He had married her a year after their first meeting, and, as Willy Schwartz had told him, he'd had plenty of warning about what to expect. There had been sudden absences from New York, missed appointments, sullen silences, a continual and destructive urge to satisfy her ravenous self. She had no interest in his business, except as it served as a manifestation of his "creative energies." The material success that continued to come to him during their courtship, and after their marriage, seemed to matter very little to her; it was Jonathan who'd urged the move to the luxury apartment, who'd wanted two sports cars, who'd insisted on fulfilling his dream to own a house on the eastern end of Long Island. Eddy spent money on dope, but her tight student-budget habits prevented her from becoming a cocaine hog—she still took it only as a gift at a party, limiting her purchases to Mexican marijuana and Indochinese hashish. But it wasn't her dope or her art that had come between them. It was the maddening fact that in more than five years of marriage there had been no growing closer, no greater appreciation, no communion—and Jonathan had expected and longed for all these things. She had married him only because he had urged something permanent on what was always threatening to vanish into thin air. Of course she loved him, but, as she often explained, she loved herself more. Anything that denied the fact of this love of self was hypocritical and wrong. There were days and weeks when her desire was to be alone with her painting, or simply alone. To deny this desire for the sake of marriage was impossible, perhaps immoral, for Eddy Singer. She could not love him at all if she did not love herself first, and he would have to learn to put up with her depressions, her ecstasies, her absences, her silences, with

75

everything that was part of her, because she would never hold back or disguise anything that was true. Jonathan didn't understand how he had fallen in love with her, except perhaps it was in the way he fell in love with the beach and the sun and the sea when he was a little boy. Eddy presented something vast and unknown, something that was attractive enough to be deadly, something that was satisfying in limited doses, and always untamable. When she was gone, taking a car and some cash and her credit cards, leaving a note—"Gone to S.F. to exhibit, miss you"—he would resent her, feel himself abused, mistreated, unloved. The affairs he had throughout their courtship, and continuing with greater frequency throughout their marriage, would be matters of no importance to Eddy, he knew, and he was driven to fits of wild jealousy during her absence—certain that she had the same attitude towards any affairs of her own.

"You drove three thousand miles in two days?" he said, becoming angry now, feeling the fact of her fatigue through his own vague sense of sleepiness.

"No," she said, suddenly laughing. "I'm talking about loving you and you're getting mechanical. Hey, I figured it for sixty-five hours' driving time. The French cassettes were three hours, and the Italian two and a half. I listened to each of them at least five times. I thought it was two days, but maybe it's three. Tomorrow I'm going to eat a lot, after I sleep. Tonight I want to be light, because I feel very good, very gossamer and dreamy. I want to make love tonight."

She was too weak to stand up without help, but she wanted to make love. He wondered why. There had been no talk about the paintings, just a hint of self-criticism in the statement that she was to stop taking dope—a statement that he'd heard before. She'd been gone for more than a month now, and he had news for her, news he'd like to be able to blurt out, happy as a child with his new adventure with Valerie Holmes. But he knew in advance that the news wouldn't interest her. She'd simply be listening for the sound of joy in his voice, and react to his own sense of achievement; she herself had no judgement to make on the craft and skill necessary to pull a Valerie Holmes off the vine and into his business. Worse, she'd feel nothing, he thought, about his own attraction to Valerie. Eddy loved him, and her love wouldn't change according to the way he handled his private parts. For a moment, knowing of her desire, feeling her light weight in his arms, sensing the hunger for food, for sleep, for love running through her frame, measuring the strength of the drug in her body by the unnatural fire in her green eyes, he had to hold back an urge to rebel, to turn his feelings inside out and dump her on the floor, leave her to an instantaneous, ignoble sleep on the carpet. But the moment passed. Once again, she'd told him that she loved him. If she'd rushed back, endangering her health, threatening her life in the speeding car, it was because of this moment, however absurd, however meaningless in the day-to-day routines of their lives. Like a warrior, she was home from a battle and had appeared now, fatigued, and weary of the outside world, wanting only to make this declaration of love.

Jonathan picked her up, carried her to the bedroom, undressed her, and place her in their bed. This woman was his wife, and when he loved her, his love was sure and violent and desperate, and he forgot everything else in the world except Eddy, Eddy and the mad longing to reach her soul.

7

It was Willy's voice, and it was talking trouble. Jonathan pulled his legs out from under the covers and carried the phone into the bathroom, shutting the door after him. "Tell me again, Willy," he said.

"Immigration was here, three cops, they got our boys."

"What do you mean cops, what kind of cops?"

"Immigration cops, no uniforms, just badges and papers, and they didn't want to be kept waiting at the door. You've got to get down here, Johnny."

"They arrested them?"

"That's what I'm telling you."

"All four of them?"

"Yes."

"Christ," said Jonathan, and he slammed his elbow into the bathroom door. "What kind of fucking bullshit is this? I pay the fucking union through the nose, I got my bucks ready every time they're selling tickets to the sergeants' ball, I got the best crooked accountant on Broadway, and just because I go out of my way to help a couple of broken-down aliens with a little work now and then—"

"Johnny," said Willy Schwartz. "Save that stuff, OK? You gotta get down here. The whole place's shaky. And Valerie's in your office now, talking on the phone—she was here for the show, and just maybe she didn't go for it in a big way."

"I'll be right there, Willy," said Jonathan. "Hey," he said. "Don't hang up. You know your daughter's back?"

"I know, Johnny," said Willy. "On top of everything else."

Valerie had dressed for yesterday's work in a Ralph Lauren blazer, Cacharel shirt, and jeans. She'd wanted to talk to Jonathan early yesterday afternoon, after she'd managed to extricate herself from mother and brother, and to walk crosstown from Beekman Place to the garment center. But the mad activity along Broadway had changed her mind. Now that she was on her own, there was no point in rushing to Johnny—he'd assume, correctly, that she was there for sympathy and for solace. Already she could see him pulling out his checkbook, or reaching into the safe for some of that unaccountable cash, all the money derived from "backdoor" sales, in which neither buyer nor seller had any inclination to record transactions. Whatever her percentage of "Valerie Holmes for Lorelei Paris" would be worth, she wasn't going to see any money until the line was completed, made up, shown to retailers, and—they hoped—ordered in quantity. Jonathan would certainly be happy to advance her money on his faith in the new line, but she didn't want to ask him for that until she'd accomplished something, until she'd gone a step further than he'd asked. Leaping into the gutter to avoid an onrushing hand truck, she hailed a cab with the two-fingered whistle taught her by Jonathan, and went the mile uptown, on the East Side, where *Nouvelles* magazine rented space for its New York office.

Nouvelles was the only magazine in the building. Valerie remembered being rude to staffers from *Nouvelles* on at least two occasions, when questions about her impending divorce had been coming in fast and furious from all the junk tabloids, and she had made no differentiation between the glossy sort of magazine in which her mother loved to find the Holmes name and the pulpy weekly sold in supermarkets. She held her fresh copy of the magazine, in which she'd found their address, under her arm, and examined the people waiting for the elevator. Three men—talking loudly about the quantity of Scotch they'd consumed before lunch, hitting each other in the arm to accent salient points in their conversation—all had very lawyerly looks about them: the dull suits, the duller shoes, the twenty-dollar ties, and the two-dollar haircuts. They weren't directing their low talk at her; it was primarily for the benefit of three gorgeous young women, younger than Valerie and between four and seven inches taller, all of whom carried large model's portfolios. When the elevator arrived, there was a sudden rush of people to catch it—various secretaries in unattractive pants suits, bad makeup adding five years to their features; a tall, sleek black messenger, elegant in corduroy jeans and a pressed plaid shirt; a career woman carrying a Louis Vuitton bag, wearing shoes she recognized from the window at Charles Jourdan, and a heavy unflattering tweed suit with a too-short skirt, a badly fitted jacket, and a tired-looking turtleneck the same color as her flamboyant shoes.

Jesus, do they need help, she thought, trying to think like Jonathan. The models shoved her into a corner of the elevator, making her feel like an unattractive dwarf. Two of the girls wore jeans, and Valerie couldn't help but wonder why. Obviously, the girls were stunning, with long legs, tiny waists, terrific curves; and though their business called for directing attention to precisely these assets, the jeans and Guatemalan sweaters they wore did their best to hide everything. Valerie followed the models out of the elevator and up to the *Nouvelles* receptionist, a pretty college girl in steel-rimmed spectacles who wore two army shirts—one green, one blue, the blue one functioning as outer shirt.

"Hi!" said the first model cheerily. "I've got an appointment with Cheryl—"

"Yeah," said the college-girl receptionist, cutting her short. "I know." She pointed to a grouping of chairs about a huge coffee table piled high with copies of *Nouvelles*. Every chair was already occupied by a gorgeous girl, and there were perhaps another dozen seated on their portfolios on the floor. The other models didn't even bother to check in. They followed their compatriot to the waiting area and slumped against a wall, under a row of framed *Nouvelles* covers.

"Yeah?" said the receptionist. It was Valerie's turn, and she wondered if perhaps she should've called the friend who worked at *Vogue* or written a note to the *Nouvelles* editor.

"I'd like to see Mrs. Michon please."

"Mrs. Michon?" said the receptionist, instantly alert. "Do you have an appointment?"

"No. I thought she might be able to spare me a couple of minutes. My name is Valerie Holmes."

"Valerie Holmes," said the receptionist, in tones that indicated quite clearly that Jonathan's characterization of her as former full-time celebrity, the girl whose name was on everyone's lips when she and her husband traipsed through museum openings and charity galas, each dragging the other, was far from apt. "May I ask what this is in reference to, Miss Holmes?"

"I'd prefer that you just ring Mrs. Michon's office and tell her I'm here," said Valerie, exhaling her high-society tone.

"Does Mrs. Michon know your name?" The receptionist was trying to decide whether to follow a rude or respectful route.

"Yes," said Valerie, hoping it was true.

"Just a minute, please," said the receptionist. She pressed a button on her intercom. "Hello, Clara? There's a Miss Valerie Holmes to see Mrs. Michon. She doesn't have an appointment, but says that Mrs. Michon knows her."

That was not what I said, thought Valerie, we've never had that woman in our house. The receptionist held the phone and continued to give Valerie her noncommittal look. Finally she said: "Nice blazer."

"Thanks," said Valerie. She refrained from complimenting her double army shirts.

"Whose is it?"

"It's Ralph Lauren's," said Valerie, a statement that rather surprised the receptionist, who had a vague idea of the designer's prices—usually far out of reach of any girl in her early twenties. But before she could continue this interesting line of conversation, she was treated to the sight of Mrs. Michon's secretary emerging from an inner office with a concerned look on her face. She gestured to the receptionist, and the receptionist shrugged at Valerie.

"Are you Miss Holmes?" said the secretary.

"Yes."

"Excuse me, I'm only asking because of Mrs. Michon's schedule today—I don't recollect your face—Mrs. Michon wanted to know if—"

"I'm the Valerie Holmes whose father is the grandson of Samuel Holmes."

"Yes," said the secretary, looking sharply at the receptionist who had gotten to her feet for a better look. "Would you please come with me, Miss Holmes?"

Valerie followed the secretary, a slightly overweight young woman dressed in gray flannel slacks a size too small, through an outer region of cubicles, along a quiet corridor leading to shut-doored offices, and into a surprisingly sun-filled private reception room, where a Cory was in the process of brewing some lovely coffee.

"I know that Mrs. Michon would very much like to see you, Miss Holmes. She's in a meeting right now, and I expect it'll be finished quite soon. May I get you some coffee while you're waiting?"

The secretary to the editor-in-chief of *Nouvelles* magazine, whose lead story that month was "The New Red Reds—Wow Clothes for Now," spoke in clearly articulated phrases, poured coffee with a delicate touch into a fragile little German china cup, and smiled showing all her even white teeth. But now that Valerie had a chance to further examine her, she found her lacking in just those areas in which she should have been most strong. The girl had no sense of fashion.

It was not just that the slacks were a size too small.

They were simply the wrong style for her, perhaps for anyone. Perhaps a stick-thin girl who was quite tall could get away with wearing them. They were obviously man-tailored, and the girl's problem was that she looked too much like a man to begin with. If only nice, simple, classic dresses were in style, thought Valerie, this girl could get away with a lot. She could hide about ten pounds easily.

"Do you like Hugh Robertson?" said the secretary unexpectedly. She'd poured herself a cup of coffee and taken a chair opposite Valerie's, and was apparently following orders to keep the conversation flowing until Mrs. Michon was ready.

"I don't know him," said Valerie.

The secretary hesitated for a moment, wanting very much to laugh at this, and she finally did, letting out a titter that was nine tenths sweetness. "I didn't mean that," she said. "It's funny. If you asked anyone else if they liked Calvin Klein or Pierre Cardin, they'd always assume that you were referring to their clothes."

"Of course," said Valerie. "I didn't realize that's what you were asking."

"Yes, I know. That's what I thought was funny," she said. "I'm sorry if I've offended you."

"Of course not," said Valerie. "As a matter of fact, I like Hugh Robertson's clothes very much—or, at least, the things of his that I've bought I liked." But suddenly Valerie had remembered Jonathan's dismissal of Robertson's clothing as fake, a rich man's version of what poor people wear, and appropriate only for society balls. This girl was wearing a modified work shirt tucked into the waistband of her gray flannel slacks—the slacks for office-girl solidity, the "fake" work shirt (fake in that it was not for blue-collar sweating, but for white-collar work, then off to the laundry for careful pressing) for the phony sense of fashion prevailing everywhere. If the receptionist outside wore two creased army shirts, and the roomful of models wore jeans, why so was she, heiress and fledgling fashion "designer," wearing jeans under her rich blazer.

"But sometimes," Valerie added, impulsively, "sometimes I think a lot of that look is useless, if you know what I mean."

"I know what you mean, Miss Holmes. I certainly can't wear Hugh Robertson, even if I could afford him. It's just that it all looks so great in the magazine." The secretary leaned a little closer. "The only reason I've mentioned Hugh Robertson is that he's the one in there with Mrs. Michon."

Suddenly an awful grating sound flew their way, a sound something like laughter, but not at all unrestrained. If it was a laugh, it was mechanical, self-conscious, mocking. The secretary was already out of her chair as Mrs. Michon entered the room, followed by a man with beautiful brown hair, which he wore straight back in a well-cut gleaming shock. Valerie had time to take in the perfect cut of his pin-stripe suit, which fell about his athletic frame as if it were being worn for the first time.

"I'm Mrs. Michon, dear," the woman said, and she took the man with the beautiful hair by the elbow and pulled him closer to Valerie. "I'd like you to meet Hugh Robertson. Hugh, this is Valerie Holmes. There was a picture of her somewhere wearing something of yours—I don't know what or where."

"Very nice to meet you, Miss Holmes," he said, "whether or not you wear my clothes."

"I do," Valerie blurted out, a bit awed by the designer. He didn't sound like a gay, that was for sure. But of course that meant nothing. More important was the fact of his face, features more pretty than handsome, fingernails manicured and covered—she was sure!—with a clear polish, the slight feminine roll to the collar of his pretty shirt, the foppish red silk square in his lapel pocket. And, of course, the very fact of his being a designer—not a factory man like Willy Schwartz, but as close to a *couturier* as an American operating from New York can be. Of course, she thought, this could mean only one thing.

He had taken her hand, very lightly, and she imagined

she could sense the utter indifference to her physical being that she thought must be the natural condition of gay males with regard to her own sex. She wondered how old he was. Older than Jonathan of course, older than Tom, but his dress, and his manners, and his hair obscured his age, put it in what was for her the never-never land of "over thirty-five."

"Margaret and I are old friends," he was saying. "I don't just say that for the sake of present company," he added to Mrs. Michon. "We've gone through the wars together."

"Your mother," said Mrs. Michon, "has done more good for the entire American fashion industry than you might think. If people like her hadn't started buying our Americans up front, I think we'd still be little better than Paris copycats."

Valerie had never seen a smile more false, a mouth more evil than that possessed by Mrs. Michon. The mouth was painted a glossy red, and her red-tinted hair, her black eyebrows, her pale skin dabbed with red blotches of makeup all shaped the smile into something demonic, something unfeeling, something all-powerful in its perfect artifice. But Valerie smiled herself, a charming, natural smile, realizing that she was where Jonathan couldn't yet venture, and that she would soon be allowed to speak. Hugh Robertson was bowing almost imperceptibly, and Valerie had a sudden revulsion toward the entire scene: the elegant fag-designer, the bitchy fashion editor, the meaningless talk about fashion, inflated by the talkers' sense of importance and grandeur. "We've gone through the wars together!" thought Valerie. She imagined that to mean that her hysterical mother had needed a different gown for her daughter's coming-out party, after one of Mr. Robertson's spies had discovered that some other *belle dame* was about to wear something similar to what she'd already prepared. What a crisis!

"Do remember me to your mother, my dear," he said, and he pressed her hand once more in parting. Mrs.

Michon walked him a few steps into the corridor, followed by the secretary, then scurried back to Valerie.

"Now this *is* a surprise," she said.

"Actually for me too," said Valerie. Mrs. Michon smiled her fake smile at this, and Valerie had an intense desire to skip all further delays. Small talk would only bring on an endless repetition of that terrible imitation of enjoyment, and the chance that the smile might turn into the grating laugh. "I'm here because I've got something to tell you that I think might be of interest to the readers of your magazine."

"If that's the case," said Mrs. Michon, her eyes greedy, "I'm more than happy for the chance to listen to it."

"I'm going into the fashion business."

"Yes," said Mrs. Michon, as if this were the most ordinary statement in the world. She was wearing a leather suit that Valerie had noted with dismay the last time she was in Gucci's, wondering who on earth would wear such a thing.

"Well," said Valerie, "I'm in the process of developing my own line of junior sportswear." Mrs. Michon was looking at her with unfriendly sort of curiosity, and Valerie felt the urge to explain herself further. "I've gone into business with a small established manufacturer in New York—"

"Just a moment," said Mrs. Michon. "You've become a designer?"

Valerie hesitated. She couldn't call her "adaptations" of existing styles new designs, even if Jonathan could. "Well—" she began.

"And you want some publicity for the line," interrupted Mrs. Michon.

"Yes," said Valerie.

"And you think because of your name, we're just going to go right ahead and give it to you?"

"No," said Valerie. "I don't know what you're going to do. I only know what I'm offering you."

"You're doing us a favor?"

"I really don't understand," said Valerie, standing up, her royal past coming to the rescue of her dignity. Who on earth did this clumsy woman think she was? "I was under the impression that your magazine likes to keep its readers informed about changes in fashion."

"Sit down," said Mrs. Michon, "and if you want the free space, you can drop that society-girl tone with me right now." Valerie hesitated, then sat, clutching for her cup of coffee. "If you think that you're the first rich girl to try and break into the fashion business, Valerie, you're very much incorrect. All of a sudden, it's become the thing to do. Pick up the phone, call a few friends, get a mention in *Vogue* and *Nouvelles*, have a few styles made up and placed in Bendel's, and if you ask her nicely, you'll end up with a shot of Bianca Jagger wearing your rags in *Women's Wear Daily*. Listen, I don't know a thing about you as a designer. I don't know if you took a correspondence course in pattern making, or hung out at FIT, or, as is much more likely, you're simply fronting for some vagabond black boy with a flair for sketching ladies' dresses. All I know about you is that your coming-out party cost more money than I'll make here in the next fifteen years, if I last that long. I know that you were married and divorced, that you got your face in the papers when you went to parties, and that you didn't want to be bothered by *Nouvelles* for our issue on the new divorcées. Our readers aren't especially interested in seeing photographs of your new line of sportswear; they'd be a lot more interested in seeing shots of one of the Holmes apartments or houses, and with a retrospective article on the girl whose debutante party cost her parents a half million bucks. If you really have a line of clothes you're trying to hawk, you and I can make a deal. You'll get some publicity if you give us some of the things we want to see."

Valerie finished her coffee and looked for a long time at Mrs. Michon. All the reasons that her brother Tom had for wanting to keep their name out of the garment business came back to her as she thought over Mrs. Michon's proposition. It infuriated her to be thought just another in a line of spoiled dilettantes looking for publicity for some inconsequential—or counterfeit—achievement. Worse still was the large kernel of truth in the midst of Mrs. Michon's broadside: Valerie was not a designer; Valerie was capitalizing on her name; Valerie did enter into the fashion business on an impulse propelled from the outside.

"I'm terribly sorry, Mrs. Michon," said Valerie, rising, "but we couldn't possibly have someone with your manners come to our house, with or without a complement of photographers."

"I wasn't trying to be rude, my dear," said Mrs. Michon, getting up after her. "Merely realistic."

"I'll try *Vogue*," said Valerie.

But rather than taking her story to another magazine, Valerie spent the rest of the afternoon walking along Fifth Avenue in the Fifties, Madison Avenue in the Sixties, Seventies, and Eighties, trying to pick up the thread of an idea that had been building slowly in the back of her mind since she had begun to put together her line for Lorelei Paris. She was alternately excited about her line and depressed by it. So many women she saw were so sloppily dressed, with such a display of thrown-out money—designer initials on shirts, bags, belts; expensive fabrics in colors more shocking than new; three-hundred-dollar riding boots absurdly coupled with billowing peasant skirts. Valerie's line would be guilty of none of these transgressions. She'd coordinate everything—sweaters and shirts and jackets and pants—and outfits would be sold as entities. The last month had been filled with shopping expeditions—raids, really—finding her separates in Bloomie's and Altman's, Saks and Lord & Taylor, Bergdorf's and Bendel's, Bonwit's and I. Miller and Anne Klein. Outfits had been put together and taken apart, shown to Jonathan and Willy, tried on by Valerie, exhibited to salesmen—the big question always being how much could they copy it for? Fabric salesmen had extolled their wares, exhibiting synthetics meant to duplicate the feel of silk and cashmere, leather and suede, pure cotton and pure wool. Valerie learned, and worked, and felt gratified, but what was missing was made evident today in the offices of *Nouvelles*, listening to Mrs. Michon, seeing Hugh Robertson, looking at the overweight secretary in the gray flannel slacks: Valerie had discovered nothing new.

She could not have told Mrs. Michon: "Ah, but wait until you see *these*." Because the novelty of her line would simply be its classic look economically presented and coordinated, all wrapped up in her socialite name. And every bit of it would be derived, a continuation of someone else's thoughts, a replication of what the fashion world already possessed in abundance.

Mrs. Michon had a right to be resentful. It would be Valerie's marketing that would be new, and nothing else. Rich girl uses name to sell Same Old Stuff. And, looking at the afternoon parade of women, Valerie was tired of the Same Old Stuff, sick of it in fact—she had a sudden desire to throw out all her jeans and wear something— something *else*.

"Have you got a nice, simple, sexy dress in my size?" she asked in a little boutique near Eighty-first Street.

"Dress? Did you say *dress*?"

"Yes."

"What're you, about a seven?" the saleswoman said, and quickly began to show Valerie pants and skirts and fake-leather tops with fringed hems, always answering Valerie's complaints that these items were not really what she'd asked for with, "But these are Hugh Robertson's," "These are Milton Brommel's"—until Valerie's ideas began to pick up speed, enthusiasm, and confidence.

She spent a good part of the next two hours in search of a simple, sexy dress, and all she found were complicated arrangements of pants and skirts, except for the half-size departments. Valerie didn't know what kind of dress she wanted, but she wanted to talk about it with Jonathan, with Willy. She wanted to tell them that she'd found something lacking, something needed, something that they could pick up on and market in a way that would put her present imitative line to shame. Even a simple little shirtwaist dress, in the right fabric, for the right price, could be perfect, she thought: perfect for the overweight secretary, the pretty college-girl receptionist in her absurd double army shirts, the gorgeous models hiding their legs in rumpled jeans.

By the time she'd arrived at Lorelei Paris, Jonathan was already occupied with a buyer. "It's a pleasure to meet you, Miss Holmes," she'd said, as if she were relieved to know that Jonathan hadn't made up the story of his new business associate.

"Johnny, I've got an idea," she said softly, but the whisper didn't convey her excitement to him, and he simply patted her hand and said, "Good, good, keep 'em coming," so that Valerie realized she'd have to wait till the next morning to tell him what was burning through her. After he'd gone off with the buyer, she spent an hour watching Willy Schwartz work late cutting a pattern, and she kept up the barrage of questions that he'd come to expect from her at all times, whenever she was in the factory.

"I hope he knows," said Willy, "what gold he's got working here."

"I'm not gold, Willy. I'm just trying to learn enough so I can take over," she said. For a moment she was about to tell him about her day: about the quarrel with the family, the temporary loss of allowance and parental blessings, and, above all, her sudden revelation about the need for a simple, sexy dress. But she decided to wait for the morning, for the next time she'd see Jonathan.

Because it was an important occasion, she got up early enough the next day to put on makeup, find a three-year-old jersey wrap dress, and slip on her highest heels. She waltzed into the office at nine-forty-five, but instead of finding Jonathan barking orders into the phone, she found Angelica, the sloe-eyed receptionist, crying hysterically over her desk, and a young Puerto Rican shipping clerk pounding his fist into his palm and screaming in rapid-fire Puerto Rican Spanish at a tall oblivious man in a gray suit as the man scrutinized the contents of a plastic wallet.

"Valerie," said Willy Schwartz, coming out from the back room, his face ashen, "Valerie, get into the office and stay there until I tell you to come out."

"What's going on here, Willy?" she said, and then she saw two more tall men, dressed in the same sixty-dollar suits as the first tall man, lead out the four Colombian packers from the back. All four were handcuffed, and one of them, the youngest, was in tears.

"Valerie, please," said Willy. "Johnny's not here, I've got to take care of it—please go into the office."

"But why on earth are those men arresting our—" she began, but she let the sentence drift into the air. "OK," she said. "I'll be in the office."

Valerie had not simply understood that the tall men were officers of the Immigration Department, that the four Colombian packers were illegal aliens, that four lives and one business were being threatened by forces outside their control—she understood what had put those forces in motion. She understood, and she was so furious she began to cry.

Closing the door to Jonathan's little office behind her, she called the bank that bore her family's name and asked to speak to her brother.

8

It had begun to snow at four o'clock in the afternoon on the first day of November, and the chauffeur had to rush the limousine out to the garage in Long Island City to have snow tires put on; he'd been called specifically for this purpose by some executive's secretary, a Miss Thomas. She had a beautiful voice, he thought, very gentle and obliging, but with a sharp crack to her periods. Apparently, his evening's tasks were to involve at least one VIP, but he'd so far neglected to look at any of the names on his list of pickups, except for the very first, and that was because the address was so perfectly astonishing! Eight o'clock, 74-14 35th Avenue, Jackson Heights, Queens.

Why for Chrissake, *he* lived around the corner, on 34th Avenue.

And he certainly never got invited to anything at the Plaza.

For a moment, he thought of pulling up in front of his own apartment and buzzing his wife. She always liked a chance to sit in the car, and he was a good half hour early. What a joke to be so close to home. Whoever this Mr. Schwartz was, he must either be getting some very unusual favor—or else be the cheapest bigshot he'd ever picked up. No, he wouldn't go home. The small fry were always ready early, and he could use the extra time to get back into the city—he had a stop on East Eighty-fifth and another on East Sixty-fifth—and if he was going to be kept waiting in the car, he might as well have the joker from Queens in the back seat with him. Carefully, he double-parked the limousine in front of the entrance to the tired-looking building, six stories of fake Tudor frontage, just like his own. Naturally, there was no doorman. As he paused to check the name on his list, two small boys wearing hooded sweatshirts under jean jackets, their red, ecstatic faces squinting at him through the falling snow, approached the limousine. The chauffeur noted with satisfaction their sense of wonder at the machine that was his to command—a quiet, climatized, immensely powerful center of luxury in a shabby city, a brutal world. He patted his thin hair, put on his sober cap, and hesitated a moment more before venturing to open the door.

Incredibly, he saw a man running from the building through the snow, a black raincoat held over his head. Giving in to his sense of duty, the chauffeur jumped out of the car, even though it was perfectly likely that this particular passenger would be more than happy to tear open his own door, all the while apologizing for getting the seat wet.

"Mr. Schwartz?" said the chauffeur, his hand on the door latch. It was an unnecessary question, as the man in question was wearing a tuxedo and heading directly for the back seat of the limousine.

"Yeah," said Willy Schwartz. "Waiting long?" And he let the chauffeur open the door, and fell into the first limousine he'd ever sat in. The chauffeur had left the glass partition between compartments open and didn't even think to offer to close it, as he was certainly supposed to do.

"Yes, sir," said the chauffeur, jumping into his seat and starting the car forward. "Quite a night we're having." He studied his passenger, and he was pleased to see that this was a man struggling to keep the conversation alive, someone who felt obligated to talk to him, to the faceless driver.

"Thank God, we're in this," said Willy Schwartz. He was looking all about him, at the familiar streets—but, dashed by this early snow and seen from this sheltered vantage point, it was all new, and dreamlike. Willy couldn't hear a thing from the outside world, not even the jolting of the shock absorbers as the tires drove through potholes covered by snow. He closed his eyes and hoped that Eddy would wear the dress that Jonathan had brought home to her, that she wouldn't find it repellent or bourgeois; he would hate it if his daughter disappointed them all in the face of a near-stranger. Idly, he wondered if there'd be music he could dance to. He hadn't danced more than half a dozen times since his wife had passed away, and then only at weddings, with clumsy relatives. His wife had died before she was forty, and he remembered how she'd looked, before the illness, turning and turning under his extended arm on the little dance floor of some big hotel in the Catskills, the waves of her hair swinging madly about her glowing face. He had a sudden pang of longing for her; there had been too much time spent talking about what they'd do when his success was achieved. But he had never taken her for a ride in a limousine, he had never dressed her in mink, he had never taken her to Sardi's. Willy forced back the happier image: out of the sickroom and onto the dance floor, when the music was fast and loud, and they both forgot about what they wanted and remembered only the moment of the dance. He suppressed a rising shudder of tears and clenched both his fists as the driver said: "You want to hear something funny, sir? I live in Jackson Heights myself."

"What?" said Willy. There was something about the driver's face in the rearview mirror that irked him—some lurking presence of mockery that struck him like a spur. Perhaps the driver had seen him start to cry.

"I said," said the chauffeur, exhibiting a condescending smile in the glass, "that I live here, too. In Jackson Heights, just around the corner.

"Yeah?" said Willy.

The chauffeur didn't understand the shift in tone. "I mean it's funny, if you know what I mean, that I get a

94

chance to pick up someone in my own neighbourhood."

"Why?"

"Because," said the chauffeur, suddenly afraid that he might be overstepping his bounds, "the company usually has me picking up executives in the real ritzy sections, if you know what I mean." He waited for those words to register with Mr. Schwartz, but his passenger seemed to have fallen back into his reverie. Some kid in a white Chevy blew out of the snowfall and passed him on the right, sending a filthy splash of mud and snow along the limousine's side, and the chauffeur spent a few moments concentrating on the task at hand—getting into the quiet right lane and maintaining an easy dignified pace along Northern Boulevard as they approached the wild interchange before the Fifty-ninth Street Bridge. After all, if he'd been called specifically to remember his snow tires for this evening, he'd better look sharp and make no mistakes with his passengers. Any one might turn out to be the big cheese, and then he'd have his head handed to him if he'd stupidly insulted him. "If you're too cold or too warm, sir," said the chauffeur, "there's a climatecontrol knob in the door handle."

"I'm not with the company," said Willy Schwartz, returning slowly to the driver's previous remark. "And I'll tell you something else. Twenty years ago, Jackson Heights was a beautiful place, nothing to be ashamed of."

"Yes, sir," said the chauffeur. It was too late to offer to close the glass partition. He took the upper level of the bridge for the sake of his passenger, and hoped that the sight of the city's towers, glittering through the storm, would lift his spirits. He couldn't tell if his passenger was angry or about to cry. Shaking his head, he turned on the map light and looked at the next address, a good one on East Eighty-fifth. The severity of the storm decided him against taking the Drive, and, as he turned east on Sixty-second Street and north on First Avenue, he thought for a single frightened moment that the name that went with the address was Holmes.

For a full minute he couldn't return to his sheet of paper. The cabs were jockeying for position around Adam's Apple, and he had to lean on his horn to avoid being crushed by an oncoming hippie's van, painted with glowing orange figures of a long-haired man, a short-haired woman, and a shaggy dog. Past Sixty-sixth Street, he maneuvered into a break in the traffic and drove in an easy line, waiting for the next red light. Mr. Holmes was in California, as his driver, George, had told him only yesterday. George had had the honour of carrying Mrs. Holmes around town the last two weeks, and he was very tired of the task. Mr. Holmes, at least, never burdened him with shopping bags. George much preferred a good detective novel, read in a lazy afternoon sitting in one of the canyons of Wall Street, waiting for his august employer to finish lunch. As for the younger Mr. Holmes, the one who never kidded, he had his own car, a Buick Electra; and his driver was an old Irishman who never spoke a word to the other chauffeurs, in a ridiculous imitation of his employer's seriousness.

The light went red on Seventy-third Street: *Valerie Holmes*. The driver extinguished the map light and sat up a little straighter in his seat. Why the hell wasn't George driving her? He accelerated with even more caution and looked nervously back at the middle-aged man from Jackson Heights. How was he supposed to guess that he'd have anything to do with a Holmes? Now he knew why he'd been called about the snow tires. Jesus, what an ass not to look at the names. George had even said something about her the other day, something about her moving out of the Beekman Place apartment. But was he supposed to remember every little bit of gossip? Wouldn't it have been a lot better if that dumb bitch of a secretary had just told him who he was picking up, and that he'd better be on his very best behaviour?

The doorman's eyes were very bored with the limousine, and very grand with the repetition of the Holmes name. The girl herself was pale, blond, petite—

and pretty, if you liked that type. She didn't notice his face as she climbed into the back, not allowing Mr. Schwartz to get to his feet to help her in. There was a kiss, but not an amorous one, and by the time he'd gotten round the back of the limousine and into his own warm seat, someone had shut tight the glass between compartments and both passengers were talking without a pause. Carefully, he read both name and address of this last pickup a short mile downtown.

Mr. and Mrs. Jonathan Singer. Well, at least he'd never heard of *them*.

"Hey, Mr. Singer," he heard their doorman say, "you gotta car down here bigger than a house." And he had to wait for them for fifteen minutes, standing outside the car, wanting to look sharp for the Holmes girl. Mr. Singer looked like the kind of guy you like to see get his head handed to him in the movies—big, and dark, and conceited. His wife was something else though. The chauffeur thought she smelled like soap as she passed him by, entering the car with an amused look, as if all this door holding was something of a joke. She was probably a model or an actress. He glared at the back of Jonathan's head as he ducked to follow his wife inside.

"Hi, Daddy," said Eddy to Willy Schwartz, and Valerie watched as daughter kissed father.

"You OK?" said Jonathan.

"Sure," said Valerie. "All the surprises are on our side."

"Nice car."

"All the advantages," said Valerie. "As soon as I make up with the family."

"It's not too late to stop this," said Jonathan. But she could see that he didn't want to stop it any more than she did. On that terrible morning two and a half weeks before, when he understood what she was telling him, understood the words and was made to believe that what they meant was possible, it seemed as if the only thing left for him to do was find her brother and kill him. For Jonathan, it was a personal affront. The notion that someone would deliberately set out to destroy his business, simply as a means of disciplining a younger sister, represented an egotism larger than anything he'd thought possible. That destroying Lorelei Paris was incidental to a larger purpose was far more terrible than if Thomas Holmes had set out to settle some personal vendetta with Jonathan; Jonathan was too small to be a direct enemy—he was to be simply the unfortunate bystander in a dispute outside his experience.

Thomas had used the Family Influence to send out the immigration authorities. He had used the Family Influence to begin an Internal Revenue Service investigation of the firm. He had used the Family Influence to persuade two great midwestern department store chains to discontinue their business with Lorelei Paris. He had used the Family Influence to effect a cancellation of the firm's insurance policies.

"I'm surprised the son of a bitch doesn't have the CIA come down here and just kill us all," said Jonathan. If he had been slow to believe what Valerie told him, the events of the few days following the visit of the immigration authorities had more than convinced him. Valerie had been unable to reach Thomas on the phone for a full three days; his apologetic secretary explained that he was out of town and there was a problem getting messages to him while he was in transit. Her mother was correct with her on the phone, sorry for any difficulties she was having, and unable to forward any messages to Tom at all. When he called her, the three days had vanquished her.

"I quit," she told Tom. "You win. Just call off your dogs."

"I don't know what on earth you're talking about," he said. But the next day the insurance policies were reinstated, the papers of the Colombian aliens were found to be in order, the tax audit was called off, the department store chains from the Midwest replaced their standard orders.

"I don't want you to quit," said Jonathan.

"It's done, Johnny," she said. "No more 'Valerie Holmes for Lorelei Paris.' "

"No," he said. "I know you better. You're not quitting. You're not about to give in without a fight. I didn't ask you to leave." But he didn't have to. There was certainly no other way to stop the destruction of the firm. Willy and Johnny took her to lunch at Lino's, and they'd all three tried to act like they'd somehow managed to come through a war without much damage. But the damage was there. Johnny couldn't do anything but grimace into his food, unable to discover a site to focus his fury. Willy was sad, sad at being familiar with the feeling of failure. Valerie's remarks about the strength of their new season, the healthy orders coming in for the regular Lorelei Paris line, the idea that what she'd so far put together for the Valerie Holmes line could be built around another figure—perhaps an actress or a young TV newswoman— merely added to the deadly pall over their table.

Unable to fake happiness, Valerie had finally given in to their mood. "I might as well tell you," she said. "It's even worse than you think." And then she'd let fly her marvelous inspiration earlier that week, telling them of her interview with *Nouvelles* magazine, her plans for creating a totally new line built around the need for a classic, simple, sexy dress.

Jonathan immediately attacked her idea as being ten years old, an upper-class notion of what the middle class needed. "Fashion used to come from the richies down to the slobs, with every little shopgirl trying to wear the colors that the Duchess felt were right for spring. But now—now, we follow Louella, we watch what the pimps are wearing to see what's going down on Madison Avenue in the next couple of years." He began to expand on his theme; forgetting to ignore his food, he began to eat and drink, talking all the while, hitting the heel of his hand on the edge of the table to emphasize his points. It was a familiar habit of Jonathan's to try and decimate any idea that wasn't his own, as long as it dealt with the rag business, and as long as it excited him. This idea excited him, and it was Valerie's. She didn't answer any of his attack. It was a pleasure to see him diverted from the wake.

"Just a minute, Johnny," said Willy, talking for the first time.

"Shit," said Jonathan. "I know it's brilliant, Willy. It's wonderful, it's just exactly perfect. It's been a few years since I've seen any leg in this town."

Then she told them more: about the sloppy office girls, the models in jeans, the Madison Avenue housewives in diamonds and pants suits.

Willy wanted to know more, much more. What sort of dress did she have in mind? In what price range? From what materials? For what occasions? For what season? And there, in Lino's, as they all drank another bottle of wine, Valerie's idea grew; the hostile soil left by her brother proved fertile, if not to reality, then at least to imagination.

And rebellion.

There were two weeks before the Winstons' ball. Two weeks for Valerie to effect a reconciliation with her brother, to procure tickets for the four of them, to work with Willy on the sketches, to fight with Jonathan over the fabric. Two mad weeks in which Jonathan's wife came into her life, offering her suggestions, refining Willy's sketches, agreeing with her—and fighting Jonathan and Willy—about going with the simplest first, the shirtwaist, in the stark geometric print. The two samples, the statement to the press, the two amateur models at the society ball—all these were Valerie's ideas.

If she was quitting, it was only to rise again, battened by the strength of her own idea, and the fact that she would start, not her own line, but her own company. The family might attack Lorelei Paris; they wouldn't dare attack her, especially not after tonight.

"How're the shoulders?" Willy was talking to her.

"You're a genius," said Valerie.

"My wife never even needed a pattern," he said. "A manufacturer once sent us a couple of tickets to the opening of a play he was backing. She didn't have anything to wear, only about eighteen hundred dresses. I got her a piece of black crepe de chine—even then it cost fifty bucks, just for the fabric. She draped it, she stuck some pins, she cut. One-two-three. She had a knockout in less than five hours. I mean a knockout."

If she was anything like her daughter, thought Valerie, she must have made any dress look great. Willy had worked on the patterns for the shirtwaists in size nine and cut the dress for Louella. He didn't want the first pattern to be Eddy's—and Valerie's—size seven; it was bad luck for him. He stuck with his familiar production pattern size, and when he had it ironed out to Louella's satisfaction, he made two special numbers in the smaller size. The fabric was the most expensive ever used in the Lorelei Paris factory, and they'd gotten the bolts with some difficulty. The fabric salesman who'd shown it to Valerie weeks before had picked it up in Paris. It was an acrylic soft as cashmere. His own fabric house was planning to copy it, but only if the manufacturers were wild for it, wild enough to pay the twenty-five-percent increase over the cost of any other acrylic fabric in their line. Jonathan, at Valerie's insistence, paid extravagantly for four bolts of the fabric, in four different prints. She wasn't crazy about any of the prints, but liked the geometric one best; and when she saw it on Eddy, saw how it transformed the obvious late-sixties hippie-princess into a subtle young beauty, she knew that she was not about to turn back.

Even Eddy said: "I hate what it says, but I love how you say it."

If Eddy wasn't ready to join the establishment, the rest of her generation was. Her generation, and the preceding one, and the one before that too. When Jonathan's lovely wife returned to her jeans and her work shirt, she was still beautiful; but the beauty was hidden by a silly intransi-

101

gence, an unwillingness to come to grips with the changing world. The shirtwaist was not new, or overwhelming, or politically conservative, or a symptom of hard times; it was simply appropriate. It was simply to be worn when nothing more was to be said with clothes other than: Here I am, attractive, not afraid to reveal the shape of my body, and certainly not afraid to be a serious woman. If Eddy's wardrobe said, "Screw the establishment," Valerie's dress said, "I'm just a dress—if you want to know the person inside me, you'll have to get to know her without preconceived notions."

Of course, thought Valerie, none of that would be apparent tonight.

It took thirty minutes to crawl through the half mile of snow and traffic from East Sixty-fifth Street to the Plaza Hotel. Their chauffeur delivered them to a doorman's umbrella, and all four scurried through the storm into the bustling main lobby.

"My first time in the Plaza," said Willy.

"You see what you've been missing?" said Eddy. A silver comb nested in her black glossy hair, and as she turned about the lobby to show Willy precisely what she meant—silly tourists, sillier socialites dressed in flimsy, expensive clothes, perfumed and pomaded, wearing mincing grins and frightened eyes—her frail frame, wrapped in a raincoat, became the object of a hundred stares and desires. Eddy took her father's arm, allowing Valerie to take hold of Jonathan's.

"Maybe we shouldn't go upstairs," she said. "Maybe we should wait for the dinner."

"No," said Jonathan. "Willy wants to dance."

Eddy's coat was off first, and because they were still in the lobby, still mingling with ordinary guests of the hotel, people in transit, her daytime shirtwaist dress wasn't shocking. Still, when she retook Willy's tuxedoed arm, only her beauty prevented her from looking absurd.

"Somebody knows you," said Jonathan, before Valerie could take off her coat and hand it to the checker.

102

"Where?" she said, and then she saw Julie Winston, the *grande dame* Martha Winston's only daughter, striding their way. Trying to keep up was another young snob, Arthur Beach, who had already looked Jonathan up and down without recognition.

"Valerie," said Julie, and she was already pulling her forward for a quick double-peck to each corner of the mouth, breathless with anticipation.

"My God," said Arthur, "the last time I saw you must've been two years ago. Newport, I think. You were with Phillip, of course." He seemed to be struggling with some difficult memory. "His mother's. Yes, I think it was at Mrs. Raymond's."

Valerie introduced Jonathan Singer, and they looked at him with curiosity.

"Can I help you with your coat, Val?" he said roughly, and she quickly removed it and handed it to him. As Jonathan in turn handed the coat over to the checker, he could feel the shock start up behind him.

"Valerie," said Julie Winston. "What on earth—?"

Valerie returned her incredulous stare without animosity. "Oh, you mean the dress."

"There's a girl with Eric Porter upstairs," said Arthur, "and she's dressed in feathers." But he didn't think it was funny either.

"It's a long story, Julie," said Valerie. "I'll tell you about it sometime." Willy and Eddy were coming back for them, and when Julie and Arthur saw the other girl, in the same daytime shirtwaist dress, they let their mouths hang open.

"You guys ready?" said Eddy to Valerie and Jonathan.

"Sure," said Valerie. She felt like an incipient hoodlum.

"Both of you," said Julie, trying to reach across her daze for an explanation.

"Excuse us," said Jonathan, taking care to let his powerful right shoulder hit into Arthur Beach's dandruff-flecked upper arm as he steered Valerie away from them

103

and to the stairs. As they walked, the ratio of hotel guests to party-goers dropped dramatically, so that with each step closer to the reception desk, the shirtwaist dresses grew more and more inappropriate.

The man at the reception desk was a short-haired black, wearing an English school tie and a blazer. Presumably, he was to sit outside the festivities for the evening. His accent was Oxford, and he didn't look at Valerie's dress, or notice her last name as anything other than something to be checked on his typewritten list.

"Four, are you?" he said, and he looked up at Willy, Eddy, and Jonathan.

"That's right," said Valerie. Julie and Arthur had whisked past them, certainly to entertain friends and relations with the shocking news. As they walked past the reception area, a flock of photographers followed the lead of the man from *Women's Wear* and began popping their bulbs at Valerie and Eddy.

"Holmes is the blond one, right?" said one of the photographers to Jonathan. He told him yes, and they went on into the predinner dance, where everyone who'd paid two hundred and fifty dollars for the privilege of attending the Winstons' ball, and thereby aiding future research into the dire effects of some favorite disease, eagerly awaited the arrival of famous faces, whose appearance would validate the ball's success.

Jonathan recognized Robert Crowell, Sheilah Tait, Mick Damson, and with Eddy's help, Eric Porter. But aside from the presence of these society-kept artists and writers, it was simply a large, heavy-drinking, loud crowd. The clothes were a bizarre mixture of years-old *haute couture* and the very newest *prêt à porter*. There was not a single black or Oriental in the throng. The bland band beat out a monotonous fox trot, and the red-faced dancers shook their shoulders like penguins, in a hopeless attempt to convey a sense of rhythm. But Valerie saw much more than this.

"Oh, Jonathan," she said. "*Everyone* is here."

104

Willy and Eddy began to dance, and for a moment Valerie could do no more than bask in the glory of her creation. "Look how that dress *moves*," she said. "I don't like the pattern, and we've got to make an evening version, but the idea—Johnny—I really think it's going to be OK."

Jonathan spotted Julie Winston coming their way in the company of a squat basketball of a woman, her hair hammered into a solid copper helmet, her face masked with green paint. "Let's dance, pal," he said. "I think I see the Queen of the Apes." Jonathan wrapped his arms around Valerie and began to shuffle his feet. As they turned, she let out a little gasp.

"It's Mrs. Winston," she said.

"Let me lead," said Jonathan, and he danced her out to the center of the floor, to a zone of comparative refuge.

"Johnny, I have to tell you something," she said.

"I can't dance—I know it—I'm watching out for your feet."

"No," she said. "Something else."

"The ape lady's parked herself at the edge of the dance floor," said Jonathan. "Apparently, she wants to talk."

"I'm going to Paris tomorrow," said Valerie.

"Tomorrow?" He turned her around, so she could face Mrs. Winston for a while. "I thought we'd decided on a week. I can't get away before then. We've got to make the most of tonight, and that means lunches with editors, meetings with the buyers, finding out just exactly what your big brother's going to do to us this time around—"

"Johnny, I mean alone," she said.

"What?"

He was holding her closely, a real hooligan's embrace that she supposed was natural, and not deliberately meant to assault her body. Willy smiled at her over his daughter's head, and she returned the smile, sick with an envy that she despised. All the talk of his wife had never prepared her for Eddy. She'd expected someone bigger, closer to his own size, with a sharp tongue. Perhaps she might have been pretty, but never in the way Jonathan talked of her—certainly not in the luminosity of her features. She walked lightly, as if afraid to ruffle her innards. And she was a girl who'd been told all her life she was beautiful; her confidence was quiet, self-effacing, almost apologetic for the heads that would surely turn at her entrance. Whatever terrible problems there had been between them in the past, Valerie could see no evidence of a strain in Eddy's and Jonathan's relationship. If she was at all "odd" in the way he sometimes chose to speak of her, it was an oddness associated with her art, her silence. If a little distant, she'd certainly been polite, helpful with sketching the dresses, agreeing to appear in one of the two models, alongside Valerie. Valerie wondered if anything could shake the smooth beatitude of Eddy's face—if she were to go up to her right now and tell her that she loved her husband, that she wanted him.

"I want to go by myself," said Valerie.

"But if you wait a few days, we can go together."

"That's just why I'm going tomorrow." He still didn't get it, so she sucked in her breath, waited for the music to stop, then whispered as he relaxed his embrace, "I don't want to fall in love with a married Jewish businessman."

She spoke so evenly that Jonathan had to look into her eyes, his hand catching her chin, to check the meaning of her words. There it was, all right. She was ready, his for the taking.

Whatever desire he'd nurtured for her suddenly vanished. She was no longer elusive, forbidden flesh; she was simply another too-young girl, ignorant of him and his world. "Don't worry," he said. "I'm not easy to fall in love with. It'll never happen."

"Johnny," she said, but he pressed her hand for silence as Willy approached to change partners for the next dance. Jonathan found Eddy looking out the window at the falling snow.

"You want to dance?"

"No," she said.

106

She looked happy, and he asked, "Miss smoking?"

"Oh, no, not now," she said, and she turned to face him, eyes bright, so happy, she was at the verge of tears.

"It's very pretty," he said, but he knew what he said or felt about the storm couldn't approximate what his wife experienced at the window; but he enjoyed the reflection of what she felt, and threw his arm about her shoulders and looked, not at the snow, but at the whirling figures of the fancy ball mirrored in the window glass. He wondered which of the figures might be Thomas Holmes, and he wondered if this dress on Eddy would be the beginning of something enormous, grand, something big enough to lift him high above these unattractive, unhappy people whom too many of the world envied and loathed.

"You're thinking about business," said Eddy.

"What? No—I'm looking at the snow."

But she was smiling. "It's cool, Jonathan," she said, "you and business. I can feel the excitement running through you." And she pulled his head down to hers for a lingering kiss, ignoring the commotion at the edge of the dance floor. But Jonathan wasn't oblivious. He waited for the kiss to end before pulling his neck back, swiveling about, and going for the source of the commotion.

"Eddy," he said, "come on, it's Willy." And she followed him then, turning from the window and taking quick little steps on her new high-heeled pumps, bought solely to enhance the appearance of the dress. A pale young man in an old limp tuxedo stood within a circle of inquisitive party-goers, wagging his finger at Willy Schwartz, while Valerie stood to one side, trying without much success to intervene.

"My name isn't Singer, that's first of all," Willy was saying.

"*This* is Mr. Singer," said Valerie as Jonathan pushed through the knot of people. "And that's—" Valerie said this with relief—"that's Mrs. Singer with him."

Thomas Holmes turned first to Jonathan, then to Eddy; his eyes were too angry to register the additional shock of her beauty, or the more significant shock of seeing her wearing the same dress as his sister. "I suggest," said Thomas Holmes, "I suggest we all go downstairs and have a talk."

Jonathan had been hoping for something else. He'd been prepared for a longer evening. First the dancing, the drinking, the casual introductions, the first shock of Mrs. Holmes seeing her daughter in the presence of her former business associates, dressed for the day in an acrylic shirtwaist. Then the sit-down dinner. Mrs. Holmes and escort, and Thomas Holmes and escort, and Valerie Holmes and Willy Schwartz and Mr. and Mrs. Jonathan Singer, all at the same table, sipping nonvintage French champagne, while all the time Valerie would spin her tale.

"You have no right to act like this, Thomas," said Valerie. "These are my friends."

"First time I've ever seen them," said Thomas.

"I'm happy to go downstairs, Val," said Jonathan. Everything was getting faster now, going the too-easy downhill route that invites speeding, disaster. Thomas had interrupted Valerie and Willy in the middle of their dance, had demanded to know what Valerie meant by "this stunt," referring to her dress, to her choice of escorts. He presumed that this "gentleman" was the "famous Mr. Singer." Jonathan had missed most of this, but he'd seen the stung look on Willy's face. Thomas Holmes would get away with none of it. Jonathan could feel the future in the lusting of his clenched fists. He smiled easily at the grotesque Mrs. Winston, wrapped Eddy's arm in his, and followed Thomas and Valerie through the tight knots of chattering couples, with Willy Schwartz bringing up the rear. As they began to exit from the Terrace Room, two photographers came their way. One of them had been tipped off by Jonathan earlier in the day, and he dropped to one knee as Jonathan maneuvered Eddy around to Valerie's free side.

"OK, girls," said Jonathan. "Free publicity."

Valerie turned to Eddy, and the two smiled into the air

108

over each other's heads as the photographers shot their prey. Thomas didn't know where to srike—at the photographers or at Jonathan. Tomorrow he'd read, if he took the trouble to search the trades:

Mrs. Margaret Winston's oh so social ball was the scene of an unusual debut last night: Valerie Holmes, the half-million-dollar deb, every fortune hunter's favorite divorcée, took one giant step toward INDEPENDENCE, when, flouting the traditional family low profile, she chose to announce the creation of her new dress company, Valerie Holmes, Inc., by showing up at the ball in one of her first creations. Next to Ms. Holmes is one of her designers, doubling, like her, as instant mannequin. Ms. Holmes has been working quietly at 1407 Broadway for one of SA's smaller manufacturers, just to get her silver-slipper feet wet. Rumour has it that the Holmes family takes a sour view of the heiress dabbling in trade, though Mother, Mrs. Margaret ("Happy") Holmes, is a well-known U.S. designer-booster. Valerie Holmes, Inc., will be designing and manufacturing here, from European fabric. The line will be shown sometime in the spring.

"Keep walking," said Thomas to Valerie. "What are you doing, *posing* for that man?" He turned to Eddy and snapped at her: "Get away from here!"

"Thomas," said Valerie, "this woman is my friend, and she's wearing my dress. If you'd think for a minute, you might realize that I want to be photographed, that I want us both to be photographed."

"So this isn't over," said Thomas. "You've already progressed to going back on your word."

"No, not at all," said Valerie. "And if you'll have the courtesy to listen to me, I'll be more than happy to explain." Eddy dropped back from brother and sister, and took hold of her husband's arm.

"Take it easy," she said.

"I'm easy," said Jonathan. "Now he's managed to insult father-in-law and wife." They walked quickly through the ever-thickening crowds of people about the reception desk; the snow had made them late, but it seemed everyone was determined to show up. Valerie stopped Thomas at the foot of the steps to the lobby, and Jonathan watched as brother and sister approached a pretty blond woman who looked not a bit older than forty years old.

"This is my mother," Valerie said, as Mr. and Mrs. Singer and Willy Schwartz joined the Holmeses. Mrs. Holmes's mouth was open, and she was nodding her head faintly. Jonathan smelled her Bal à Versailles, his favorite perfume, and one that he'd always associated with youth. Mrs. Holmes was looking at Valerie's dress and saying something about the fact that there was a ball going on; and then her eyes riveted on Eddy.

"This is part of a scheme, no doubt," she said to Valerie.

Thomas asked her to join them in the Oak Room, but she was waiting for the return of her escort, Lord Clayton, the British tabloid king. Their stopping had allowed a fresh flock of photographers to group strategically about them, getting shots of mother and daughter together, of Eddy alone, of Thomas raising his fist into the lens, of Mrs. Holmes smoothing her hair and posing with bored, regal eyes. Jonathan allowed Thomas to pick up the pace, leaving Mrs. Holmes behind. Soon he found himself looking across a comfortable table at Thomas Holmes in a nearly deserted Oak Room. Drinks were ordered and brought. The snow continued to fall. Jonathan drummed four fingers of his right hand on the tabletop. Valerie didn't touch her drink. Thomas's cummerbund was graying with age; Jonathan always wore a vest with his tuxedo. Eddy stopped listening to Valerie's explanation before she'd reached the second sentence; there was too much defense in it, too much of a tone of begging to be understood.

110

"Let me get this straight," said Thomas to his sister. "You expect me to believe that you've quit your association with this man, only to go into business for yourself."

"I have a name," said Jonathan.

"Pardon?"

"It's not polite to call me 'this man.' I don't like how it sounds."

"I see," said Thomas.

"Thomas," said Valerie, "I'm only telling you the truth. You were against having the Holmes name exploited by a company you didn't know anything about—"

"What do you mean I didn't know anything about?" said Thomas, smiling. "I know a great deal about this man's company."

"Excuse me," said Eddy, getting out of her seat. "I can't listen to this." Jonathan got up and walked with her to the door. "I want you to stay," she said. "This part isn't for me. I did my part, didn't I?"

"Yes," said Jonathan.

"Can I go home in the limousine? I'd like to go home in the limousine all by myself."

"Of course you can."

They retrieved Eddy's coat and sent a doorman off after their limousine. "This is your thing," she said.

"What is?"

"This night. What's happening. The fight. The chance for big money."

"That's not all there is to me either," he said.

"I'm not criticizing," she said.

"Did you like dancing with Willy?"

"Yes," she said. "Jonathan, I'm going to be working tonight."

"OK."

"It's not that I'm not interested," she said. "But tonight, the snow, the way that Valerie looks at you, the way you talk to her brother—it's all for you, and I don't want to interfere with it." He knew better than to try and contradict her. She wanted only to follow her true in-

111

stincts, and for him to do the same. While he was always searching for compromise, for a means to draw the two of them into the same orbit, she was always looking for separate stars, different destinies. Tonight she'd be shut up in her studio, trying to paint, or simply thinking about it, smoking cigarette after cigarette on the bay window's padded seat. She was forced into this desire for activity in her own sphere simply because of the excess of energy in his. She could not allow his life to overwhelm hers, because what was true for him was not true for her. "I know you don't want to come home tonight," she said.

"I do," he said, speaking truly. "To come home to you."

"No, Jonathan that's not true," she said, and for a moment the whole perfect length of nights and days since her return from San Francisco threatened to skid to a halt. It was maddening to be in love with a woman whose jealousy was inverted, twisted around to a desire for her husband to pursue every fleeting notion of infidelity that entered his head—if only to remain true to his wife in the sense of wanting her along with every other desire, rather than the alternative of a shut-up world of forbidden lusts. "I want you to have your night," she said. "The way you want it to be, not the way you think I'd want it to be." Eddy's eyes were looking past him, closed to argument, thinking only of her own night, her own work, the long stretch of silent time. He kissed her cheek, handed her over to the doorman, and walked slowly back to the Oak Room.

Mrs. Holmes and her escort—bald, trim, hook-nosed Lord Clayton—had joined the table, and when Jonathan approached, Lord Clayton got to his feet. "What do I call you?" said Jonathan. "Not your lordship, I hope."

"Just nod your head in my direction and clear your throat when you want to speak," he said.

"Your wife is feeling well, I hope?" said Mrs. Holmes. Then she added something about Eddy's beauty and apologized for seeming abrupt before on the steps. Valer-

112

ie's explanation—or Lord Clayton's presence—had done something to change the wind speed.

"I take it then," said Jonathan, "that your daughter's plans meet with your approval, Mrs. Holmes?"

"Wait a minute," said Thomas. "You're jumping."

Jonathan just looked at him—the careless look of a bully who doesn't even need to take the measure of the man he's about to throttle.

"Mother likes the fact that I'm going to be in Paris, and staying with some friends of the family, and getting a chance to meet some designers that she knows very well—"

"We understand that there's no possibility of your joining my sister in Paris," Thomas interrupted her, "due to the extent of your work here in New York."

"Maybe," said Jonathan.

Willy gave him a "Do you have to always be an asshole?" look.

"I've already told you that he won't be coming," said Valerie. "We don't have to get him to sign a paper, do we? The company's in my own name, isn't it? I did what you asked me. I dropped my association with Lorelei Paris, and I've started on my own."

"I didn't ask you to start on your own," said Thomas.

"You should be proud of me."

"I'm not," said Thomas.

Lord Clayton interrupted. "My dear," he said, "I'll be in Paris in three weeks' time. I'll call you, if I may? See how things are going? Maybe we can talk about some newspaper coverage?"

"Wonderful," said Valerie.

"You don't want to get involved with a man like this," said Mrs. Holmes, about Lord Clayton. But then she wanted to hear about everything: about the idea for the shirtwaists; about the fact that the finest fabrics were still more available in France and Italy than they were in New York, especially for small purchases; about the editor of *Nouvelles* magazine; about her plans to break into *Vogue*

113

and *Bazaar* and *Town & Country*. Thomas Holmes let his eyes drift from his mother's happily engrossed face to the empty glass in his hands. Valerie had been right, of course. If her mother could see her daughter's new venture as something to be proud of, something to gain her a few extra social points, Thomas's chagrin at having a sister involved in a world inhabited by climbers, hoodlums, and homosexuals could be easily overridden.

It irked Jonathan that Valerie had apparently so flagrantly dismissed the need for his presence in Paris. Did she really think that she could find and purchase all that fabric alone? He remembered with annoyance her too-easy acceptance of their new business relationship: a paper charade, wherein Jonathan was now working for her, instead of the other way around—at least as far as Valerie Holmes, Inc., was concerned. It was a charade because Lorelei was to handle all of Valerie Holmes, Inc.'s, manufacturing, and because Valerie's silent partner in her company was Jonathan Singer. Still, Valerie's acceptance of the arrangement had been signaled by a pleased little smile, a sudden confidence. No, thought Jonathan, he didn't mind the charade of working for her, as long as she'd take care to remember that, compared to him, she knew *nothing*. If *he* thought she could do the job in Paris alone, that would be one thing. But there was no way that she could tell him where he had to be, what he had to do. After all was said and done, she was still a twenty-three-year-old princess, with no experience, and that was what he planned to tell her at the very first opportunity.

"Excuse me, Mother, Lord Clayton," said Thomas abruptly, and he got out of his seat so quickly that the waiter who'd rushed over to help pull out his chair was sent sprawling over it and made an undignified landing on the carpeted floor.

"I wish you'd speak to him, Mother," said Valerie.

"Don't worry, don't worry," said Mrs. Holmes. "I won't let your brother do anything nasty this time. Even if

I have to speak to your father."

"Willy," said Jonathan, "you dance with Val. Eddy's gone home. I'll be back in a while."

They were all getting to their feet now, prepared to face the figures at the ball, bolstered by the knowledge that Valerie's dress was not a sin, but an object of conversation, a mark of achievement. Jonathan left a large bill with their waiter and walked very quickly out to the lobby.

It was an easy guess that Thomas wouldn't be coming down to the dinner, not with Valerie's guests at the same table. Jonathan tried to breathe easier now, to remember how Valerie had smiled at him—a thin, secret smile of triumph—before he'd scrammed out after her brother (only she didn't know that, of course). Perhaps, by her strange code of ethics, Thomas had done nothing for which he must be repaid. After all, she was being allowed to go to Paris, to keep her limousine privileges, to dance with Willy Schwartz at the Winstons' ball. What was all that nonsense about not wanting to fall in love with a married Jewish businessman anyway, but a flattering way of telling him to stay put in New York? Jonathan looked around. The son of a bitch wasn't in the lobby, and he wasn't on the Fifty-ninth Street side, buying a cigar—only another clod, in another faded tuxedo.

The man at the reservation desk looked up at him, as if he had been expecting him all along. Jonathan took one last look down the long north corridor, then retreated to the desk, opening his wallet, his hand full of credit cards. "I don't think we're going to fight the storm," said Jonathan.

"Yes sir, Mr. Singer. A room for you and your wife?"

"Yes. A suite. And I'd like some flowers sent up, and some champagne." And then, before the key was even in Jonathan's hand, before Valerie had been found and seduced. Thomas Holmes came out of an elevator, his eyes on the floor. Jonathan took the key and followed the brother out for a breath of air in the snowy night.

"Now I suppose you want to beat me up?" said Thomas

Holmes as he turned to face Jonathan on Central Park South.

"Let's cross the street," said Jonathan.

"All right," said Thomas Holmes, suddenly full of pre-school courage, remembering the boxing lessons that had plagued his childhood in California. There was little traffic as they skipped and slid across the street, then entered the snowy shadows flanking the park. Jonathan, impervious to the cold, noted with pleasure his adversary's involuntary shivers and runny nose.

"This isn't for what you did to my business," said Jonathan.

"No?" Thomas had squared himself up against the stone wall that girded the park and was prepared to tuck his chin and lead with his left.

"This is for the way you insulted my wife," said Jonathan, and he didn't bother to feint, just let the right fly into the side of Thomas Holmes's head, then battered the falling face with a double jabbing of his left. At the last moment, he decided not to let the pale man's chin bounce off his extended knee—he didn't really want to break any bones or teeth, and besides, Thomas Holmes was no longer listening to the lessons he was giving. Jonathan wrapped the light man's arm about his neck and carried him quickly back across the street. In the lineup of limousines, he found the driver who'd just carried Eddy home, and now he gave him a graver burden.

"This is Thomas Holmes," said Jonathan. "You know where he lives?"

"Yes, sir!" He was already cradling the master in his own arms, letting his nose bleed on the collar of his uniform, placing him gently on the cold leather cushions of the passenger compartment.

"Well, take the schmuck home," said Jonathan.

Now there would be dancing and drinking and eating, plans would be spun, victories imagined. Mrs. Holmes would be flattered; Willy would dance; Lord Clayton would beg to be called by his first name; Eddy, at home,

116

would dream. Jonathan walked out of the snow, into the Plaza. Eddy was right, he realized. It was his night, and he didn't want to go home. When he caught sight of Valerie Holmes, lifting a glass to her lips at a far table, he felt a thrusting of desire that was as intense as it was expected. In a night of victories, he must have her too.

Part Two

Paris

9

This is how Jonathan made love to her:

"How do you like it?" he said, exhibiting the large sitting room, the Dom Pérignon in a silver ice bucket on the low table before the couch.

"Can we look at the snow?" she said.

"Take off your raincoat."

"My raincoat?" She laughed once—a bright, hollow laugh. "I don't remember putting it on."

"Here," he said, and he came up to her at the window and helped her, with surprising gentleness, out of the coat. The glass was cold on her forehead as she peered out at the park from the high floor. She felt the warm weight of his hands take hold of her neck, and this touch, joined with the drifting of snowflakes into the window, the cracking of ice about the cold bottle of champagne, and the late-night music of a too-loud radio filtering through from some other room in the hotel, all combined to expand the moment, to enlarge and suspend it, to reserve a silent space for it in her memory of nameless times, ineffable feelings.

"It's late," she said, or something equally foolish, for his hands had turned her head to his, and his eyes were open wide, and his lips moved closer, for after all she had driven with him in the limousine through the snow in the dead of night, holding hands while the chauffeur dropped Willy off in Queens, and had returned, not to her apartment nor to his, but back to the Plaza, where he told her very simply that he'd reserved a suite for the night, and now his body was against hers, no longer in her imagination, but with her shut eyes and open mouth, her shoulders pressed against the window glass, one foot out of its pump, her toes driving into the carpet for some flimsy support.

"That's the first time I've ever kissed you," he said, and she looked at him, dark and confident, his black bow tie askew and absurd against the sensual background of his muscular frame. A shock of sexual excitement began to run through her now, an excitement at the inevitability of what was to unfold. She had not made love since the separation from Phillip more than two years ago, and it bothered her that the lovemaking had not proved to be something very much missed. There were times when she felt herself to be asexual—or, worse, a deviate whose particular fancy had not yet been discovered. But if she had not understood her attraction to Jonathan in the weeks of working with him, she understood it now; it was not a case of admiration, or a happy pull to a kindred soul. He was different from her concept of a romantic man in almost every way—coarse, bullying, undereducated, with little or no interest in art, literature, in anything save business, his business. Yet she fancied herself falling in love with him; and she was thrilled finally to be allowed to believe that this love was predicated on sexual desire—a desire to possess and be possessed by this dark, handsome man, whose notion of romance was a hotel suite, flowers, and a bottle of champagne. What ran through her body now was the sure current of lust, and she was glad to feel it, glad to understand that it was something that might not be denied her, like too many other aspects of the ordinary world.

"Valerie Holmes," he said, and his hand was on her backside, and on her belly, and on her breasts. They had moved to the couch, and he wasn't smiling, and so she leaned forward and tore off his tie and opened his stiff blue shirt. And again he said her name: "Valerie Holmes." And he thought that it wouldn't be half as much fun if she weren't Valerie Holmes, weren't the girl and the

122

family and the fortune and the name, and he kicked off his shoes, and bent low to remove her other pump, and picked up her legs and placed them across his lap, and, as she nuzzled closer, her dress riding high up her thighs, he popped the champagne cork clear across the room and poured the wine sloppily into chilled glasses. There was no toast. They drank, and then he refilled their glasses, and they drank again, and there was talk about her legs, laughter about her dress, and there was enough champagne left for a half glass more for each of them, enough to set the room and the night and the beating of his heart and the flash of red flowers and the flushing of her face into a twirling, mad consonance.

"Stand up," he said.

He didn't help her, and she got shakily to her feet, feeling the smudged mascara about her right eye. "I'm cold," she said.

"Come closer," he said, and she moved her knees up against the couch, and he cupped his hand under her dress and took hold of the waistband of her panty hose and began to pull it down, while she awkwardly tried to retain her balance.

"Wait," she said, and she started to reach her hands under her dress to help him, but he told her to stop.

"Let me," he said.

She remained as still as possible, and he pulled the panty hose down to her ankles, and then, slowly, laboriously, he pulled it off each leg, as she leaned tipsily against him, her hands on his shoulders.

"Now turn around."

She did as he asked, and immediately his hands ran slowly up the back of her legs under the dress, caressing her backside, easing up to her back, where they unhooked her bra and slid if off her little breasts. Now that she was naked under the dress, he bent low to find her pumps, and he put them back on her feet, while she stood silently, alternately on each foot, allowing herself to be shod like some complaisant ghost in a silent dream.

123

Jonathan got up, tall, smiling, sharing the secret of her nakedness. He opened the shirtwaist's buttons, all the way to her waist; then he put a rose in her hair.

"I like the dress," he said.

He held her closely, and they began to dance in slow awkward circles, her hands reaching for his chest, his waist, the hard line of his jaw. They danced until the room began to wobble in a haze of exhaustion and desire, until behind their shut eyes they shared the same desire, the same pointed dream. She remembered waking once in the bed, in the early morning light, and, without thinking, turning to him, arousing him while he still slept, rubbing her lips along his chest, drawing her knee across his groin, kissing him softly back to a demi-consciousness, and then straddling him, placing him inside her without even being sure he was aware of their lovemaking, and finally driving both of them back to ecstasy, and to a sleep that would last into the early afternoon.

"Where the hell am I?" she said only half-seriously when she finally woke and remembered that he hadn't shown her the bedroom of the suite until she was too far gone to notice it. Jonathan came out of the bathroom, wet from his shower, his freshly washed hair slicked back from his rested face.

"Just a minute," he said, and he ran into the adjacent sitting room, the naked muscles of his back reminding her of what they'd been to each other the night before, what bridge of intimacy they'd crossed, irrevocably. She eased herself up against the headboard as Jonathan returned in triumph, holding aloft her dress. "Look at this," he was saying, "look at this. Not a wrinkle—it looks just as good as when you first put it on."

But she wasn't responding to this enthusiasm. The smell of coffee from the next room prompted her to take the painful steps from bed to bathroom. "Oh, Jesus," she said, in response to seeing the now-angry makeup she'd left on the night before—a long, long-time ago. Suddenly, she was laughing, laughing so hard that Jonathan crossed

124

through the bedroom and into the bathroom to find out if she was all right. "It's only that I just remembered," she said.

"Oh," he said, smiling.

"I mean—about the dress."

"The dress," he said. And then he smiled too, because of course he hadn't forgotten how they'd made love the first time, in search of a symbol, too tired to stand up, too drunk to do anything but allow themselves the luxury of this, their only point in common. "And still no wrinkles," he added. "No spots either."

They didn't leave the Plaza till nearly four o'clock in the afternoon, and then they separated, Valerie rushing about to find her passport, pack a suitcase, gather the sketches (some, the best, by Eddy) and her credit cards, call her mother, call her father's secretary (to forward her fond goodbyes), wait for the swift messenger from Jericho Travel to drop off her plane tickets, and then finally sitting in the quiet limousine, crawling hopelessly through traffic all the way to Kennedy Airport. And if she'd expected him to show up at the airport, the expectation didn't reveal itself in her joyous look of surprise when she spotted him, slouched against the Air France counter, waiting for her. He swept her into his arms as if they had not had simply an evening of drunken sex, but had begun an affair. Valerie was idiotically glad. She felt herself perfectly stupid under the spell of his handsome figure, flamboyant gestures, booming voice carrying his message of love

"Last night I thought it was Valerie Holmes, I told you that, but now it's still Valerie Holmes—I'm not making any sense—I mean that I meant I figured I wanted you because I wanted to sleep with the Princess of the Goyim, if you know what I mean, Holmes this and Holmes that. Here, I brought you something. You told me you get scared shitless on planes."

She took a pill from the palm of his hand and swallowed it then and there, without water. "You love me?" he asked.

"I don't know," she said.

"Maybe it's the pill—it takes a while to work," he said slyly. "Now where the hell did I put this thing?" Jonathan rummaged in the pocket of his leather sport jacket, finally coming up with a small lumpy object wrapped in gift paper. "Here," he said.

"Jonathan," she began, ready to be touched by any gift. As with a lot of the very, very rich, she almost never received gifts from outside the family. Everyone was scared off by what the Holmeses already possessed.

"Wait," he said, pressing it into her hand. "I want you to open it on the plane."

"Johnny—"

"Like in the movies."

"This feels like—" she said. "Johnny, you didn't get me jewelry."

"On the plane. That's when you find out. Kiss me."

"I do love you," she said.

"That's how easy it is, huh? A little gift wrapping?"

Maybe it was, she thought. They'd laughed then, and remembering the moment, Valerie laughed again two hours later, laughed out loud in the closed confines of the Air France first-class section, on the 9.00 P.M. flight to Paris. Dinner was served, and the Valium Jonathan had given her at the airport relaxed her enough to get through the takeoff, and the overly reassuring smiles of the stewardesses. (Had her mother phoned Air France with special instructions: Watch out, she flies bad?) For a moment, in the darkness of the cabin, she thought she must have actually been sleeping.

But of course, she never slept on planes.

Valerie conjured up Jonathan.

She admitted that she would have liked to be with him right then, that second, on a beach, or in a cheap cabaret, or in the tiny office at Lorelei, naked under her proper clothes. But Jonathan's image started violently when a man sleeping two seats behind her let out a sudden terrible cough, and, as she turned around automatically in

126

the dark of the cabin, she felt the still-secret gift rattle in her pocket.

She flicked on her overhead light and opened the paper. Wrapped in tissue was a long diamond bracelet, and it took her a full five minutes to realize why it was too big for her wrist—it was an ankle bracelet. A diamond ankle bracelet. Oh, my God. She couldn't imagine what it cost; or, knowing that, imagine what the figure meant to Jonathan Singer. But the idea. Rushing home to shave, change, talk to his wife, check in with Willy, find a taxi, find a jeweler, find *this*. He'd told her about his high school, his days of athletic glory, his first girl friend—too quiet to be a cheerleader, too shy to fit in with his friends. She wondered if he'd given her one of these, in silver plate, with his name (JOHNNY) engraved on its flat surface.

Very touched, Valerie Holmes quickly unfastened the clasp and bent low to place it around her right ankle. With her gray high heeled shoes, black pants, and white silk shirt, this touch of the gun moll was eminently decadent, and she sat back in her seat, very pleased with her gift, and herself for wearing it.

Then the plane shuddered.

Turbulence, thought Valerie, remembering that she'd taken the Valium, that she'd slept, that they were certainly almost there, that if anything was the least bit wrong the seat-belt light would flash on, and the captain would make an announcement at once, in two languages, very calmly.

This time the plane seemed to stop suddenly in midair, and, try as she might, all she could think of was cinema images, long fuselages erupting in flames of destruction. Johnny, she thought, trying to lose herself in the simple syllables, Johnny, Johnny, Johnny. But the plane truly seemed to have slowed down. Surely it wasn't her imagination—God, let it be her imagination—that the great big hunk of metal in the sky was losing momentum, losing power, maybe out of fuel, maybe with malfunctioning engines.

Maybe if I think about the ankle bracelet, she thought. Imagine a high school with Johnny at seventeen, his hair greased and swooped back over each ear in a "duck's ass." Bump, shudder. "Jesus," she said out loud and looked round for signs of life in the other passengers. How could all these sons of bitches just lie there and sleep?

Another bump, and then it was official. First the safety-belt lights went on, and then, just as the mechanical clunk signifying the beginning of an announcement sounded, the light to extinguish cigarettes went on too. Oh God, oh God, she thought. ". . . some minor turbulence . . . belts . . . and . . . worried about . . . thank you . . ." said a young woman's voice, filled with boredom, in two languages.

Why hadn't the captain spoken?

Not important enough for him to break his reserve? Or was he perhaps too busy at the controls, fighting the disaster? Or was something wrong with *him*? Had the captain of this jet suddenly had a heart attack, and the copilot gone blind?

She knew one thing. She'd better put a stop to this at once or she was going to make a god-awful fool of herself. But, still, she had to know one thing, one simple, blessed thing.

Who were all those sons of bitches behind her in the first-class cabin who were still slumped in their seats, fast asleep? Who the hell did they think they were anyway? If only they were all awake and screaming. Or just awake, period. How the hell was she supposed to know if she was overreacting again, like that terrible fit of near-hysteria on the flight to Los Angeles over last Christmas. Maybe the stewardesses were all drunk, the pilot and copilot dead, and she alone of all the passengers knew the terrible truth:

They were on the way down, down.

"Are you all right, Miss Holmes?"

"What? What did you say? What did you call me?"

The tall man in the gray flannel suit sat down next to her and smiled. "I didn't say hello earlier because I know how some people like to have their flights all to themselves. I'm like that myself, actually."

She knew this man, of course—very handsome, a slight affectation to his American accent, very pretty mouth—but for God's sake, didn't he feel *that bump*?

"Hugh Robertson, we met at Mrs. Michon's office," he said.

"Is something wrong with this plane?" she said.

"No, no, not at all, Miss Holmes." He smiled again—the doctor reassuring his patient. "I was afraid you might be—"

The plane, she was sure, let out a flash of light. She could see that clearly through her window. Either that or she was completely mad.

". . . all the symptoms," he was saying. "The twisted head, the almost getting out of your seat, the hands on the ceiling—"

"What?"

"If I'm wrong, please do forgive me, my dear," he said. "But if I made a mistake, it was an honest one."

"What are you talking about?"

"I was saying that I thought you might perhaps be a bit worried about the turbulence."

"You feel it too?"

"Yes, certainly, but—"

"*Why don't they do something? Please, why doesn't it stop?*"

"It'll stop," he said, and the smile had gone out of his face. This wasn't simply a pat-on-the-hand job. Real hysterics round the corner. His voice was now dull and authoritative: "Listen. Stop it."

"What?" she said, angrily, but her eyes had turned away from the window, and its flashes of light against black.

"There's absolutely nothing wrong with this flight. There's a minor bit of air turbulence. Quite minor. I know because I fly all the time, and this is nothing. Absolutely insignificant."

129

"What—" said Valerie, trying to enunciate clearly, feeling her throat constrict, her tongue thicken, like the twin symptoms of some fearful ailment— "What are you doing here?"

"I expect much the same thing as you," he said. "Flying to Paris."

If I don't concentrate, she thought, I will never understand what this man is talking about. She knew exactly who he was, a handsome fag designer, famous and chic, a friend of her mother's, and trying to make her believe that this plane wasn't about to burst into flames. "Flying to Paris," she repeated, and then there were those flashes again, flashes and a double bump, and she couldn't keep it to herself anymore, not for another second.

"Jesus Christ, we're on fire," she said.

"Miss Holmes—"

"Look," she said, and she grabbed the lovely flannel sleeve of his jacket and pulled him towards her window, and there were more flashes, yellow and red, and a stewardess walking by was suddenly jostled by the movement of the plane, and Valerie thought for sure that she'd fall, fall head over heels, and at once the plane would duplicate her movements, twisting and turning and screaming through black space.

"It's all right," Hugh Robertson was saying. "She's just a bit upset by the turbulence."

Someone was telling her to put her head down between her knees. There were smiles, calm voices, hopelessly faked. First the stewardess, then Hugh, looked at the flashes, and both explained that it was lightning, that they were nearing Paris in a little thunderstorm.

The seat-belt sign flickered, perhaps the electrical system was about to go too; all she knew was that something was rising in her gorge, and she swallowed and shut her eyes, and kept her head down, and then she didn't care. What did it matter if she threw up when the whole plane was going down, and they'd all be covered by fire and explosion?

The voices seemed to cease for a space of time. Someone applied a wet cloth to her head, and she heard her name—*Miss Holmes, Miss Holmes*—and there was an airsick bag removed, and a gentle pressure at her shoulders to sit back, to sit up and sit back and be brave.

"Now, it's just another minute, my dear," said Hugh Roberston, looking at her with the same easy smile, his handsome club tie perfectly knotted, not a lock of hair out of place, not a bead of sweat on his ageless brow. Where was she, and what the hell was happening? "Just the landing," he said. "Sit tight."

She looked at the long aristocratic fingers on his right hand as he patted her double-clenched fists and finally gripped them. Valerie remembered the polish on his nails—clear polish, on perfect half moons. He leaned back with a barely perceptible sigh. If she wasn't dead and dreaming, she'd once again made a fool of herself on a plane, throwing up, screaming, the whole works. Oh, my God, she thought, hearing the wheels emerge from the wings, forgetting everything but the need to think of the ground, the car into the city, the lights of Paris, the bath at the hotel. Landing knocked the wind out of her. A sudden enormous release of air, coupled with the instantaneous realization that her worst fears of self-embarrassment had been realized, left her pale and breathless, even as the lovely first-class stewardess rushed back to her side, to see how she'd made out with the landing.

"I'm terribly, terribly sorry," said Valerie.

"Please," said Hugh Robertson. "Don't mention it." He asked her whether she was being met and then offered her a ride into the city. She walked with him through the famous transparent tunnels of Charles de Gaulle Airport, now swept by rain, and allowed him to take charge of her suitcase, and shepherd her through customs, and outside, to the rainy Paris morning.

"There's Milt now," he said, and she saw the designer wave to a strikingly handsome young man, with long bleached blond hair, wearing a silk scarf outside his shirt, flowing over the front of his blazer. Hugh put down the bags and stood still as Milton Brommel ran up to embrace him, kissing him on both cheeks, French style. As Hugh made the introductions, a small, silent chauffeur whisked away the bags and opened the rear door to a black Mercedes 600. Milton, she saw, wore makeup, and did nothing to disguise the fact that he was pretty, flighty, flirtatiously gay.

"Wait a minute," he said. "That's fabulous. I love it. I think it's perfect, I think it's wonderful, I think it's divine."

"What?" said Valerie, as meekly as possible. The compliments were aimed her way, and if Milton Brommel was not as famous as Hugh Robertson, he was still a stellar attraction in the world of fashion. The chauffeur remained poised at the open door. Hugh waited for Milt's answer.

"The bracelet," he said. "Look, Hugh, an ankle bracelet! Could you just die?"

"Where to?" said Hugh once they were inside, and he forwarded Valerie's destination—the Ritz—to the chauffeur and settled back for a comfortable talk. Valerie didn't know quite where to look. She was flanked by the two of them, and, as she followed their talk, she felt as if she were watching a tennis match. Hugh's scent was subtle, something masculine and soapy, but Milt's was familiar— he was wearing Calandre, the full-strength perfume. After a while, she stopped looking at their pretty faces and just concentrated on the wet road to the city, trying not to fall asleep.

"Oh, it was a bit bumpy," Hugh was saying.

"Oh, Gawd, glad I missed that one. Next trip we sail, honey."

"Miss Holmes, if you'd like to close your eyes for a while and try to catch a few winks, that's fine with us."

"I'll guard your ankle," said Milt, thrusting a dramatic hand through his long blond hair, "with my life."

"No, I'm fine," said Valerie. "Just looking forward to

132

my bath."

"We didn't really get a chance to exchange the essential small talk on the plane," Hugh said to Milt. To Valerie he said, "Do you have any idea how long you'll be staying in town?"

"Several weeks. I'm not quite sure."

"Then you must come for dinner," said Milt, and she saw Hugh nod his approval. "We don't cook but we have a little old Portuguese lady who loves to feed our prettiest friends. And she's one of those people who don't discriminate against women." Milt laughed at his own joke, then went on: "And believe me, my dear, neither do we."

Valerie didn't laugh at this, feeling herself being baited, suspecting that the two men were homosexuals of two very distinct species. At the Ritz, Milt said goodbye to her with a bob of his head and kissed his own fingertips to punctuate his regard.

"I'll be right back," said Hugh to Milt. And before Milt could offer to join them, Hugh had followed her out of the car, and the chauffeur had closed the door.

"I just want to thank you again," said Valerie.

"Miss Holmes—"

"Not just for the ride, I'm talking about the plane. If you hadn't been there—I don't know what I would've done. Now please, you don't have to take me inside—"

But he did, following her into the famous lobby, turning his head away from a guest who seemed to have recognized him. "Listen please, Miss Holmes, I just want to apologize."

"Apologize?"

"For my friend. He's not always so piggishly rude, and I hope you'll forgive him for his behavior, and myself for letting you in for it."

"There's nothing to apologize for. I didn't even think he was being rude."

"Please."

"You're forgiven of course."

"You see," said Hugh Robertson, "I didn't want to leave you with the wrong idea about us. We're simply friends, and when I'm in town, I share his house in Neuilly. Where you simply must come and dine with us."

"I've already said that I'd be delighted to."

"Good," he said, and for a moment the elegant gentleman seemed to be fumbling for words. "Well then, I hope to be able to show you around town a bit too. I remember Mrs. Michon mentioning something about you being interested in the fashion industry." He stopped short, looked about the lobby of the Ritz Hotel, looked out toward where the chauffeur waited for his return. "I hope you'll forgive me for saying this so bluntly, Miss Holmes, but my friend often finds it amusing to put me in this position, and then there's no way out of it but to explain quite clearly: I'm not homosexual."

Valerie, still stunned by the incomplete night of sleep, the terrible plane ride, the idea of her new lover, simply looked at Hugh Robertson with as polite an expression as she could manage. "Yes," she said stupidly. "That's OK."

"I just wanted that clear, Miss Holmes. It's something that too many people assume, and it's a wrong assumption. In my case, at any event."

All right, so you're not a faggot, what am I supposed to do now? Tell you that I'll spread the word? Inform my mother? Explain to the fag clerk at the counter that the man with the polished fingernails is actually straight as an arrow, and that the fruit in the back seat of his limo is only a friend? "I see," she said.

"And, again, if I've embarrassed you or—or made you uncomfortable in any way, Miss Holmes, I apologize."

"That's not necessary."

"Prove it to me, then," he said. "Have dinner with me tomorrow night. Just the two of us."

She found herself agreeing to be shown a "charming little bistro" near St.-Germain-des-Prés, and then Hugh Robertson smiled, as if some urgent little task had been accomplished and he could now relax. "It's just that I find

you so very appealing, my dear," he said, and he squeezed
her hand once more in parting and walked off, very erect,
and manly, to the waiting car.

10

The buyer's name was Allard, and he was a very big buyer, and he liked to buy from Jonathan Singer for one reason, and one reason only. "It used to be money," he explained to Jonathan one day. "I mean here we got this incredible situation. Your Lorelei is knocking off what some other jerk's knocked off from some other jerk who designed it in the first place. Only you do it cheaper than the designer, and cheaper than the first luxury knock-off, so we can afford you. But that still don't make you special. You know why that don't make you special?"

"Yeah," said Jonathan, who knew, but the buyer preferred to do all the talking when he was in his cups.

"That don't make you special, because over in 1407 Broadway everybody's knocking off everybody else. You got a hot number you're pushing for eighteen ninety-nine, so big shit, everyone knocks off the same thing, in the same fabric, for the same lousy fucking eighteen ninety-nine. I mean in this building we got a little Lorelei, a big Lorelei, a medium-sized Lorelei, we got all the Lorelei Parises you could ever need. So why buy from you and nobody else? Why, eh?"

"We do good work, and fast, Mr. Allard."

"Kenny, Kenny."

"Kenny."

"Bullshit, good work and fast. That's no answer, and you know it, you lying son of a bitch Jew, just like all the rest of them. Lying son of a bitch Jew."

"Do I insult your religion?"

"Fuck religion, *I'm* talking."

"Just don't call me a son of a bitch Jew," said Jonathan, grabbing the buyer's throat. Another drunk at the bar on West Thirty-fifth Street glanced at their table with approbation.

"Fuck you, can't a man talk?"

"Talk, Kenny."

"What the fuck was I saying?"

"You were calling me a lying son of a bitch Jew."

"Then I shit sure had good reason, you bastard." The buyer patted Jonathan's hand. "I've always thought you were a tough little shit, Singer."

"Thanks."

"But that's not why I buy from you either." He slapped his hand down on the table and picked up his empty glass. "Shit," he said, and he waved the glass at the waiter. "I mean what'd you say—you do good work? You all do the same bundle-shit work as everyone else. A bundle of right sleeves, a bundle of left sleeves, a bundle of tit pockets—I tell you, Singer, you're in a very fucked-up business. Like I said, you all rip off the same design, you all pick up on whatever's hot, you all got just about the same goddam line in the same goddam price range, so why the fuck does anyone buy from you and not from someone else? I'll tell you why."

"Sir," said the waiter, putting down his Scotch.

"Bribery," said the buyer. "Pure unadulterated fucking bribery." He sucked up half the double Scotch through the hollow swizzle stick. "And even when some lucky bastard picks something that no one else gets and it turns into a hotshot best seller, you know— What's it called? When it's hot?"

"A runner."

"No, shithead, I mean when every son of a bitch goes ahead and copies it. When I see something in your place that I see in fifteen other showrooms I know it's a runner, but I mean it's got a name because it's so copied—"

"A ford."

"Yeah, a ford. I'm talking about a ford."

137

"Except," said Jonathan, relishing his expertise, "a ford isn't the same as just a knock-off pure and simple. A ford can be in a few different price lines, like when culottes got hot, they became a ford; from budget to designer, there were knock-offs and runners in every range."

"Bribery, asshole," said the buyer. "You keep changing the subject. The only reason a buyer's got to buy from Mr. A instead of Mr. B is because he fucking feels like it, because Mr. A and Mr. B are selling the same shit for the same price. So how're you gonna make him feel like it? That's your business. I never heard of such a lousy business. All bullshit, bribes, and lies. I don't have to be drinking this shit with you. If I went next door, I could make three grand tonight. Like that. With one order. You bastard, what the fuck did you ever give me?"

"You sure you want another?"

"Yeah."

"You won't be good with much more of that crap."

"What's the matter, Singer, afraid to pick up the tab for a lousy few drinks? We're gonna run to twenty bucks here? If we push it and you leave a decent tip? Do you know what I'm talking about? I'm talking about three grand for letting you have the order. I'm talking about holding you up for three grand, and you'd pay, you'd pay because you don't have a prayer otherwise. You wouldn't get a single dress into my stores."

"What are you trying to say, man?" said Jonathan, finishing his own drink. "What the fuck are you trying to say? Are you trying to tell me you don't want to get laid tonight?"

"Jesus," said Kenny.

"Answer me, man. Answer me, you drunk son of a bitch."

"I didn't say nothing about that."

"What the fuck are you trying to do, bust my balls?"

"Hey, cut it out. I'm just putting it in perspective man."

Again the drink was empty, and the buyer made a feeble

attempt to look for the waiter. But his mind was on something else. "Bribery," he said. "Everyone else offers me money. But Johnny Singer, you go another route." Again, the pat on his hand. From aggressive to defensive, from tiger to pussy. "Johnny Singer, Lorelei Paris. Everybody wants to know why I buy Lorelei Paris." A secret smile. "But I don't tell them. Oh, no, I wouldn't. I couldn't."

The house was on West Forty-third Street, near Tenth Avenue, but this part of the city signified nothing frightening to the buyer, who made his home in Skokie, Illinois. Besides, the whores had benefited from a local beautification program that had renovated many of the block's brownstones and brought in ad execs and English professors to leaven the wider population of youthful Latin Americans and aging Poles and Irishmen. Jonathan helped the cabdriver look for the number; it was just another nondescript brownstone.

"Don't give me that attitude," said the buyer. "I know this ain't costing you no three grand. I know when a guy's got a good thing going."

"Right here," said Jonathan, and he paid the cab, as he'd paid in the bar, and he'd pay later on in the restaurant on Eleventh Avenue while the buyer would tell him, in painstaking detail, everything, absolutely everything. Some buyers liked a good phone number, and all they'd say about it afterward was thanks. (Especially since he'd be paying for the call girl.) But a few, a very few, like Allard, were still reliving their college fraternity days. It was impossible to do anything quietly, without fanfare, without an escort. Some wanted a quiet blonde to take to dinner and a show, for company. Others wanted red lights and loud music and bad liquor and bad girls—but always together, always with Johnny.

"I'm not drunk no more," said the buyer, grinning.

"We'll fix that," said Jonathan.

A black man with a shaved skull and a red silk shirt opened the door for them and smiled at Johnny. "How ya doin', man? What's happening?" The buyer glowed in the warmth of a greeting that included him, the friend of the regular. They followed a red carpet along a hallway lit by bronze electric sconces, and, at every step, the sounds of WBLS-FM and laughter and ice cubes rattling in glasses grew louder.

The "parlor" was on the basement level of the narrow little four-story building and, like the rest of the rooms in the house, had green-glass windows covered with climbing plants and thin steel bars. It would be just as hard to break out as to break in.

"Johnny, Johnny," said the buyer, growling with appreciation at his first sight of girls. He hadn't been to the house in a year and there was a considerable turnover of employees. Jonathan assumed that their shaved-headed maitre d' had set things in motion for their benefit when he'd gone to answer the door. Four black girls, two white ones, all with dopey eyes, sarcastic smiles. Two girls danced, their arms wrapped about each other in a display of desire; one girl was dressed in a long slithery evening gown—it looked like Qiana—but her partner was nude, except for very high heeled slippers. A girl in a bra and panties lolled on a chair, sipping a cocktail, waiting for instructions. Another girl stood at the bar wearing a knock-off of a Fernando Sanchez negligee and enough makeup to paint a barn.

"What're you drinking?" said the shaved-headed man.

"Jesus," said the buyer. Jonathan hoped he wouldn't get a heart attack before he'd placed his order. Their maitre d' had once been an actor, or an aspiring one, and the house was run with an eye for the porno-theatrical.

"Do a dance," he told one of the white girls, who got up slowly from her chair and, her bare feet rooted to the carpet, began to shake her upper torso. The buyer knocked back his first drink, and Jonathan asked him if he'd made up his mind.

"I want to see," he said.

He knew there was more to the house. They went

140

upstairs with their drinks and heard male voices, other patrons, laughing and slapping from behind closed doors. There was a billiard table, deserted under a naked light bulb, at the end of a hallway, and a door with a locked padlock in a recess at the head of the stairs. "Is somebody with her?" said the buyer.

"You been here before, man?"

"You bet."

"He's cool," said Jonathan, going along with the joke. The black man winked, took out his key, and slowly unlocked the padlock and removed it from the door latch. When the door was opened, they could see nothing at first, for the room lights were out. The maitre d' entered the room with fake caution, switching on the lights with a sudden wary motion.

"Wow," said the buyer.

On the bed was a dark Puerto Rican girl, no more than fifteen, her hair peroxided a dull orange. She wore a transparent black nightshirt, and around her neck a studded dogcollar, which was attached to a very long chain, linking her to the brass headboard. If the buyer read in her frightened face a young chained-up virgin, that was his problem; he was no drama critic, and he'd be very happy with his fantasies of rape. To Jonathan, it looked like the poor girl had had quite a night already. Weeknights were always busy, entertaining the out-of-town businessmen.

"This the one you want?"

"Yeah," said the buyer.

"See you around," said Jonathan. He heard the chain rattling as he followed the maitre d' out the door.

"And you my friend?"

"I don't think so," said Jonathan.

"I don't remember that one."

"He's a fast fader."

"Good, it's getting late. For a Tuesday. What about a drink?"

"Yeah," said Jonathan.

141

Downstairs no one was dancing. Two more girls had come down from their rooms, and a very drunk man, dressed in a very expensive, very rumpled dark suit, was stroking a girl on his lap, telling her over and over again that he was sorry. She gave the maitre d' a look as they entered the room: How much longer do I gotta put up with this shit?

Sometimes Jonathan felt the same way. He sat on a stool next to the maitre d', and the negligeed bar girl poured their drinks.

"So, how's business, Johnny?"

"How's the girl upstairs?"

"A screamer and a crier, but she don't scratch—she goes limp at the right moment."

"Then business might be OK," said Jonathan.

"He's important?"

"In my little world."

"Funny."

"Why funny?"

"They all look like such assholes, man, I mean the VIPs. They all got that pussy-whipped look. I know it when I see it."

"What about me?"

"Not you."

"That a fact?"

"You're bad," said the maitre d'. "I can always tell a bad dude."

"I'm not so bad," said Jonathan. They weren't using the word in the same sense, but Jonathan meant it in both ways. He wasn't so bad, he wasn't so good, he wasn't so tough, he wasn't so hard and cool and wise. Not at all. He had no desire to ball the teen-ager upstairs with the chain around her neck, but neither did he plan to enter into a moral argument with his buyers about frequenting low rather than high places of ill repute. Jonathan knew perfectly well he was willing to sacrifice a hundred name-less Puerto Rican fifteen-year-olds on the altar of good business. And the one upstairs was no china doll, after all.

142

But still, if he could have it another way . . . If buyers didn't have to be bribed. If clothes didn't have to be knocked off. If life could be a bit simpler.

"I fucked her three times," said the buyer in the Landmark an hour and a half later. Jonathan finished his cheeseburger and ordered another, and another beer. The restaurant was crowded with a troupe of actors from a nearby experimental theater, still wearing their grease-paint, eating chili with quiet exhaustion. "Three times," he repeated. "Jesus, you get my order cheap, Singer, but what the hell—you make me happy."

"You want another?"

"No, I want coffee. Get me a coffee, and we'll talk some business."

"Good."

"I mean you may not be so happy with what I got to say," said the buyer, "but after you think on it, you won't be so mad after all. You'll see I'm doing right by you."

The coffee came, and the buyer sipped, and the alcoholic haze lifted somewhat, more from the business at hand than from the caffeine. Allard bought for a chain of stores in the Midwest and California—the California part of the chain tried out "newer" ideas more readily, and this was where he'd preferred to direct Lorelei's goods. Jonathan assumed that he was getting maybe a sixth of Allard's business in the junior sportswear line—and that if he didn't have that business, Lorelei would be in a very shaky way.

"First of all, Singer, let's be honest about one thing." This was the warm-up, nice and easy, a joke and a smile. "You make me a very happy man, every time I come to town, you make me leave a little less horny in spirit."

"We try."

"And I'm grateful, you know how grateful."

"And I give you good work, and fast."

"Don't sell me clothing, Singer. I'm not interested in clothing. I told you already. Clothing you don't got no monopoly on."

"So you buy Lorelei 'cause Lorelei gets you laid."

"Yeah, that's it, Singer. You pimp real good."

"Thanks."

"And I figure it costs you something. I mean, those broads don't do it for love."

"For money, Kenny."

"It's not a thousand bucks."

"We don't have to discuss that, Kenny. It's never the same, it's tough to take as a tax deduction, there's always the tips to consider—"

"You didn't spend a grand tonight, Singer. No way did you spend a grand."

"OK."

"But I give you a grand, OK? I mean, maybe you spent two, three hundred bucks, maybe it was more, I don't know—but I'm giving you the benefit of the doubt, I'm being generous, I'm saying a thousand bucks you spent." He finished his coffee, looked in disgust about the room. "I mean, this isn't Sardi's."

"The Landmark's got the best cheeseburgers in town. You wanted a cheeseburger."

"Look, Singer, let me get to the point. I know what order you're expecting. I know what the order's worth to you, and I know what it's worth to the ten other guys I can go to tomorrow morning, and still be home finished tomorrow night in Illinois. Now, I just want to tell you what it's worth to me to give you that order."

"Yeah?"

"Yeah, and don't give me that face, Singer. If I say three grand, you ought to remember something. Even if I'm picking up that kind of change for my order, that doesn't mean that just any son of a bitch can come along and plunk it down and—pow—he's got me."

"Right, it's got to be a very special son of a bitch that's allowed to bribe Kenny Allard."

"That's right."

"And I'm one of the fortunate few."

"Right again."

"How much are you holding me up for this order?"

"Let me tell you about the order first," said the buyer. And he drew it out of his pocket. For all his seeming indifference to buying, the style numbers he'd picked from Jonathan's line were smart, and going to be hot that year. And he wouldn't respond to any suggestions once he'd made his choices. "Don't try to sell me shit," he said. "The order's here, and that's what I want, if I want anything."

"Like I said, we do good work, and we do it fast."

"You want the order, Singer?"

"Sure."

"It's going for three grand."

"Three grand."

"But for you—two grand—since you got me laid."

"I used to think the lay was worth more than that to you."

"I got smart, Singer. I want a swimming pool. I like to have a good time in New York, but I can't afford to give away so much of my stores' money without bringing home a little bacon for myself."

"And what," said Jonathan, "does Mrs. Allard think about all this?"

"She doesn't ask where the money comes from. She just wants to know that it's coming."

"I'm not talking about the money, Kenny. I'm talking about something else entirely. I'm wondering how Mrs. Allard likes the idea of you going to New York to get laid."

"That's enough Singer. You shut your mouth about my wife."

"Sure, sure," said Jonathan. "We got too much to talk about as it is. Like the order, for example. It's not big enough."

"I didn't realize I was dealing with Jonathan Logan."

"We got a very impressive line this year, Kenny. Classic. You can buy twice what you're buying now and put me into the Midwest. I'm not just a California line.

145

They'll buy Lorelei in the sticks, you wait and see."

"I'd like to help you out, Singer, but I've got other plans for the rest of my orders. And you're not California. You're not anything until you tell me what you're going to do about the cash I got coming."

"OK," said Jonathan. "I'll tell you." And with that he took his glass of beer and splashed it into the buyer's face. No one else saw the movement, only its aftermath. "Oh, my God," said Jonathan, jumping out of his chair and rushing over to the stunned buyer to help him out of his chair.

"You must be crazy," said the buyer. But the waiter had come over now and asked what the problem was, and Jonathan said that there was no problem, just a little accident, and the waiter brought over a stack of napkins. Jonathan took the buyer's arm.

"Come on, let's go to the toilet," he said.

"I'll kill you, you bastard."

"I slipped man," said Jonathan, and the buyer, still trying to mop his face and chest, allowed himself to be prodded to the bathroom, where he stumbled to the mirror and tried to wash his face.

"My price has gone up, you asshole," said the buyer. "This little stunt's going to cost you another grand."

"No, it's not," said Jonathan, and then he grabbed the man's shoulder and turned him away from the mirror and slapped him very hard, twice, across the face. As the buyer put up his fists, Jonathan reached under his guard and slammed into his belly. "You son of a bitch, you don't pull this kind of shit on me, cocksucker." Allard went down, very slowly, holding on to the wall, still very much conscious. Jonathan, fully awake and furious, sat down next to him on the bathroom floor. "First of all, asshole, you don't go back on a deal. The deal was to give me that order. Now you're trying to hold me up. That's robbery, and I don't let myself get held up. Here, I want to show you something. You like to fuck fifteen-year-olds, let me show you what you look like in the act." It was a Polaroid,

146

but big and clear, and it showed the buyer, the girl, and her chain. "Get up," said Jonathan.

"Jesus," said Allard, very scared.

"I'll take this shit to Skokie personally, just for the fun of it. You sober enough to understand me, you faggot?"

"Yeah."

"That order's not big enough. You're not giving Lorelei an even break. I want to get us into all your stores, the Midwest too. I want us to show you how good we can sell, you understand?"

"I understand."

"Tomorrow morning, Lorelei gets a new order—that's double what we've got now. I don't care how you work the numbers, that's your business. You buy what you need. Just as long as you spend twice as much as you thought you were going to get away with."

"OK."

"I know it's OK, Kenny, you don't have to say shit. Just be there. Nine o'clock, 1407 Broadway." If he was really bad, as he knew he wasn't, Jonathan could've made him pay for the cheeseburgers and drinks, for the cab ride back over to the East Side. But he felt sorry for the big slob. Blowing six grand in bribes for fast-fucking a pro. On top of everything, he'd probably give his wife the clap. In Skokie. Jesus.

It dawned on Jonathan as he was taking his hot shower a half hour later that the great order would mean that he'd be free to leave Lorelei in Willy's capable hands a lot sooner than he'd thought. He'd be free to leave the whole dirty garment business and fly to Paris for his chance to break forever out of the small time. Suitably cleansed, cologned, and deliciously tired, he slipped into bed beside his sleeping wife and allowed himself the luxury of thinking about the little princess on the other side of the Atlantic—the poor little rich girl who just might make his fortune.

Jesus, if I'm such a bad guy, he thought, how could a broad like Valerie Holmes fall for *me*?

147

11

"*Ici*," said Valerie nearly a month later, spotting the address ignored by the speeding cabdriver. The house was in Neuilly, equidistant from the Seine and the northeast tip of the Bois de Boulogne, on a block of four- and five-story apartment buildings, distinguished by a pair of Le Corbusier houses partially hidden by old trees and a new high fence. Their house was much newer, built by one of his disciples almost ten years after Le Corbusier's death in 1965. It was a three-story square of glass and red brick sitting on a flat plane of grass, fronted by an enormous steel sculpture touched intermittently by tiny threads of light. Getting out of the cab, Valerie approached the sculpture slowly, trying to discover its source of illumination. Suddenly a huge Harley-Davidson screeched to a halt outside the gate, and she heard a series of giggles and kisses. Then the bike turned into the courtyard and roared past her in first gear, screaming to a dramatic halt near the front door. She walked faster, leaving the sculpture, trying to get up to the door at the same time as the two men on the motorcycle.

"*Bonsoir, bonsoir*," said the driver as Valerie approached. His rider, over six feet tall, flat assed, narrow hipped, dressed in a jeans jacket with a mink collar, bowed very low at her and straightened up, flashing capped teeth in the yellow light from the electric lanterns over the entranceway.

"*Bonsoir* Bonwit's, *bonsoir* Bergdorf's, *bonsoir* Bendel's—*bonsoir à toutes les américaines*," he said.

"You left out Bloomingdale's," she said.

"But they are not coming—are they not?" said the rider, still prepared to flatter or insult, and not to recognize her existence except as an object to win over or ignore.

"I'm not a buyer," said Valerie.

"Not a buyer," said the rider, trying to mimic her American accent without success. They all heard the sound of several cars pull up outside the gates and then a series of car doors opening and slamming shut. "But if you are not a buyer, then how come, why is it, that you are here?"

"I'm a friend," said Valerie, and she walked past them to the front door and rang the bell.

"A friend?" said the driver. "A friend of Milt or a friend of Hugh?" He pronounced the names "Meelt" and "Oogh." But Valerie didn't have time to answer, as the door opened to a smoky foyer, a pretty maid bobbing her head in their direction, and the sounds of very loud, very new Donna Summer disco music. She excused herself from further baiting and walked into the mass of people, mostly men.

"My dear Miss Holmes!" said Milton Brommel, spotting her instantly. His voice was as sarcastic as ever, but tinged with a sense of injury that she didn't quite understand. Long silk scarves with tassels seemd to be the accessory of the hour at the party, and Milt was no exception. His was white and looked like antique silk, the bit of flash worn by an aviator in pursuit of the Red Baron. He touched her cheek with the tips of his fingers and made a loud little kiss in the air. "You look superb, my dear!" He looked down; she wore Jonathan's ankle bracelet; he let out his high-pitched little laugh. "Ah, you've got it on! Decadent to the end! I love it!" He grabbed a passing muscleman, dressed in a black tee shirt, and said to him: "Jean-Loup, look at this—*regardes-le*— did you ever see such a thing?"

"A foots?" he said, practicing his English.

"Excuse me," said Valerie. "I'd better go find Hugh."

149

Milton put his arm about Jean-Loup and laughingly kissed him twice, at the corners of his mouth. A woman with badly dyed red hair and a Missoni cowl-neck sweater made her way through the jammed foyer and into a large living room. Valerie followed her and watched the way she turned to stare at the sights: old queers kissing young men, some not much more than seventeen or eighteen years old; a famous French designer sitting on an ottoman surrounded by a small court of pretty men and mannequins so thin, with such exaggeratedly geometric haircuts and photogenic white makeup, that they were positively ugly next to their male companions; an Italian designer and a young South American beauty on her fifth marriage, snorting cocaine through a rolled-up hundred-dollar bill and a rolled-up five-hundred-French-franc bill, comparing the merits of the paper; a lovely transvestite mincingly protesting about the state of his/her hair to a famous crew-cut haircutter; a call girl on the arm of an aggressively heterosexual American buyer, terrified lest he be mistaken for gay; lithe men dancing the hustle together, and badly; a German movie star, famous for his bisexuality, contemplating a group of male and female mannequins supposed to mix with the party-goers to exhibit some Italian's new ready-to-wear line, but who had remained together, shyly staring down at the floor or at the intricate details of the wainscoting.

The red-haired woman seemed to enjoy what she saw, much as if she'd paid an admission fee to a sideshow and was now getting her money's worth. She seemed capable of ignoring everything about the people she saw except their deviation, there for her to look down upon from her precious vantage point of normality. When her eager eyes lit upon Valerie, they just as quickly turned away; here was nothing worth gloating over—just a girl, an ordinary girl.

"Are you Miss Holmes?" said a very handsome man in his early thirties. He was wearing the ubiquitous tasseled

150

scarf, but his voice was smooth and friendly, and his eyes were not prepared to mock her. "Hugh is trapped over there," he said, gesturing to where Hugh stood, surrounded by a crew of serious women in serious suits. "And so he asked me to introduce myself. Just until he can get away. He wanted us to meet anyway. Serge Marandino. The 'Serge' for France, the 'Marandino' for Italy. I was born in Brooklyn, but I've lived in Paris since I was one year old, except for four terrible years in New York."

"Serge!" said a young man with a chiseled face, grabbing his shoulder and turning him about for a kiss. Valerie kept on smiling: Ho hum, doesn't bother me, I've seen it all, and am not simply tolerant—I'm weary. Serge disposed of the young man without, thank God, bothering Valerie with another introduction.

"Hugh says you're a designer," he said abruptly, politely trying to resume their conversation.

"Not yet. I don't even know if that's what I plan to be."

"But you are interested in the fashion business?"

"More than interested. It's just that my forte may be business, and not design—and my ideas aren't so terribly original."

"Well, that's good to hear," he said. "Originality kills in this business. Or at least that's what they used to say in New York. What's your first name, Miss Holmes?"

"Valerie," she said, happily realizing that he was one of those who didn't recognize her family association.

"Valerie," he said. "Did you ever hear of me?"

"Maybe," she said. "Serge Marandino does have—"

"It's got a ring to it, no?" He laughed. "Come here and have a drink." He steered her to an unoccupied couch, to the right of an unnecessarily blazing fire, and sat her down while he went after a couple of cocktails. When he returned, he told her. "Hugh says you've got a head on your shoulders."

"He's always a bit prone to exaggerating my good points."

"You don't talk Garment Center, Valerie. You mind if I ask you something?"

"No."

"Just why are you going into this thing?"

"You mean the business?"

"It's not a business. It's more like a sickness."

"Let's just say I find it exciting."

"The rise and fall of Valerie Holmes—or shall I say, fall and rise? That sort of thing?"

"Maybe not so dramatic, but along those lines."

"You know this stuff that Hugh's pushing now, this peasant look? You think that's dramatic?"

"Yes."

"I mean the success it's having. The buyers are jumping into his pond like there's no one else in town with an idea worth looking at. I mean that's pretty exciting. Pretty original."

"I think you want me to say yes, so you can jump down my throat."

"Hugh's right. You do have a head on your shoulders. I won't jump. I'll just tell you that this whole peasant thing is a crock of shit. It's all marketing. And it's all glued on to Hugh's name. Like I said, originality kills. I know at least four designers who had elements of Hugh's peasant influence—so called—in their lines over the last five years. That's in Europe and the U.S. The same shit, and the buyers wouldn't touch it. They were original, and that's why the designers wouldn't touch them with a ten-foot pole."

"But Hugh's told me—" she began, but the handsome man cut her off.

"I know what he's told you. The same thing he always tells the magazines. It's true that other people may have had similar ideas at earlier times, but that doesn't matter. The true innovation is to innovate when the time is right."

"That's exactly how I feel."

"Let's see how you feel after your first line is killing

152

space in somebody's rented warehouse. You ever work on Seventh Avenue?"

"One block over—1407 Broadway."

"A sportswear house?" He didn't let her answer. "I'm surprised you're not a little more cynical then. Hugh Robertson can afford to talk about innovating when the time is right. That's because if he does something new, that's an innovation. If someone else, some small guy, tries something new, that's being too daring—the buyers will tell you that the public may not be ready for it, and they won't touch it. Only a Hugh Robertson can launch something big, but not because he thought it up all by himself. He can launch something that eight other guys tried to get off the ground, and he'll be the first to succeed, because he's got muscle." Serge Marandino had long since finished his drink, and now, for the second time, he was tilting back the empty glass. "I don't think it's a good idea to confuse originality with muscle, or design talent with good connections."

"Can I ask you something?"

"Sure."

"Are you one of those eight guys—"

"I said I only knew about four—in this particular peasant fake-out promo. All hail *Vogue* and *Nouvelles*, arbiters of good taste, sharp-eyed spotters of everything trendy."

"You *are* one of those four."

"Sure, sure, OK—but I'm not mad at Hugh. I'm crazy about him. I think he's very talented. He's standing right behind you, Valerie."

There were his hands—dry, cool, handsome, reaching from behind the couch to rest on her cheeks, over her eyes, on top of her head. "Is this man telling you lies, my dear?"

"That remains to be seen," said Valerie.

"I can prove everything I said," said Serge. "Do you want a drink, Hugh?"

"Please. A Scotch, no ice."

Serge left them. "He's one of my dearest young friends," said Hugh.

"Is he a good designer?"

"He's a good, paranoid designer. Always afraid his ideas are being stolen. As if that's the whole point of the business."

Valerie nodded politely at this pithy understatement. She was pleased with her weeks in Paris, because she felt on the verge of understanding something about the fashion business that wasn't simply dictated to her by Jonathan or Willy Schwartz or Hugh or a buyer or another disgruntled designer. Hugh was a tremendous influence, of course. His success, his intelligence, his selfless help had been invaluable; but, even where he was concerned, she was beginning to be able to read between the lines of his various proclamations. Jonathan had often told her about the secrecy of Garment Center manufacturers, and their fears didn't seem at all paranoid. There was the story of the night watchman with the spy camera who, for a very fat fee, would photograph the competition's line during the night, so that their competitors would be able to duplicate anything promising—having it ready at the same time as their competitors, without going to the expense of styling or designing. The stories of fast-sketch artists who could quickly outline the dress coming down the runway (in less than a minute) at the couturiers' shows, with enough detail so their employers could skip the prohibitive expense of buying all the dresses they planned to copy, were accepted facts of the fashion world. The stories of used-up once-talented designers milking their assistants for the ideas that would further old careers and old fortunes were heard every year, every season. If Hugh didn't care about the copies of his clothing that existed in every price range in every country "civilized" enough to have department stores, that was because his fame was enough to guarantee the supposed "inimitability" of a true, sanctioned Hugh Robertson. If people bought his copies, there were many other people who would buy nothing less than a garment that bore his name, regardless of the garment's place of origin, workmanship, or relationship to the real original that Hugh had made up for himself in Paris or New York. Copying Hugh simply enhanced his name, his self-perpetuating publicity. And more and more firms chose not simply to style their line after him, but to ask him for the privilege—that is, ask him to license them to produce a Hugh Robertson shirt or skirt or slip or scarf—and it was from this form of "copying" that Hugh Robertson made the major part of his immense fortune.

Hugh continued his analysis of Serge. "If he didn't spend so much time agonizing over missed opportunities, and the possibility of having every new idea of his stolen, I think he'd hit the jackpot. If he could only let go. Not be afraid. Right now he's got some beautiful designs he's trying to push—I've just been talking to a couple of buyers about him, and I'm sure they'll meet later tonight. But I know what they're going to tell him. They're a little uncommercial, and he didn't follow through—he's got a few items in his line—and that's all because of his fears. All because he's bottled up."

Valerie spotted the red-haired sightseer catching sight of Hugh and heading their way. She was a buyer, and Hugh excused himself for a moment from Valerie, allowing her to get back to Serge, who had returned with fresh drinks and had nothing uncomplimentary to say about Hugh. "After all, he's my patron in a way. God help me. Yours too, I suppose."

Valerie traded stories with him, but kept hers pared to a few essential details: She was a friend of Hugh's, had some money of her own, and was planning to start her own line of medium-priced to expensive dresses for the mass market.

"What do you mean by dresses?" he said. "Just dresses?"

"Trying to steal my ideas?"

155

"It's just that women have outgrown their dresses—or haven't you noticed?"

"I've noticed. I'm putting my money on the notion that they want them back."

"How much money?"

"I don't know yet. That's one of the things I'm trying to discover."

"But you said you have some money. Don't you know how much you have?"

"No," she said. "Because it's tied up with family right now. And I'm not sure how easy it's going to be to get how much."

"I wish I had your problems. The only money my family's got is tied up in the wholesale lasagna business, and I'm afraid Marandino's not a very big name in lasagna." Serge told her about his new line. Instead of trying to put together a multifaceted collection, he'd concentrated on items that best showed his themes; his direction was to very soft, unstructured clothes, so simply shaped that they hardly revealed a seam. "I know I'm going to be compared with Hugh again, or Saint Laurent, but this is my direction, I started it, and I'm taking it a step further. I'm sticking to ponchos and kerchief dresses."

"Kerchief dresses? Hugh's got them this year."

"Mine aren't like his, at least not the ones he's let out so far." Serge's rueful smile implied that, yes, it'd be simple for Hugh to pick up on the new trend and make it his own. "And my colors are fantastic—the deepest green, the coldest blue. You'll have to come see what I've got."

"What fabrics are you using?"

"Angora, cashmere, silk—"

"I can see we're playing in different ball games. I'm strictly into synthetics. What kind of prices are you going to have on those things?"

"It's a lot of fabric—kerchief dresses and ponchos, you know. I've got a coat that used up fifteen meters of angora."

"A little rich for my blood," said Valerie, talking as tough as she knew how. Perhaps Hugh's greatest contribution to her education was his introducing her to Joseph Weintrob, a fabric manufacturer with a plant outside of Paris, and an infinite capacity for fielding naive questions. Valerie had begun daily visits to the plant for on-the-spot observation of yarning, discharge, and pigmentation printing techniques—and a month's study had served notice of how very much more she had to learn. With Joseph's help, she'd begun selecting and testing fabric for use in her shirtwaists, trying to find something as durable and luxurious as the fabric used in her first dresses in New York, but within as inexpensive a price range as possible. "I'm trying to sell retail for eighty, ninety bucks," she now said to Serge.

"That's what I'd sell panties for," said Serge. "But then I've always had a soft spot for panties."

"*Miss Holmes*, said a sharp voice behind her, and, as she turned round, she saw the red-haired buyer smiling at her in a way that suggested she was about to be sucked up to. "I had no idea you were here," she continued. "My name is Amelia Vogel, and I've been curious about your whole little adventure ever since the spread in *Women's Wear*." Hugh moved in to take Serge for a walk. The red-haired woman, who apparently had been sent by Hugh, took Valerie's arm and began to walk her into an adjacent room.

"Where are we going?" said Valerie. "If you don't mind my asking."

"I can't stand being among so many gorgeous fairies another second. It's such a *waste*. Such a waste to the world." Valerie let herself be led into the library, a room she'd passed through once before, when she'd finally come to dinner at the house as she'd promised Milt and Hugh when they first drove her into Paris from the airport. The dinner had been awkward. She and Hugh had been seeing each other practically every day since she'd come to town. He'd not only taken her to the little bistro

157

near St.-Germain-des-Prés, as he'd promised, but also along the Faubourg St.-Honoré to see the couturiers' ready-to-wear outlets, to the rue Tronchet to see some of his favorite boutiques, to the Deux Magots Café on the Left Bank to point to what was fashionable and what was not among the tourists and residents parading in front of them. They discovered a fabric shop on the rue de Buci whose geometric prints led Hugh to take her to Joseph Weintrob and which marked the beginning of her education in fabrics. She visited Hugh's offices in Paris, and he gave her her first lecture on the licensing business, as she sat in a Windsor chair in his large inner chamber and he lectured her from a standing position, punctuating his remarks with his finger.

It was all heady, and friendly—a mad trip getting to know the town's ready-to-wear sources, warehouses, creative shops, people. Aside from that first bizarre statement on the morning he'd dropped her off from the airport—about his not being a homosexual—the subject had never again come up. If she thought about it, she had to admit that he had many of the other characteristics of a nonflamboyant, discreetly elegant gay: everything perfect, from sideburns to fingernails, to color of handkerchief in breast pocket. Of course, these were hardly proofs of homosexuality. There were some heterosexuals who were that neat, that preoccupied with clothing and hair, that sensitive to color and tone and taste and style. But there was more than this, of course. His touch on her hand was never more than friendly; and the friendship was something that seemed to exclude forever the possibility of sexual involvement. It was not simply that the handsome man didn't excite her; she was quite sure that she didn't excite him—at least not in that ordinary fashion.

But obviously she excited *something* in him. He wasn't quite old enough to be her father (unless it was a very, very young father—he was forty-one to her twenty-three), and his interest in her education could not simply be described as fatherly. It was too enthusiastic. He wanted

158

her to feel the way he did about fashion and the fashion business, to understand the way he did why his life in this trade was a good life, a civilized life. He wanted her to share the distance he'd traveled from a boyhood in Waterloo, Iowa, to an adolescence in Manhattan, living with a miserly aunt and uncle while he attended the High School of Art and Design; to FIT; to design apprenticeships on Seventh Avenue, in Rome, in Paris; to the founding of an empire in New York City under his own name, under his own ubiquitous designer's logo—the darling of American fashion, with tentacles in France, Germany, Italy, and Japan. Hugh wanted her to share this distance, not so she would join in the singing of his praises, but because he wanted her to see the value of traveling. She had a distance to go as well: from socialite dilettante to student-designer, to inspired business-woman. Both could share the experience of leaving the expected confines of their lives for some different course, a course inextricably linked to style and grace.

None of this was clear to Milton Brommel, of course. During the dinner he made a hundred references to homosexuality, to bitchy dykes, to dangerous unions. Hugh had told her (enough times to make her suspect the truth of what he said) that Milt was a dear friend, the youngest American to ever get a toehold in French ready-to-wear, a brilliant designer who chose to live abroad, and with whom he shared the house in Neuilly whenever he came to France. That was all.

"And when Milton comes to New York, where does he stay?"

"Well, I naturally try to put him up at my house—there's plenty of room."

If they were sleeping together, that was their business, and during the dinner she imagined the two of them together in bed, hard and handsome and trimly masculine; and this didn't make any sense either. If Milton enjoyed brushing Hugh's hand when he poured champagne into his glass, Hugh didn't seem to reciprocate the joy of

159

touching. But neither was the dinner a crossing of swords between two sexual rivals. It was more like something out of her childhood, when she'd gone to a best girl friend's house in Rye, New York, only to come to grips with this friend's *other* best girl friend—and Valerie had felt herself under attack all afternoon by the jealous friend, a girl of nine with blond curls and a desperate, injured expression.

Hugh had discovered something in Valerie that Milton didn't see, and Milt's resentment and his confusion at the intrusion of a new friendship—a dangerous male-female friendship—were evident throughout the meal.

Mrs. Vogel, the red-haired buyer, sat Valerie down in the library, under a wall arrangement of framed stills of Milton Brommel's latest Paris ready-to-wear collection, and said, "Now, Miss Holmes, the fact is, I want to buy you."

"I beg your pardon."

"My store does, that is."

"Buy what?"

"Why, the Valerie Holmes line, of course."

"But I haven't got it. I mean not yet. Not for months. Maybe longer. I don't know when it's going to be ready."

Now the red-haired woman looked very perplexed. "I was under the impression you'd be showing your line in the spring. For next fall. Your sales representative in New York has been in touch with us."

"My sales representative?"

"Quite a persuasive young man," she said, smiling. "And very handsome. And not a fairy, thank God. Did you ever see so many fairies under one roof before, Miss Holmes?"

"I'm still getting over the shock of learning that I'm already being sold in New York," said Valerie. "I think my—my sales representative is being a little premature."

"He didn't give me that impression," she said. "He seemed to be right on top of things. When I told him I was going to Paris, he gave me your number." She began to search for it in her Louis Vuitton bag.

160

"Whether or not Mr. Singer has given you my number, Mrs. Vogel, really doesn't make any difference, because the decision as to when we'll be ready to show and to produce dresses is going to have to remain with me."

"Oh, my," said Mrs. Vogel, looking over to Valerie's right, as if she'd just seen a ghost.

"Are you all right?" said Valerie, but she followed the direction of the buyer's stare and reacted with even more violence than Mrs. Vogel.

"For a second I thought I was seeing things," said Mrs. Vogel as Jonathan Singer spotted them from across the room and came their way with great athletic strides.

Valerie slowly got out of her chair, and Jonathan pulled her to him and kissed her once on the lips. "What in God's name are you—?" began Valerie.

"Steady, girl," he said. "I've missed you too."

"Hello," said Mrs. Vogel feebly. "Hello, Mr. Singer."

Jonathan folded Valerie's arm in his, explained the need for an emergency sales conference to Mrs. Vogel, and quickly stifled all incipient protest from the girl on his arm. "Let's get the hell out of here," he said. "I didn't come all the way to Paris to make chitchat with buyers."

"How did you find me? What are you doing here? Why didn't you tell me you were coming? How did you know how to get to this party? Where are we going?"

He was walking her briskly through the jammed living room, and she was glad that they didn't run into Hugh, glad that he wouldn't give her a chance to say goodbye to her hosts. "I met one of your hosts, a blond fruitcake who's trying to learn how to lisp," he said. "And no questions. Not now." A white Peugeot cab was parked outside, the *compteur* already on ninety-five francs.

"Back to the hotel," said Jonathan.

"*Pardon, Monsieur?*"

"Zee hotel," said Jonathan, trying to put a French accent on his English. "Hotel Intercontinental, dig?"

"A *l'hotel?*"

"Drive, man. *Allez*," he said. As the cab lurched

161

forward, he sank back in his seat and took hold of her, and she looked into his blue eyes, wondering what Hugh Robertson would think of her business associate. "I don't know about you, kid," he was saying, "but all I want to find right now is a big soft bed." His smile allowed no possibility of misunderstanding or argument, no reproach or refusal. Jonathan Singer had come barreling into town, and she was to be allowed no natural rights and privileges. As the cab tore up the avenue Charles de Gaulle toward the Arc de Triomphe and the Champs-Elysées, she wondered for the first time whether Jonathan might not be yet another form of tyranny over her sheltered, structured life. No matter what terrible symbol he might represent to her parents, he might turn out to be simply another alternative to freedom, to discovering her natural impulses.

But now he was kissing her, and he'd come three thousand miles, without a warning, and with evident joy. "Look," she said, "look what I'm wearing." And she showed him the diamond ankle bracelet, and he took hold of her little foot and pulled it across his lap, and kissed her neck and crushed her to him, and all about them were a thousand little cars with yellow lights, and ten thousand strollers walking past Fouquet's, and five hundred tourists waiting to see the Bluebell girls at the Lido, and scores of newlyweds weaving back to the grand hotels, drunk with the city and its wine; and suddenly she didn't care if she was being taken, didn't care if she was being overwhelmed, didn't care if she didn't love this man, didn't want to really think about it all.

"A nice soft bed," said Valerie. "Sounds good to me, Mr. Singer."

12

Jack Jacobson, that's who he reminded her of.

Immediately, she felt guilty for even thinking it, Jack Jacobson was number one in his Columbia University class, picking up a triple major in English, philosophy, and sociology. He was a member of whatever the remnants of the SDS were calling themselves at the moment—she always got them confused with the Progressive Labor Party and the Young Marxist Alliance. Before she'd married Phillip, he'd introduced her to Jack Jacobson in the John Jay cafeteria, that great democratic meeting hall in the center of the university, where all tuna sandwiches were created equal, equally bad; and in a moment his blue eyes—they had that in common, besides their Jewishness—were drilling into her, plainly fascinated by what they saw. Phillip left them to go to a class, and she walked with him out into the quadrangle in front of Hamilton Hall.

"How responsible do you feel for what your family's done to this country?" he asked. It was not an attack. He was mild, curious.

"I don't feel responsible for what they've done at all," she said, without thinking. It wasn't so long since her coming-out party, since her immersion in an "intellectual" milieu for the first time.

"You know," he said, "the Germans, the young Germans, don't feel responsible for what their parents did either."

"What has that got to do with me?"

"I'm not sure. You see, most Americans don't feel

163

responsible for what their parents did, either. In the case of my parents, they don't feel particularly responsible for the sins committed against the black man by white southerners generations before their parents came to America."

"You don't know what it's like," she said.

"What what's like?" he said. Jack Jacobson had a kindly face, until it erupted in anger. Now he was mild, questioning, fascinated by this unformed girl he had just met. Valerie sat down on a bench, and he stood over her, one foot resting on the edge of a trash can.

"Being a Holmes."

"No," he smiled.

"You talk about whether or not I should feel guilty, but—That's the whole point," she said, making no sense, wondering whether to go ahead with what she believed so intensely to be true, or whether it might shock or anger him if she said it. She dared. "Sometimes I feel like a black," she said.

Only the intensity of her expression convinced him that she wasn't being flippant. He waited for more.

"Even when I was in grade school, even in third grade, they all knew my name, they all used it in expressions—'Rich as Holmes,' you know what I mean. One little boy asked me if my father used to light up cigars with hundred-dollar bills, like it said in the comics. I wasn't the same as them, I was different because of my name. I said it's like being a black, because with a black man, people tend to look first at their color, then, only afterwards, at who they are. With me, they never usually got much farther than my name. No one could see me or relate to me, because they didn't see a person, they saw a symbol. I was rich, but I had it rough, if you can believe me. I had a childhood that was lonely, with no one who could relate to me as just another kid, except my brother. That's why I've always been sympathetic to the problems of black people."

It hadn't been a smart thing to say, she could see that in

164

an instant. As she'd tried to explain further, his eyes had grown colder and colder, with incredulity fighting fury, and fury winning the match.

"Come on," he said. "I'm going to show you something. Since you're so sympathetic to the problems of black people." And he hadn't even offered her his hand—just grabbed hers and yanked her to her feet. He had an old VW, appropriately red, and scarred up from the years of city parking. He let her open her own door, and drove north and east, straight into the heart of Harlem.

"I'm sorry if you think that I—" she began, but he asked her to refrain from speaking.

"Please," he said. "Just look. Just open your eyes, and don't bother to comment. You can think about it afterwards."

Either he knew all the worst streets by heart (from a Marxist crisis map of Manhattan), or it didn't really much matter where he turned once he got off 125th Street. A hundred times she began to say that it looked like the aftermath of a war, like the scenes from old newsreels of bombed-out cities in Europe; she wanted to say that she hadn't known, she never would have believed it to be this bad, this hopeless and forlorn. But she said nothing, having learned her lesson. She kept her eyes open and tried not to look at the intense pain in his. Someone threw a rock at their car when they were parked on East 116th Street, on the "wrong side" of Morningside Park. A big old Cadillac cut them off, and several hooting black faces smiled at them, whooshing by and reveling in their sense of territory. She remembered the colors of the street: the natural browns and grays and blacks of grinding poverty, interspersed with the gaudy finery—reds and oranges and hot pinks and shiny purples—of young people refusing to find themselves drab. She remembered the garbage rolling from the piles along the cracked walks to the potholed streets. She remembered the rocks and the rubble of the old tenements, the incredible, mad ugliness of the new housing projects, with their terrifying bleak fronts. She remembered the old women's split shoes, stuffed with newspapers, the packs of hungry dogs roaming the hungry streets, the fires in the garbage cans, burning for the benefit of frozen hands.

Jack drove around Harlem for what seemed like hours, starting and stopping, crawling along in the VW's second gear. Back at Columbia, he'd gotten out of the car first, and waited for her to get back her legs, to open the door and walk out in the fresher air of hopes and aspirations. He hadn't lectured her, but the lecture had been implicit in everything she'd seen; and she always felt that he despised her after that, despised her for the fact of her wealth, and for the fact that she didn't realize what the wealth meant in relation to the poor.

"What happened to him?" said Jonathan, to whom she'd told a piece of the story.

"He died."

"For the cause?"

"No, nothing like that," she said. "An automobile accident. Driving home to see his parents. I don't know what would've happened to him, to him and his ideals."

They were sitting up in bed in Jonathan's suite at the Intercontinental, and all the serious calls remained to be made. Valerie had moved out of the Ritz after her fourth day in Paris and moved into an enormous apartment on the avenue Foch—the apartment of her mother's very dear British cousin, Lady Oliver: very dear and very fussy and very ancient. Luckily, she'd been in London for the first week of Valerie's stay. But then she was back, filled with family gossip, dropping hints about the latest rifts in the perennial war between Mr. and Mrs. Holmes. Though she was anxious to gossip about the men in Margaret's life, Lady Oliver would allow nothing improper in Valerie's—not without a struggle. She was frantic with the mission given her by Mrs. Holmes: to see that no harm came to her little girl in the City of Light. Still, it was free room and board, and staying there kept Valerie in the family's good graces. She was hardly swimming in free and easy cash. Her credit cards could be canceled by a flash of Daddy's pen, and, as her brother had so recently shown, her allowance and living quarters could be pulled out from under her.

Pleading poverty and fright to Jonathan had brought on an angry outburst. He was sick and tired of her moaning and groaning, of her starting a fight only to leave it in the middle, of her sketching out a plan only to rip away the diagram for fear that someone would think she meant business. "Jesus Christ, I wish you'd learn to shit or get off the pot," he'd said, and his eyes, and his fury, and his absolute incomprehension of her peculiar status in life all took her back to the incident with Jack Jacobson—and she'd told him the story, late in the morning after his coming to Paris.

"You know any other Jews while you were at college, honey?"

"What is that supposed to mean?"

"That I'm not exactly prone to driving heiresses around Harlem to teach them how the *shvartzes* live."

"You're very kind to black people," she said. "No matter how you pretend to be tough now. Look what you did for Louella, turning her into a pattern model instead of a whore.

"She's still a whore, Valerie. She comes on to the buyers and then she gives me the bill."

"If I believed that, I'd be very angry with you."

"Call your mamma's friend and tell her you've found yourself another apartment."

"I've already told you I can't just do that—"

"Sure you can. And then you can tell me what the hell's going on here, why you're all of a sudden dragging your heels like there's no tomorrow. Because I'll tell you something—there is a tomorrow, and it's coming closer every second, and we can make it pay for us in a big way, or we can just let the opportunity die. Come on," he said, and he gave her a playful little punch. "Let's get out of here. We can't stay in bed all day, no matter how much

167

After he'd flown in the night before and dropped his bags at the hotel, he'd called Lady Oliver and demanded to know where Valerie was—it was a matter of life and death, he'd told her. She wanted to know *whose* life and *whose* death, but Jonathan had still managed to get the address of the party from her, and to pick her out of the mob in a short time. He was here, he said, to get her act together. All this studying of fabrics was very well and good, but they wanted a line, didn't they? She was supposed to have made her decisions, picked her fabrics and designs, and be ready to roll by now. He was quick, he was efficient—why on earth couldn't she be?

"Unless it's because you're second-thinking every-thing," he said. "If that's it, why don't you just tell me?"

"Second-thinking what?"

"Me. This Jewish Jacobson story, the guy I remind you of. Maybe you suddenly realize that it's not cool to have me at the Newport yacht races."

"That's disgusting."

"Well, I doubt if I'm mentioning something that's never come up. With your mother or—better yet—with brother Tom."

"Stop it, you don't know what you're saying."

"I just thought you liked me, that's all," he said. He got out of bed and made for the shower. "I didn't think you were sleeping with me just to prove yourself a liberal."

"Stop it," she repeated. He crossed back to the bed, and his anger rose to fire his words.

"No," he said. "I won't stop it, because it's obvious that some part of the reason you're sleeping with me is because I'm forbidden flesh, kosher meat to Christian skin. It's certainly part of the reason I'm sleeping with you. But it's gotten to mean a little more than that to me. A little bit more, enough to get me to Paris, to leave my nice little business and come here and try to do something exciting with someone I care about. And now it's becoming a little bit obvious that you're not exactly as thrilled with me as I am with you. That my being bad and lower middle class Jewish somehow isn't enough for you. Maybe you'd rather hang out here for the next ten years until Mr. Right comes along, and maybe he'll be one of those blacks you identify so strongly with. Think of that. Wouldn't that be a lovely way to piss off your parents?"

And then the shower was running, and she was left alone with the telephone. He had called her weak, but that wasn't a fair description, she felt. If she knew, really knew, what she wanted, she'd follow her desires without flinching, without deviation from a straight-line path.

But what did she want? To finish her apprenticeship with Joseph Weintrob, to study the new fabrics, the new ready-to-wear, the empire of Hugh Robertson? Or to make up her mind, grab a few designs, a few fabrics, place her orders with the Weintrob factory, and return to New York, to 1407 Broadway, to sleeping with Jonathan, to following his great schemes for her own dress company?

"*Allo*?" she said into the hotel phone. "*Je veux téléphoner aux Etats-Unis.*" The operator asked for the city she wanted, the phone number, the person to whom she wished to speak. Then she said it would be thirty minutes, and Valerie put down the phone and began to brush her hair.

Almost instantly, the phone rang, once, twice, with urgency.

"*Oui*?"

"Who the fuck is this?" said a deep, grouchy voice, newly torn from sleep.

"Oh, the time difference," said Valerie.

"Valerie?"

"Hi, Daddy," she said. "It's eleven A.M. in Paris—I'm sorry."

"That's OK, it's only two A.M. in California. It's almost time to get up and do my morning run."

"Yes, Thomas says you're really fit these days."

"I got your letter."

"I didn't get yours."

"You don't know what it's been like," said her father.

"I can imagine. The governor, the president, the bank; the golf at the Del Monte Lodge."

"Guilty as charged. you've got a hell of a father. What can he do for you now that he's almost awake?"

"I can call you later, Daddy, I mean if you're not really all awake."

"You'd better tell me now, don't you think?" he said. For the first time, his voice was serious, acknowledging the mystery of a call from his daughter, to whom he rarely spoke on the phone. When she was in California and their paths crossed on the estate, he was always loving, if he had the time. He was not one of those men who sacrificed family for great affairs of state and finance; her father was a man who sacrificed nothing. His life was simply a series of pleasures interspersed with various decisions, usually already made for him by a battery of law firms. Once he'd been in love with his wife, and there was a part of him that was still in love with the idea of a decorous marriage; one didn't bruit about the respective affairs of husband and wife. He was a man who preferred a different sort of society from that of his wife—the society of ex-political leaders, aging captains of industry, old school chums of various sorts, all revolving about the sunny outdoors. This Mr. Holmes lived for golf, swimming, and the rejuvenating experience of the Del Monte Lodge health spa. He insisted on correct behavior from his family, on proper filial and wifely respect. He was not especially unhappy if he didn't see Thomas or Valerie or his wife for six months, even a year; his life was full, self-contained. Thomas was in touch with him almost daily for endless talk about the bank, quick political speeches, lectures on the responsibilities of the Holmes family. When he'd acceded to Thomas's demands to cut off Valerie's allowance, it was not because he was Thomas's stooge nor because his son was the favorite child; it was simply because, from the evidence presented to him, it was apparent that his daughter was not acting in a seemly fashion. She was being misled, the Holmes family was being taken for a ride—all very incorrect, very feminine, very deplorable. So he let Thomas handle it.

It was a mark of her father's automatic dismissal of matters that no longer concerned him that his mind didn't jump at once to the little fracas of nearly two months past. No, this was simply his daughter calling him: How surprising, let me hear what she's got to say.

"Daddy, I'm afraid I'm being contrary."

"Contrary to your own better judgment?"

"No, just contrary—contrary to the orders I've been given."

"What orders?"

"I'm talking about Thomas and Mother—and I suppose you had some part in it too." She paused, giving her father a chance to remember what on earth she was running on about. "The garment business—I wrote you, Daddy."

" Of course," he said. "Yes, yes. You were in some sort of fix, Thomas got you out of it, and now you've gone off to Paris to study clothing. Is that about it?"

"Well, I wasn't in a fix to begin with."

"I'm glad to hear that you weren't in a fix. Suppose you tell me what you're calling about."

"It's just that—" she began. Her father wanted to get back to sleep, he wanted to exchange telephone kisses over six thousand miles, he wanted to feel he'd done his fatherly duty, his fatherly best, and not lose so much sleep that he'd be positively sloppy on the golf course later that morning. "Listen, Daddy. You know from my letter how much I'm enjoying what I'm doing here, learning about a business, becoming involved with something interesting and useful."

"That's very nice."

"Now I don't want Thomas to interfere with me again, like he did last time."

"Did he do that?"

"Well, he didn't understand what I was trying to do. He thought I was being manipulated, used. Now that's not the

171

case at all, and I've explained it to him. I'm starting my own dress company—that's what I came to Paris for, that's what I intend to do." Valerie hoped that he was still listening, that he hadn't slipped effortlessly back to sleep. "Daddy?"

"I'm here." He coughed. "It's very interesting, all this."

"To make a long story as short as possible, Thomas hates a business associate of mine—"

"Business associate?" said her father jokingly. "Such a grand phrase for such a young girl."

"Daddy, please listen." The shower was finally shut off in the bathroom, and she half expected Jonathan to come out instantly, naked, wet, hair wild, talking loudly in the background. "It's important to me. Thomas has the idea that this business associate of mine is always trying to use me, control me. But the fact is he's a nice man, a good businessman, and he's going to be working for me, for my company. Anyway, he's come to Paris, and we're going to be going through some fabrics and designs together—"

"Valerie," said her father, "this is all very interesting, but as it's two o'clock in the morning, and as we're both straight shooters, let's have it, OK? What's the problem?"

"I told Mommy I'd stay with Lady Oliver. I want to move out of her house because she doesn't give me a minute's peace—always spying, always prying."

"Is that all?"

"I just didn't want what happened once before to happen again—"

"What happened?"

"My allowance?"

"Oh, that," said her father.

"I don't want Thomas and Mommy to make a big deal out of my moving out of Lady Oliver's now that my business associate has come to Paris—"

"On business?"

Jonathan came out of the bathroom, dried and powdered, and less angry—now that he saw her on the phone.

He retreated to an easy chair and watched and listened.

"On business, yes of course."

"Well then, why on earth should your mother and Thomas care that you've moved? Everyone knows that Lady Oliver is a pain in the ass."

"Thank you, Daddy."

"I didn't do anything. Except get up in the middle of the night."

"Thanks for understanding."

"Where are you going to be living?" said her father, remembering that it was his duty to ask.

"The Intercontinental," she said.

"OK dear," said her father. "Take care. Call if you need anything."

"I'm sorry for waking you, Daddy. But thanks for everything."

She hung up.

"Good going," said Jonathan.

"That remains to be seen," she said feeling suddenly annoyed with Jonathan. His remark seemed to be a compliment for her having manipulated her father, and for a moment she felt like correcting his error. Instead, she let it ride and proceeded to dress, allowing the resentment to fester, along with others. They had a short argument about living arrangements, Jonathan feeling it would be much simpler for her to move into his suite—there was plenty of room. But Valerie insisted on registering and taking a suite on the same floor. She didn't believe in letting everyone in Paris (that meant Lady Oliver, Hugh, Joseph Weintrob) know that she was sleeping in Jonathan's bed.

They had a short, disastrous meeting with Lady Oliver ("May I introduce Jonathan Singer?" "No, you may not. This is disgraceful. Leaving here like this. Whatever will your mother say?"), but Jonathan played the quiet gentleman, refraining from imitating her ladyship's accent and mannerisms until they were safely out of her grand chambers, Valerie's luggage in hand. The day was warm enough to lunch outside, and they celebrated the move at a sidewalk table of a brasserie on the rue Thonchet. Jonathan's impatience was held in check by a golden omelette, which he devoured with pleasure and speed.

"Now what's all this nonsense about delaying?" he said finally. She began to explain (while his mouth was full with half a *baguette*) that Joseph Weintrob was teaching her things she'd need to know not only this year, but all the years she'd be in the business.

"I know you're in a hurry to get started, Johnny, but I'm really doing so much here. Groundwork, for the future. One day, when we're big enough, we can open our own fabric plant—"

"At this rate, we won't be able to afford a closet on Broadway, much less a factory in Europe."

"It's going to come, Johnny, it really is." And she'd talked to him of dreams—some her own, some picked from Hugh's head, some from the Parisian air. It was not enough to have a simple basic-dress line, not enough to be one step ahead of all the others—they had to have a product so different, so unusual, that they'd remain totally in a class by themselves, even after the other manufacturers started trying to knock off their copies. "It's our fabric that's got to be unique. Something fine, not too expensive, easy to take care of, and absolutely exclusive to our dresses."

"That's great thinking," said Jonathan. "For a Holmes."

"What's that supposed to mean?"

"That you're thinking too big. It's one step at a time in this business, kid. Nobody likes to gamble more than yours truly, but we always like to have something to gamble with. You want to buy a textile plant, that's cool, honey. But not this year. This year Valerie Holmes knocks 'em dead with her acrylic shirtwaist dresses— simple, classic, easy to get into the stores if we keep the price right."

"Which acrylic?"

"That's what I thought you went to Paris for. How the hell long does it take you to pick out the right kind of *shmates*?"

"What's that?"

"What's what?"

"That word you used?"

Jonathan looked at her with absolute puzzlement, until it dawned on him what word she meant. "*Shmates*?"

"Yes."

"*Shmates*, you don't know what *shmates* means, that's too good. I love it. Valerie Holmes is going to take over Seventh Avenue and she don't know what *shmates* is."

If Jonathan had been annoyed with her, the annoyance was fleeing in a rush of humor—and understanding. "Is it Yiddish?" she said, and he was laughing now.

"Yeah, it's Yiddish, sure it's Yiddish— Listen, kid, *shmates* is the backbone of the industry. It's what we deal, it's what we're in—we're in the *shmate* business, and we sell *shmates*."

"Clothes?"

"Not clothes, Valerie—*shmates* isn't such a nice word for clothes—it's more like rags than clothes—it's why we don't take it too seriously, the whole couture trip, the whole Yves Saint Laurent number. When you get down to Broadway and Seventh Avenue in the Thirties, we're not selling clothes as much as we're pushing *shmates*."

She wasn't sure she understood the finer connotations of the word, but she was glad to see that his humor was changing for the better. He had a beer (a "Grande Blonde") and a Gauloise, and shut up for a while and looked at Paris. She could see that he was going to have his way, that she wouldn't stay in Paris much longer, that she'd see the advisability of "stepping it up," selecting her fabric, her prints, her designs, and getting back to New York—to the whirlwind. But she was certain that her back was becoming more and more eager to rise at any sign of infringement on her rights and inclinations.

An hour later they were at Weintrob's plant outside of

175

Paris, and Jonathan traded gossip with the manufacturers about some of the fabric people he dealt with in New York. He liked Weintrob, and Weintrob seemed to approve of him—even of his haste. Valerie and Weintrob showed Jonathan around the plant and talked over a selection of acrylics that Valerie was thinking of using for the shirtwaists.

"Which do you like best?" he asked Weintrob, and after a brief discussion the older man and Valerie agreed on the fabric.

"Like cashmere, no?" Weintrob said.

"It better be cheaper than cashmere," said Jonathan.

"It's also fast-drying," said Valerie.

"I'm not the one who's got to be sold. It's your company, kid." They were all smiles now, smiles and enthusiasm, and they sat down to talk about money and production schedules, and the number of prints she should stick to for this first test. Jonathan was for printing six or seven different designs, but Valerie wanted to stick to three prints—the only ones she was sure about.

"I'm afraid this isn't worth arguing about, Johnny," she said.

"It certainly is; we have a disagreement, we can't just leave it in midair."

"We're not," said Valerie. And there was a coldness in her voice he had never before noticed. "It's my business, my name. This isn't open to debate. It's the way I want it, and that's all there is to it."

Jonathan said nothing for a moment, just returned her stare without expression. Then he said: "That's strike one, kid."

Weintrob had left them alone for a few minutes, and now he reentered the charged atmosphere of his pleasant office. Valerie asked if he could do three very short runs of the prints she wanted, and he very gallantly said that he would do it "only for her." They wound up the meeting quickly, cordially, and then Jonathan rudely pushed out of the office ahead of them both.

In the cab going to Paris, he said nothing, until she asked him what was wrong. "Just don't forget who asked you into this business," he said.

"I haven't, and I won't, Johnny, but that's no—"

"I don't want to hear it," he interrupted.

"If we have a disagreement—" she began.

"Then whatever you say goes," he interrupted again.

"Not necessarily."

"Just in this case."

"In this case I'm right."

"You're the one who's deciding what's right and what's wrong. That doesn't necessarily mean bullshit."

"Jonathan," she said. "you may have gotten me into this business. You may have spent a long time in it. You may know more about selling and fighting and bribing and trucking—but, God damn it, I know what I want to do with these dresses, and I want to do it right."

"You know something?"

"What?"

"I took a little twenty-three-year-old pussy and put her into the jungle, and all of a sudden she thinks she knows more than the lions and tigers."

"Not all of a sudden."

"One month in Paris."

"For Chrissake, Johnny, I wish you'd stop and think for a second, and realize that just maybe I've got a brain in my head, that maybe I know something, that just maybe listening to me will help you too."

"I'm listening," he said.

She told him what she wanted to do. Have someone in Paris make up three dresses from the three prints: two variations on the shirtwaist and one wrap dress that he hadn't seen yet—she'd seen a similar style in one of the Faubourg St.-Honoré's least progressive shops and "adapted it" for her own. "It's fabulous," she told him. "The wrap's going to be sexy in that fabric, and it's going to look great all the way from six to sixteen. It's the kind of cling that shows off your figure, if you've got one, and

177

slims it down with a sash if you're chunky. Once I've got the dresses here, in Paris, I want to take them to every fashion magazine in town."

"Why can't you do that in New York?"

She told him about Mrs. Michon at *Nouvelles*. "Over here I'm interesting, a rich American on the wrong side of the water, pushing dresses. I can get to Paris *Vogue* faster than I can get to American. And when I get back to New York, if I've been picked up by the European magazines, I'll have started something that the American magazines will want to continue. Meanwhile, Willy can make up the dresses in New York, and you can start whispering about them to buyers. Something big around the corner, but not here just yet. Look for an item in *Vogue*."

"As long as we're talking so big, you ought to keep in mind that 1407 Broadway is mostly a sportswear house. Maybe you ought to move a block, get a few floors in one of the hot Seventh Avenue buildings."

"Are you trying to be funny?"

"No. But I mean—*Vogue* and fashion magazines and building up the excitement slowly and steadily . . . It doesn't sound like anything I taught you."

"Maybe it isn't."

"Then what I'm asking is: Who the hell did?"

"I learned from people here, different people," she said. Instinctively, she veered away from Hugh Robertson's name—she knew it would incense Jonathan. Not just a fag, but the richest queer in the world. "But give me a little credit too. Some things no one had to teach me. Maybe it's in my blood." And she smiled to make this into a bit of a joke, a bit of a half-truth.

Jonathan became quiet, pensive. At one point, he again mentioned the inadvisability of starting an office of her own in 1407 Broadway. The buyers were used to coming there for sportswear, not for the sort of line that she dreamed of.

"All I want is one room, Johnny," she said. "In 1407 Broadway. With my name on the door. For sentimental reasons, OK?" And for the first time that day, she relaxed and leaned into him, not with passion, but with friendly familiarity.

When he had met her, she had been less of an unknown quantity that she was now; then she was immature, outside his experience, difficult to open up. But then too, she was stagnant, a still target, not changing. But now she was very much in motion. It was becoming harder and harder to peg her. Hot and cold, aggressive and defensive, eager to make love, eager to have the bed to herself. He resisted an urge to push her away from him, to punish her independence. He tried to remember the night before, in bed, what it had been like—if he'd pleased her. He'd certainly pleased himself. Maybe that was the problem. Maybe she was trying to pay him back for starting up an affair about which she felt guilt. He placed his hand on the top of her head and slowly brought it down to the nape of her neck, gently massaging away the tightness.

"Still like me?" he said.

"Yes."

"I've an idea how to spend the afternoon."

"Do you?"

"Do you?" he repeated, but in another voice, sly and wise. She kissed him, not so much friendly as forgiving. Jonathan slipped his hand down her back and slid it under her backside on the vinyl seat of the cab.

"I've got to show you the new sketches."

"What?" he said.

She was pulling his hand away. "There's a time for everything, Johnny."

Well, that was that. As passionate as an ice bag. He tried to decide whether to act hurt or indifferent; choosing the latter, he quickly lapsed into a sullenness that made no impression on her at all. She was far too busy talking about the wrap dress, wondering if it could sell wholesale for less than $49.75, asking how much time they'd be allowed between department store orders and delivery dates, thinking out loud about whether Lorelei could handle a sudden rush of business from Valerie Holmes, Inc.

"I figure I need about thirty-five thousand dollars, Johnny," she said. "Once I know there'll be orders, I can open a shop. Until then, I'm going to have to rely on you, and a lot of credit."

"We're partners, aren't we?" Even this was said with an edge, as if she'd almost forgotten this silent arrangement.

"Not exactly partners," she said. "It's my fifty-one percent."

"Yeah, and Lorelei is my one hundred percent, so what the hell are you talking about? We're making the goods, so who else is your partner?"

"I'm just trying to keep it all clear in our minds, that's all."

"Clear in our minds," he mumbled. "Sometimes I think you'd like to hire me as a shipping clerk, and that would be the entire extent of our relationship."

She didn't answer that. She was thinking about calling her father, after carefully making sure that it wasn't the middle of the night in California, and asking him for the seed money. If she was to be independent, she couldn't rely solely on Jonathan's firm. She'd have to develop her own operation beyond the one-room showroom into a plant of some kind; if they didn't sew there, they'd have to at least do the cutting. Her grandfather had died when she was eleven, and she remembered the way he used to talk to her and Thomas—mostly Thomas—about business. The usual stuff, but it hit home, remained with her like a legacy. If you've got a buck, never spend more than ninety-nine cents. When you make big plans, try to imagine the disasters waiting in the wings and include the cost of each catastrophe in your planning. If she asked for pocket money, he always gave her 10 percent more than she asked for. He was the one who taught her how to figure 10 percent of any figure; she remembered the way he looked when he slashed the last digit of some fat number with his gold fountain pen and asked her to read out the result. Her own father wasn't like that at all. He never spoke to any of them about money. That was strictly for lackeys to handle. Things like allowances, once approved, were done through secretaries, the bank. She never saw the bills run up on her credit cards, and she doubted that her father did either; or, if he did, whether they registered.

"What do you think of thirty-five thousand"? she said.

"It's a hell of a lot more than I had when I started."

"You think it's enough?"

"Enough for what, Valerie?" he said. "Do you know what you want to do with it?" But they were rhetorical questions, she decided. Ten percent, slash the last figure, thirty-five hundred, add it on: thirty-eight thousand, five hundred. A nice loan to ask from Daddy, if he could be bothered with thinking about it. Something about Jonathan's voice touched a sore spot. Like the rest of the world, there was part of him that despised her. *It's a hell of a lot more than I had . . . Enough for what?* The sore spot was the lack of independence—still. If she was showing her colors with Jonathan, letting him understand that she was growing, had a dream of her own, a dream no longer subservient to his, she was still aware of the easy access to comfort, to money—the easy way to slide back. An entrepreneur like Jonathan—a college dropout with middle-class parents, a man with a wife and expensive habits and no profession—could never feel sympathy for her achievements. If she were to fail, her failure would mean nothing other than a return to home, comforts, protection from the world. Jonathan's failure would result in something far worse. All his comforts were based on ephemera—a rented apartment, a house with big real estate taxes, an insurance policy on two expensively garaged cars. All these had to be paid for with a continuing source of income, a source for which only he was responsible. All her comforts were solidly based on a family fortune so immense that nothing short of revolution could possibly rock the foundations of her life.

Even her own revolution, she thought wryly.

All the rich young people who'd turned away from their parents to discover truth—the ones she'd known, at any rate—eventually found their way back home, to another truth. Plane tickets to India cost money, and contributions to gurus, big and small (gurus), were gladly accepted.

At the hotel, Jonathan asked her to wait for a moment. He wanted to check for messages at the desk. By the time he'd come back to her, she'd made up her mind: She would be stupid not to ask her father for the money. She couldn't escape who she was; she could not pretend that the best thing about her line of dresses wasn't her last name; she could not fake poverty. And she wanted a business, she wanted it badly; she wanted to show herself and the world what she could do. If her father had been a candy-store owner, she would have asked for help: five hundred dollars, maybe. Five hundred dollars to the hypothetical candy-store owner must be more than thirty-five thousand dollars to the head of the Holmes empire, to the man who spent half a million dollars for her coming-out party.

"There's a message for you," said Jonathan, a bit glumly.

"For me?" She took the message—a pink slip, inscribed with a neat hand. Who knew she was there? Weintrob, Lady Oliver—everybody, then. Maybe it was her mother. There was a number to call back, a number with a 213—Los Angeles—area code, and the instruction to call collect. Upstairs, Jonathan wanted to accompany her to her suite, undoubtedly to sit in a chair and watch her make her call. But she pleaded for an hour alone, and, for once, he didn't seem eager to argue or take offense. After all, the bags that had been dropped off at the hotel on the way back from Lady Oliver's had to be unpacked. And perhaps there were calls he had to make. To Eddy, for instance.

"Is it your father's number?"

"His office," she said.

"Well, you know where to find me," he said, and he bent low and kissed her cheek. She went into her suite, placed the call, and waited.

"Miss Holmes, I've a message for you from your father." The voice was brisk, authoritative, no-nonsense-lady-prepared-to-meet-spoiled-child head-on. A new voice too, not one of the old family retainers who had taken her to the San Diego Zoo when she was a child. "We're holding back all funds from your account with the bank, and will no longer be responsible for purchases made on your credit cards beginning immediately."

Once again the decisions were being taken away from her. No need to ask about thirty-five thousand dollars, or thirty-five cents. Thomas had reexplained the situation that Valerie had that morning painted for her father, and dear Daddy had apparently realized once again that she was being bad.

The voice droned on: "When you're ready to return to New York, or to California, you are to contact this office, and your ticket and all travel arrangements will be paid for. Your father suggests that you return home immediately."

Valerie had hardly spoken. Bravely, she asked: "Could you possibly put me through to him?"

"I'm afraid that's out of the question, Miss Holmes. Your father is taking messages, of course, but he's currently in transit."

"To or from the golf course?" said Valerie, but the secretary made no answer to this. "Are you allowed to tell me what this is all about?"

"I don't know what this is all about. Perhaps it will be explained to you in New York, or California."

"Mommy or Daddy."

"In any case, if our office can be of any assistance—if you're ready to make travel arrangements right now—"

"No," said Valerie, and then she thought she heard something in the background, some interruption. After a moment, the secretary, with the same no-nonsense voice, returned to her post.

"Actually, Miss Holmes," she said, "I did neglect to tell you one thing. Your father is particularly upset about some information he's received from your brother, about a business associate of yours, a Mr. Singer. Mr. Holmes was particularly insistent on my mentioning this to you, and I regret not having brought it up at once."

"That's all right," said Valerie. "You can tell Daddy I got the message."

A moment later she was knocking on the door to Jonathan's suite. "To hell with those sketches," she said. "There's got to be a better way to spend the afternoon."

"Has he left?"

"Yes—reluctantly."

"I'm sure. Biggest one he's ever seen, I bet."

"May I sit down?"

"Since when the hell have you started asking?"

"Since when have you started talking to me like that?"

"I'm not talking to you in any way, any special way—For God's sake, must we fight before I've even brushed my teeth?" Hugh Robertson got out of the hugh white bed and walked down the three steps of the platform on which it sat—ludicrously, in his opinion, but then he hadn't been consulted when Milton and his designer had fallen in love with white rooms, and flat surfaces, and platforms, and hideaway track lighting.

"Why not take a leak first?" said Milton Brommel, sitting on a white satin-covered stool. He was barefoot, bare-chested, wearing faded jeans, waist size 29. "Before you brush your teeth, man," he added. Hugh had gone into the adjoining bathroom, and now the clear sound of his urinating made Milt laugh out loud. When Hugh emerged from the bathroom, he'd put on a robe over his silk pajamas. The pajamas were one of a dozen pairs, in as many colors, given to him by Milt on Hugh's last birthday.

"What the hell is so funny?"

"Nothing actually," said Milt. "That's what I'm here to talk about."

"Well, if you don't mind, I don't feel very much like talking. I'm late as it is, I've got a headache, I've got two appointments before twelve o'clock—"

"Hugh, I'm sorry if we disturbed you last night. I know we were a little noisy—"

"Rowdy," corrected Hugh. "Rowdy and obnoxious."

"So that's what it is. You are mad about Timothy."

"No. Forget it. I don't give a shit about Timothy, or about anyone else you feel like fucking, OK? Now may I get dressed?"

"No you may not."

"Christ, I'm not mad at you, Milt—believe me. If I was, I forgave you. It's forgotten. What else can I say?"

"I don't know. I just don't know, man. You're being very strange, you're not yourself." Milt had come over to where Hugh was rummaging in the antique armoire—one of the few nonwhite pieces in the bedroom. "Listen," he said, and he put his bare arm about his friend. "I know you're upset. I don't think it's just your usual puritanical head either. It's something else."

"I'm not a puritan, Milt."

"We don't have to discuss that now. That's not what I'm worried about where you're concerned."

Hugh had a very good idea of what Milt was worried about. So, carefully, with the natural ease of a practiced prevaricator, he pursued what didn't need pursuing rather than give Milt the chance to continue to pry. "Maybe that's what I'm worried about where you're concerned," said Hugh, "I don't have anything against sleeping with someone you love—"

"Oh, Jesus."

"—or even, sometimes, someone you feel very drawn to. Someone you love in a sexual way, more than a—"

"More than a what?" Milt interrupted again. "I love you, you love me—we sure as hell aren't going to bed together."

"That's certainly no reason for fucking every male model in Paris."

"Now you sound like Father Time."

"Thanks, that's what I needed," said Hugh, and he twisted himself out of his friend's grasp and selected a blue shirt with a button-down collar from the armoire and turned with it, crossing the room to the enormous dresser.

"What I want to know is why you're so damned sensitive all of a sudden?"

Milt followed him across the room, and Hugh didn't like the curious look of concern in the face looming behind his in the dresser's mirror. If he didn't parry, the conversation was headed back for dangerous waters. "I just don't like the idea that you have—that as long as you're queer, you've got to be a promiscuous queer."

"I don't like the word 'queer.' "

Anger would certainly get him off the scent. Hugh said, "As long as you're a faggot, you might as well fuck every faggot in town."

Milt grabbed him again, but this time none too gently. Spinning him around, he said: "There's one faggot in town I'm sure as hell not fucking. One faggot in town who's a hell of a lot more screwed up than I am, you son of a bitch."

"As I said," said Hugh, "I don't feel much like talking."

"I do."

"Get your hands off me," said Hugh, and, without thinking he slapped at Milt's arm and started to push him away. Automatically, Milt blocked the pushing hand and sent his open fist hard into the side of Hugh's jaw, knocking him violently into the dresser. "Fucking bitch," said Hugh.

"I'm sorry," said Milt. "I didn't mean—" He stooped to pick up a bottle of YSL cologne that had fallen to the floor from the top of the dresser, but hadn't broken. As he stooped, Hugh let go of his jaw and pushed him; Milt stumbled, but didn't fall.

"You didn't mean it, right?" said Hugh. "You could've broken my jaw."

"You all right?" said Milt, returning the cologne bottle to the dresser.

"Just don't touch me."

"So stupid, this. All because I wanted to talk to you."

"All because of some asinine male model trying to fuck his way into your next show."

"Actually, he wants to work in *your* next show, and in New York. That's another thing," said Milt. "Christ, I told him to call you at the office today. I guess he's going to get a hell of a reception."

"I'll tell him to plug his prick into a light socket."

"You do that, I'll plug a barbecue spit up your Miss Holmes's cunt." Milt was advancing again, but suddenly his eyes were shining. The arrow had come from nowhere, but only an idiot—which Milton Brommel was not—would fail to see that it had struck its mark. "Oh, wow," he said. "That's it."

Hugh said nothing, turning his head, letting the silence grow. His voice, when he finally spoke, was chilly enough to be confirmation of Milt's guess. "I've had enough of this conversation, and you," said Hugh. "Thanks very much for an enjoyable morning."

"I mean I can't understand why it should be it, but that's it. That is definitely it." Milt stopped a foot away from him, to stare with his pretty hazel eyes into Hugh Robertson's face. "Maybe it's because she reminds you of some pretty little boy back home in Waterloo—she's certainly no great shakes as a lady."

"You know how I value your opinion, Milt," said Hugh. "Especially in anything pertaining to heterosexual relations."

"What is it about her? The thick eyebrows, the way she shakes her nonexistent ass? You like her ankle bracelet? She sure dresses chic. With a few years' training, she could pass herself off as a girl."

"Whereas you could pass tomorrow."

"Fuck off."

"More than happy to," said Hugh. "As soon as you let me get dressed. I'll move into a hotel tonight."

This gave Milt pause. "Jesus Christ, nobody said anything about throwing you out."

"I can take a hint."

"Can I please talk to you Hugh?"

"We've been talking."

"Does she know that you're a faggot?"

"She knows that I'm a gentleman, and her friend. And I'd much prefer we end this subject at once, before whatever is left of our friendship completely falls apart."

Milt walked to a chaise longue across the room and sat on its edge with considerable discomfort. "If you'd think for a minute, you'd realize that I came in here for only one reason. I thought you looked a little down-in-the-mouth last night at dinner, and I wanted to know if you were OK. That's all. For some reason, it turned into a fight. I don't know whose fault it was, but if it was mine, I'm sorry, Hugh—I'm genuinely sorry."

"OK."

"No, more than that," said Milton Brommel, getting up. "Please Hugh. If you can't talk to me, there's no one else—really. No matter what you think."

"I'm sorry too," said Hugh, and he allowed Milt his embrace, and returned Milt's two lengthy kisses to the mouth with one short one to his clear warm forehead.

"I don't want us to fight," said Milt, still holding Hugh tightly.

"No."

"I love you so much."

"I love you too, Milt," said Hugh, and he didn't have to tell him again what that meant. The declarations weren't equivalent, at least not as far as Milt was concerned. Hugh had slept with him, but not in more than two years; and that last time had been disastrous, painful. Hugh said his love was friendship, understanding, a desire to share; but his love wasn't sexual. He didn't like sleeping with men any more than he liked sleeping with women. He was not a sexual being, he'd told Milt a thousand times, but Milt didn't believe such an animal existed. As far as he was concerned, Hugh was a bona fide old-fashioned fairy, too ridden with guilt about his abnormality to possibly enjoy being possessed by another man. He wasn't bisexual, he wasn't asexual, he wasn't neuter—he was simply frigid, locked in the sad power of his unconscious. If Milton Brommel had a hundred lovers, he nevertheless had only one love—a love whom he pitied, and wanted.

"Sit down."

"All right," said Hugh, and he held his friend's hand tightly as they walked to the chaise and sat, Milt again putting his now-welcome arm about Hugh's shoulders.

"I'd like to hear about it."

"I don't really understand it myself."

"There must be something about the last few days that made you—"

"Yes," said Hugh, glad of the opening. He turned to look at his friend's beautiful face. Yes, this was someone who loved him, and for the first time that week he felt like talking about it. "Valerie's lover's come to Paris."

And then Hugh tried to explain what he himself did not yet understand. "His name is Jonathan Singer, a small-time Seventh Avenue character."

"Good-looking?"

"If you like the wife-beater look." There was a pause. "All right, he's not a wife-beater, and he's not even that small time. He does have some interesting ideas, and he's young, self-made up to I'd guess a hundred grand a year. But obviously, compared to Valerie's background, he's nothing."

"Aren't we all?" Milt drew in his quip and attempted a serious expression. "What exactly is the problem, Hugh? You don't think that you're in love with her?"

"I like her very much." Hugh got off the chaise and turned to face him. "There's a quality in her that I admire. I don't know—a civilized feeling that's not fully formed yet. Maybe this doesn't make any sense to you. I had a younger sister, you know that. She died when she was twelve, and I was fourteen. There were things I wanted to tell her that she was never to hear. She was sensitive, easily hurt, easily misled. And also bright, brave. I played

190

football in those days; in Waterloo it's a pretty big thing. I wasn't bad either. I had a good arm, I wasn't afraid to get knocked down. But Mary liked my drawings. She wanted me to be an artist, a painter with a cape and a palette. She didn't care much for football. She was always afraid I'd hurt myself, hurt my hands. She had enormous brown eyes, thick, wavy brown hair. I loved her, of course, maybe more than I've ever loved anyone. An ideal love, an impossible love between a big brother and a sister who died before she was really grown up. I think we would have been very close if she'd lived. I would've liked to show her New York, Paris, Rome—she never got further east than Chicago."

"I didn't know any of this."

"Well, I don't think about it all the time."

"But frankly—I don't see why Valerie Holmes—I don't see the relation. I'm sure she'd gone further east than Chicago before she was twelve."

"No."

"What?"

"Not really. She may have crossed a lot of borders, but she—she's not grown-up either. I see Mary in her because they both were reaching out for something, something outside the family, outside of what people expected of them. Maybe it's because Valerie's the first young woman I've met who doesn't have to use me to 'make it.' She's already got it made, in terms of what people usually think of as making it. But she wants something else. Besides making it. She wants to define herself, she wants to take control of where she's going, understand why she's going there." Hugh sat down on the stool across the room. "I didn't like her Jonathan Singer because he's going in a different direction. I don't think she wants to go there either."

"And you want to do something about all this?"

"Yes."

"What?"

"Make her open her eyes to what he is, what she is."

"Because you love her like a sister," said Milt.

"If you don't mean that as a joke—yes."

"I don't mean it as a joke," said Milt. "But I really don't see what you're going to be able to do, short of romancing her yourself."

"She doesn't think of me like that," said Hugh.

"And you, how do you think of her—like that?"

"I'm her friend," said Hugh. "And I want to be as good to her as I can."

Milton Brommel drew his hands back through his bleached hair and lay back in a comfortable reclining position on the chaise longue. "That's what you told me once. Verbatim. 'I'm your friend. I want to be as good to you as I can.' I'll tell you something, Hugh. Sometimes I don't know how good it's been. Maybe you shouldn't go around making *friends* until you get off the fence and decide what the hell you are."

"I know what I am. As much as anyone does."

"If you knew what you were you'd be here right now, right next to me." Milt patted the chaise longue and slowly raised a hand along his chest to his throat. "Instead of all this talk about friendship."

"I'm your friend."

"Yes."

"And I don't think it's been bad. I've gotten a lot from our friendship, and I've given a lot—I think."

"And now you want a new friend," said Milt. "A girl friend. But otherwise, a friend very much like me."

"I thought you were beginning to understand."

"I am."

"Our friendship should be secure enough to allow for new relationships. I've never interfered with your—with any of your affairs."

"Maybe because they presented no threat. Just some more fairy-fucking. I never brought home anybody that I'd even put in the same sentence with you."

"Well, you can hardly say that I make a habit of picking up girls, Milt."

Milt suddenly sat up, swinging his legs off the chaise, placing his bare feet on the carpet. "All right," he said. "You like Valerie Holmes. As a friend. I accept that. Let me just give you a word of advice, as a friend, as someone who loves you." He paused, started to get up, but then remained sitting, his right leg crossed over his left, the foot swinging steadily to some interior rhythm of despair. " 'Friend' is a difficult word, a tough thing to understand. You want to play around with that girl, you keep that in mind. Maybe she's not going to understand you or your intentions. Maybe she's going to think you're coming on to her and that she's the one you've been waiting for all your life. To make an honest man out of you. Maybe that's what she's going to have in mind when you tell her you're her friend, and you want to be as good to her as you can."

"No, I don't think so," said Hugh Robertson. "She'll understand. I think she already does. What I want in our relationship."

Milton Brommel got up from the chaise longue and walked to the door. "Let's just hope," he said, "those aren't famous last words."

14

It took Valerie most of the week she spent with Jonathan in Paris to understand that he thought of himself as something of a stud.

Of course, she hardly had a wealth of sexual experience upon which to draw comparisons. Putting him up against Phillip S. Raymond III wasn't giving him much competition; she and her husband had both been young, clumsy virgins, with a fear of asking each other questions. Jonathan, on the other hand, never seemed to shut up until he was absolutely certain that she'd achieved her orgasm, however small. And he was never so pleased with himself as when he'd made her come twice, three times in a single night of pressing, pulling, prodding, and pumping.

Not that she minded.

Her body was young, delicate. Sexual attention had never been lavished on her in this way. His hands were easy, gentle, slow, in search of her pace, her fulfillment. They were strong too, and large. She liked the way he cupped her buttocks, rising to strength—near ferocity— when she began to suck in her breath, draw in his shoulders, drive her fingernails across his back; when what moved inside her of him began to meet the rushing, irreversible current of her own sexual being. And afterward, the way he had of cradling her, her face buried in his wide chest; and the loud rhythm of his racing heart.

But the "stud." That was something else, something that put the lie to all his protestations of love.

"What are you doing?" she asked him early one night, after a dinner of steak and wine in which he'd referred to "tube steak" at least three times before she'd been forced to ask him just exactly what that was. For answer, he'd grabbed her hand under the table and pulled it to his crotch.

"Lean red meat," he'd said, smiling so broadly that she knew her anger wouldn't be understood. She'd pulled her hand back. "Later, later, that's cool," he'd said. "I know when the *Shmate* Queen is hot."

"I don't like when you talk like that," she'd said, but immediately putting on a smile, to forestall any anger.

They'd shared two full bottles—seventy centiliters each—of Mouton-Cadet, and she'd been flushed and happy and sexy in the taxi back to the hotel, undoubtedly because she knew this fling was to be short-lived. Jonathan was leaving in a few days for New York, alone. Their fight over authority and decisions to be made about her own line had been swept under the rug in the wake of her father once again cutting off her allowance and credit. Jonathan had been magnanimous, of course, putting her hotel bill on his account, paying for everything with his credit cards, so he'd be able to leave her the two thousand dollars in cash he'd taken along for the weeks she'd stay on after he'd be gone. She realized that he was unafraid for her future. In the long run, if her company didn't work out, there'd be another reconciliation with Daddy and Mommy—even with brother Thomas.

What he didn't know, couldn't know, was that even then, even as they clutched at each other in the cab, rode up in the elevator to Jonathan's hotel suite, his hand reaching out to grip her backside, she was planning. And her plans were sure, straightforward, self-directed. If she didn't have much cash of her own, she still had her jewelry. She wouldn't think twice about selling enough rings, necklaces, pins, and clips to make up her thirty-five-thousand-dollar figure. Daddy didn't think she was capable of running her own life. He'd soon see. Jonathan was in a hurry to see her set up and blooming. Well, she'd show him what hurrying meant, now that the devil

195

of her own ambition had been pressed into emergency service.

They were in bed almost as soon as they were past the door, but still she was planning: the lunch with the editor tomorrow; the idea she had for her future showroom in New York as a mini-living room, filled with plants and Persian rugs and good, old furniture; returning to *Nouvelles*, armed with her sample case of dresses and friendly comments from French magazines.

"Johnny!" He had turned round in bed, was kissing her navel, with his penis practically in her face. "What are you doing?" she repeated.

"Making you relax," he said, the stud speaking.

"Johnny," she said again, but his mouth was already beginning to join his hand in a celebration of her private parts. Valerie couldn't believe it. She was unaware of the preponderance of adult Americans who engaged in what she'd always imagined to be a deviation. Her heart beat now, not with passion, but with terror—the terror of committing some ghastly, abnormal act.

Jonathan was on another wavelength. The girl was retreating again, that much was obvious. Thinking of things other than Jonathan Singer, even here in his room, in his bed. Just when he was—for some perverse reason—beginning to see something in her worthy of his respect besides her name, and his desire to "pay back" rich WASP America for trying (unsuccessfully) to exclude him from the American Dream, just when he was falling for this little girl who thought she'd learned everything she'd ever need to know about running a rag business, just when he was actually thinking of her in terms of love—she was beginning to drift away.

"Jonathan, you mustn't, I don't want you to do that," she said, but he simply raised a hand from her knee to her belly in a flat calming gesture; and, as the hand moved up to her breasts, she was already resigned. Resigned to pleasure.

All the while she was thinking it dirty, salacious,

incredibly bad and wrong. Of course, this was something that the "tube steak" proponent would have in his repertoire. But, oh, Johnny. Too good to be legitimate sex, sanctioned by organized religion. She came in great waves, thinking of no dresses, not showrooms. And then they were making love again, their bodies already exhausted, but deliciously exhausted—a frame for their burning sexuality. The only thing that marred it was his consciousness of technique—his deliberate mention of what he knew had pleased her.

"You didn't want me to go down on you, did you?" he said, a smile across his face, as if to say, "You big fool, Valerie Holmes. Just let Johnny do his thing."

"No."

"But you liked it?"

"Johnny, don't now."

"Don't what?" he said, turning to face her, ruining the perfect cradling of her head.

"Talk," she said. And again: "Please don't talk. Not now."

"Well, it's OK," he said. "I know you liked it, kid. You make it very clear when you like something. Very clear."

Was that supposed to mean that she was an inordinately heavy-breathing girl? Or someone difficult to please? Was her great fear of being asexual, or frigid, to be reinforced? She had half a mind to ask him, right then and there: Am I a normal girl? How long do they usually take to come? Do they get so wet? Are they tighter, or looser?

But of course she said nothing.

"But I'll tell you something," he said. "Just as a general rule. It's nice to say something."

"What?"

"When you like it, I mean."

"Oh."

"I mean I know you liked it, I can feel it, but it's nice for me—when I hear it. I tell you when you make me feel good don't I?"

She didn't answer, just nodded her head into his chest.

197

"Oh, my God," he'd say, his orgasm just over. "Oh, my God, you nearly killed me."

And when they came together, his commentary: "Jesus Christ, we made an earthquake, a fucking earthquake."

But she couldn't necessarily fault him for such behavior all the time. She knew her own to be lacking in many ways, and it wasn't spontaneous. Perhaps she retreated into silence because she didn't have the vocabulary with which to express her joy. She would never be the one to yell, "Fuck me, fuck me, fuck me!" as he did, "driving," as he liked to say, "her brains into the wall." But the lack of words matched the lack of depth. She was having an affair; it was illicit, it was dirty, it made her feel bad, it made her feel good. Already, she knew that Jonathan could never be the great love of her life. It wasn't simply a question of training away crassness. What she loved in him was also what prevented any love to develop more serious than their present mix of rough camaraderie mixed with sensual attraction.

But when he left for the airport, getting into the waiting cab in front of the hotel, she had a sudden pang, an instance of nonrational emotion. "Johnny!" she yelled after him—after having already exchanged ten thousand kisses that day (their week had been more like a honeymoon than anything else)—"I love you!"

"Yeah," he said, grinning at her from the open window of the cab. "Now you're talking."

That night, in bed, alone, she loved him terribly, loved him more than she'd ever loved her husband, loved him more than she'd ever loved anyone. And it was absurd because it had all been decided already in her mind: This affair was not to last. She was not to use him, of course; but neither was she to use up her energies for something so purely sybaritic, without emotional value. And of course, regardless of his weird marital relationship, he was still married. The relationship must certainly be slowly cooled after her return to New York.

But all this thinking evaporated that night.

198

For the first time, she wondered if *he* really loved her. She imagined living with him, teaching him, and letting him teach her. So what if he thought he was a stud? Maybe he hadn't attended a school where they taught you not to brag. Maybe his marriage was disposable, without creating terrible sorrows in the process. Maybe she'd marry him, and grow a bit more like him: quick to say what was on his mind, not afraid to throw a punch when one was due; and sentimental. His love for Willy Schwartz compounded out of the knowledge of the older man's sorrows, his patronage of Louella, his five-dollar bills thrust in beggars' baskets.

"There's an old saw, Valerie," Hugh Robertson told her a week after Jonathan left for New York. "They never leave their wives for their lovers."

"I'm not even thinking about that," she said.

"I'm sorry if I'm treading on *terra* not *firma*; but you did ask me."

"Not that," said Valerie. "What I asked you was what you thought of him." It was another unusually warm day, a throwback to early fall on the threshold of winter. The sun was shining, they were on the lake in the Bois de Boulogne, and they were not alone. A hundred other couples were rowing the old boats about the tiny islands, and perhaps many of them were headed for the same place as they—the café-restaurant on the island in the center of the lake, to whose little dock Hugh was now making his way.

"I just want to clarify one thing," said Hugh, again hiding from a direct answer. "What I said before. It's not that men don't leave their wives. They do, all the time. What the saying means is that men who leave their wives, and who all the while have been carrying on with someone else, never set up housekeeping with that someone else, now that they're finally free. Not just free for the mistress. But free for anyone and anything."

"I haven't even discussed his wife with Jonathan."

"Would you like to row for a while?"

"You really don't what to tell me, do you?"

"What I think of him?"

"Yes, of course."

"I've only met the man once, Valerie." He was smiling, and the sun looked good in his hair, in his face. They'd all had dinner together at a restaurant on the avenue de New York. She and Hugh had been nervous. She remembered only being able to prod the exquisite *fricassée de petits gris* with her silver fork, to hardly touch her *carré d'agneau Beaulieu*, so careful was she, trying to keep the conversation alive.

Jonathan of course had no such problem with his appetite. "Great stuff this! What is this anyway, snails?" When he wasn't talking, he was chewing; when he wasn't chewing, he was talking.

And that stuffy moment when Hugh explained that the ridiculously extravagant wine he'd ordered was a 1937 Burgundy from ungrafted vines of La Romanée-Conti—which Jonathan had followed with a smiling admission that he "didn't know what the hell that was, but if it was wet and red, he'd probably think it was wine."

In retrospect, it wasn't such a bad thing to say.

But she was looking back through loving eyes, missing him. The dinner had more than a few moments when she would've liked to kick Jonathan, if only to teach him how to behave. This was Hugh Robertson. Her friend could be their friend. They could benefit enormously from his expertise, his contacts. She wasn't asking him to put on a show for him. Only not to go out of his way to be aggressive, unpleasant.

"That peasant look is a joke," he told Hugh, while she sat there, trying to keep her lips together so that her mouth wouldn't open wide in disbelief. "All those fat broads walking around like they're on the way to pick apples in the middle of Hungary."

"Most of those clothes only run to size fourteen in the ready-to-wear."

"A fourteen isn't a fat broad? Meanwhile, I've got the

feeling that a few thousand slobs have gone and let out the seams to stretch that a bit. I was at a wedding in Staten Island last week, where I swear I thought the Cossacks were coming. Never seen so many Jewish peasants in my life. It looked like *Fiddler on the Roof*. That where you got the idea from?"

"Hugh, look out!" said Valerie in the boat. "On your left."

He started to row with his left oar and Valerie shouted, "No, right oar. Stop rowing with your left. Just the right. *Oops!*" It was a very minor collision. The other boat, steered by a young man on one oar and a young woman on the other, had been wobbling obliviously about the lake, and Valerie had taken her eyes off them long enough for the accident to take place: The boats had managed to bump their flat sterns. The fault lay mostly with Valerie, the only one who, looking over Hugh's head toward the island, had a clear sight of their course. "I'm sorry, I should have given you more notice," she said.

"I should have been looking over my shoulder."

"And they shouldn't be rowing that way."

After the mutual apologies, mixed with laughter, had been made, the young couple had continued on their way, sharing the narrow seat, dipping and pulling their oars whenever the spirit moved them. Mostly, they continued to take and give idle kisses in the lazy sunshine, and their erratic course was simply a symptom of their disregard for everything outside the pale of their love.

"Why not?" said Hugh. "It looks like fun." He smiled as invitingly as he could. "I could use a little help getting to the island myself."

"Want me to row?"

"Yes," he said, but made no movement to change places with her. Instead, he patted the seat next to his and let go of his right oar. Valerie got carefully out of her seat and, bending low, took the two steps across to his bench, and sat, taking the proffered oar.

201

"Now you'll have a taste of how hard I've been working."

"We had boats like this in our lake—in California."

"And you used to row?"

"When I was a little kid," she said. "I'd read that it was supposed to improve the size of your fists. And I'd had it in for my brother for a long time."

"It doesn't seem to have done much good," said Hugh. He took one of her hands and turned it over, grazing the knuckles with the tips of his manicured fingernails. The scent of his cologne was so strong that she was reminded of an article that warned about wearing perfume in too-bright sunshine. His leg grazed hers, and, as he let go her hand and they began to row, their arms, their thighs, their shoulders touched and separated, touched and separated.

"Please," said Hugh.

"What?"

"Don't be mad at me."

"Mad?"

"I don't like Jonathan Singer at all."

"Oh," Valerie said. She looked over her shoulder and saw that they were veering slightly off course, away from the island's little dock. "Stroke."

"Sorry?"

"We're going too right," she said. "You've got to stroke; I'll stop for a bit." But she didn't—she backwatered to speed things up a bit, and then, once they were straight, began to row again.

"I'll explain," said Hugh.

"I'm not mad at you, Hugh."

"Maybe it's not even my business."

"I asked."

"Of course I don't know the man very well. But I know Seventh Avenue, and he's it."

"Yes, that's true. But that's not all of him. No more than you're just the clothes you design."

"No," said Hugh. He sounded a bit put off, as if he

hadn't been aware that she was going to be defending him. He looked over his shoulder and suddenly placed his right hand over hers on the oar she held. "May I?"

"What?"

"We're close to shore—I'd like to get us in on an angle."

She let go of the oar and remained next to him, shrinking back a bit as he pulled the oar, his arm reaching across her belly. Because he was paying attention to the rowing rather than going on with the awkward assessment of her lover, he maneuvered very well, going into a practiced fisherman's crawl she hadn't seen him use before. As they approached the last few yards before the dock, he backwatered on one side, rowed on the other, turning the boat 180 degrees in a few easy moments. Turned about, he backwatered with both oars, so that their boat could hit the dock stern-first. As it came in for the landing, he picked up both oars and, bending over, walked over the thwarts to the stern, jumped onto the dock, and secured the boat by its chain to a thick metal ring.

"May I?" said Hugh, stepping back into the boat, extending a hand for the lady. Valerie got up and let him help her step off the boat. He was showing off, she knew, showing off in a new way, a way that surprised her. They'd been to the Jeu de Paume, to the Art Moderne, to the Musée National des Arts et Traditions Populaires, to the Hôtel Biron, to the Louvre—all in the weeks before Jonathan's visit—and his familiarity was not with periods, historical dates, and the sociological context of the artwork they studied, but with personal history. He'd told her about the first time he'd been to the Rodin Museum and seen the garden with *The Burghers of Calais*, *The Gates of Hell*, and, of course, *The Thinker*, reproductions of which he'd seen even in Waterloo, Iowa: How shocked he'd been, how the raw power of their beauty had hit him like a fist, had made him wonder about his own dreams of being an artist, had made him reexamine the quality of his own life. Or, walking through the mobs at the Louvre, he spoke of the day he first arrived in Paris, how he had walked through the Tuileries in the rain, had walked the halls of the great museums, absorbing nothing but the powerful sense of civilization—thinking how through every form of tyranny and revolution, through every redrawing of some national boundary, through every riot of man's prejudices, art had appeared, had survived, had been reached out for by the same kind of people in every age. He lectured her, of course, knew a great deal more than she about most of the paintings (except for the impressionists—she knew everything in the Jeu de Paume, knew it in a clinical, academic way that embarrassed her in the light of Hugh's very different kind of knowledge), but almost everything he was saying was showing off not an education, but a personality. And the personality he was showing off was sensitive, aesthetic, elitist—as if to say, Not all men are born to appreciate beauty.

Now he was showing off something else entirely. He could row expertly, he could jump off boats with a lithe step, he could pull her weight as if it were a pound. Perhaps he felt that if he was about to criticize Jonathan on aesthetic or intellectual grounds, he'd better first demonstrate that qualities of physical strength, athleticism, were nothing out of the ordinary; they were hardly qualities peculiar to Jonathan Singer.

"It's lovely here," she said, when they'd been seated at an outdoor table looking out over the boats to the adjacent islands. "It's hard to believe that we're in the middle of Paris."

"Actually, we're at the edge of the city," he said. "But still, it's an improvement over Central Park."

Jonathan, had he been sitting there, might have said, Why? And Valerie smiled at the thought, reveled in a quality of her lover's that Hugh didn't, couldn't understand. The hardness was there—not simply a pose, but a fact of his character. But at a time like this, it would've been good to hear Jonathan say: "Why, because they're

204

talking French here? For one thing, I'm sick of their damned coffee. Look at this—mud at the bottom. And these frogs are supposed to be some kind of gourmets. I'll tell you something, kid, the only thing this rich faggot doesn't dig about Central Park is the big black Africans swooping down on their stolen bikes. Otherwise, he'd dig Bethesda Fountain, he'd love the lake—and we got better oars on the boats in good old NYC. Better oars, better coffee, at least as many queers. Jesus, please tell this guy where to get off."

Valerie said: "Actually, I kind of miss New York."

"Do you? I suppose it's natural. When you get back, wait till you see how you miss Paris." Hugh cleared his throat. "Of course, you must miss Jonathan."

"Yes."

"I don't usually stay in Paris this long, you know. My whole organization is in the middle of shifting to new markets, Japan in particular. Don't ask me why, but for some reason I'm needed in Paris to help with the Japanese boutique openings."

"So you'll be here for a while?"

"At least another month, I'm afraid."

This was the moment for her to say that she'd miss him, and, during the following silence, she mulled it over in her mind. She liked this handsome, elegant man, but a month or two without seeing him would hardly make her heart skip a beat. They both began to speak at the same moment then, Valerie starting to say that she'd miss him, and Hugh starting to say that he was glad they'd gotten a chance to know each other a bit while she was in Paris.

"I'm sorry, my dear, what were you saying?"

"Just—I was starting to say—that I'm going to miss you, Hugh."

"I'm glad to hear that," he said. The waiter took their orders for *cafés au lait* and left them with a new silence. "I'm certainly going to miss you," Hugh said.

"And I just want to tell you again how grateful I am, for everything."

"Please, don't even—"

"I'd have to sit down and type up a list if I wanted to mention everything you've taught me. And the people you've got me to meet."

"Did the lunch go well?"

"Lunch?"

"That editor?"

"I didn't tell you?"

"No."

"Oh, Hugh, I am sorry. Lunch was wonderful. She was very, very sweet, particularly when I spoke about you—and—" Valerie smiled.

"And what?"

"Next month's issue."

"Oh, that's wonderful!"

"No photos, but my name, the New York address—1407 Broadway—what I'm doing, how chic my line's going to be. It's going to be in their 'Up and Coming' section. And she said she'll try to give me more space a month or so after that, when I've got more to show. With photos this time."

"It's nice when you're like this."

"Excited?"

"Yes."

"That's why I'm so looking forward to going back to New York. Because of everything. That's where it's going to happen, you'll see."

"I believe you. I still wish you'd give a little more thought to my offer. It's really quite a good one. I don't make them every day, you know. And we can tear up any agreement once you get back in your parents' good graces." He'd offered her money, as much as she'd need, the first instant he'd heard of her troubles. Only, to make the offer more palatable, he'd attached a few nebulous strings—a connection with the Robertson organization as a distributor of her clothing. But she didn't want the arrangement. She wasn't looking for an easy way out any more than she was looking for simple charity. And because Hugh had nothing to gain from associating with Valerie Holmes, Inc., his offer was just that—a handout.

"Thank you again, but no—this girl has got to stand on her own two feet. I've got too many good friends trying to corrupt me."

"I don't doubt that for a moment." Before Hugh could segue into an analysis of the support she was getting from Jonathan, the waiter reappeared and placed their cups and saucers down with a maximum of noise and rudeness of expression.

"Oh, this is the good kind," said Valerie. The *café au lait* had been prepared with milk that was first steamed, then whipped together with the coffee.

"Like cappuccino," he said.

"You've been to Milano, haven't you?"

"Yes?"

"I wonder if you know the Galleria there? There was a coffeehouse there I used to go to every day, when I was first beginning to get a taste for coffee—I must have been fifteen. With my brother Thomas, on one of those supervised vacations with a chauffeur who carried a gun—just to give my folks a chance to get away without us on their hands. I remember the look on his face—the chauffeur's—when we went to see *The Last Supper*. Pure, perfect, unadulterated boredom."

"Valerie."

"Yes?"

"I've been to Milan."

"Of course you have."

"And I love to listen to you talk about your childhood, about your brother, about your trips—about anything, really. But not when you're just doing it because you're too embarrassed to go on with what we were really concerned with . . ."

"I'm not embarrassed at all, Hugh. I thought you were."

"No."

"All right. No more small talk then."

"I'm your friend?"

"Yes."

"You'll forgive me for being as honest as I know how."

"I want to hear, Hugh. Tell me why you think Jonathan's all wrong for me."

Hugh paused a bit over his coffee, as if she'd punctured his balloon before he'd even begun the treacherous ascent. But he shrugged off her last statement. She was his friend, she wanted to hear. Well . . .

He told her the story of the famous British fashion photographer, a Cockney, who'd married the daughter of a lord. Her parents had been incensed, of course, and at first they refused to sanction the marriage by taking no notice of it at all. But then, all of a sudden, they changed their minds. Their son-in-law was bright, sharp, a breath of life in a stale old mansion. The newlyweds were feted, introduced to family friends, shown off everywhere. Though the accent lingered, the Cockney had lost his black hat; he was in, he was accepted. And, to her horror, the young bride discovered that he was absolutely a boor.

Valerie interrupted: "I know this story."

"*He's* wearing a black hat, Valerie. You know that."

"Even if I didn't, he always reminds me. Tells me that I love his lower middle class origins, his being Jewish."

"That's not the point of my story," said Hugh. The photographer, he explained, wasn't really a boor at all. He was witty, he was tough, he had the easy charisma of a self-made celebrity. His "boorish" qualities weren't rough or ignoble by his standards—only by his bride's, and only after she'd learned to place him on the same level of reality as she did her parents. It wasn't that the bride didn't measure up to the groom, or that the groom didn't measure up to the bride. It was simply a case of the wrong people forcing a connection in order to prove a point that really didn't have to be made.

"And what point am I proving?" said Valerie. "After all, the man is married. We're hardly shouting out news of our affair to my family. Why can't it simply be a question of the two of us, different though we may be, having simply fallen for each other?"

"This is the hard part, Valerie. That you don't know how you're different. In what way you're from the other side of the tracks. It's not just the family, the money, the social position—it's something more fundamental."

"What?"

"He's a sensualist." Hugh let the word roll off his tongue as if it were going to be an unpleasant surprise. And it was. Valerie's ears pricked up, and she felt the color rush to her cheeks. A flood of insecurities assailed her. What did he mean? How could he know? How dare he say such a terrible thing? She couldn't know, in the heart of her anger, that his conviction was predicated on desire. If he believed that she was not a sensualist, it was because he wanted her to fill out the fantasy figure he'd carried in his heart: a sisterly creature, loving, sentimental, sympathetic. She listened to him repeating his words, and continuing: "He's a sensualist, Valerie. And you are not. That's what I think. That's your point of difference, that's the point you're trying to ignore—or to bring up and attempt to deny."

"I don't know what you're talking about Hugh. Honestly, I don't." She was angry, very angry. His beautiful hands had reached out for hers, which now framed her empty coffee cup.

"I think you do," he said, and there was a sad look in his eyes, a defeated look, as if what she was denying hurt him as much as—or more than—it hurt her. "I think you see more to life than crawling between sheets with a hot man."

"Now you're trying to insult me."

"No."

"I'd like to go back now, Hugh."

"I haven't finished," he said. She pulled her hands away from him and placed them on her lap. What an incredible statement, she thought. This handsome fag telling me that I don't want a "hot man." As if reducing Jonathan to a fairy catch-phrase would somehow lower his esteem in her eyes.

"I want to tell you what I think of Jonathan Singer," he said. "He's very handsome, he tries very hard, he has good fists, and probably would have had them with or without rowing boats on a family estate. But if you were a man, a young man in love with Jonathan's female equivalent, that female equivalent would be pink and voluptuous, with bow-shaped lips and long slender legs, and a face so sensual that no one who met her could think her anything more than someone to sleep with. Not beautiful or fine, but vulgarly sexual. A whore. What I think of Jonathan Singer, Valerie, is that no matter how smart a businessman he might be, no matter how well he may or may not fit into what's left of your parents' sort of society, whether or not he divorces his wife and gets rid of his New York accent and clumsy manners, I still think he'll remain Jonathan Singer. And Jonathan Singer is a whore."

"Well," said Valerie. "You've made that clear."

"You asked for it."

"Yes."

"It's that I've been with you. I've watched you, I have a notion of how you feel—and that man—"

"I've got the message, Hugh," she said. But of course she hadn't, not all of it. She'd taken in the insult to her: that she wasn't capable of understanding human nature, neither hers nor Jonathan's; that the man she loved was a vulgar boor, a sensualist, a whore. And she herself—this was perhaps worst of all—was not a sensualist, not in the all-important estimate of Hugh Robertson. Not a sensualist, but a creature of the mind, of frail sexless feelings. A creature like him. On the way back across the little lake, she watched him row, slowly, effortlessly, his eyes hooded with sadness. Not for a minute did she stop to think that his criticism was influenced by a selfish dream, a dream inhabited by the two of them, by longings for a union whose chaste bonds would be stronger than marriage, stronger than the wistful memories of brother-sister love.

Her anger clouded clear thinking. As they glided over the placid surface of the lake, her mind was roiling with the attempt to reject every part of his statement, to allow no kernel of it to penetrate unchallenged and lie festering in some recess of her soul.

Valerie knew what she was. Or at least, what she wished to be: free of any outside control on her life.

And, for the moment, that independence seemed to include another vision of self: a businesswoman, a lover, a breaker of conventions, a seeker of money, power, sensual gratification. She longed for everything at once, because such longing seemed to underline the fact of her independence, the fact of her deviation from the past sheltered life. If Jonathan was a whore, then so would she be a whore. Not because she loved him, only him, and blindly, but because she loved the anticipation of change, the anticipation of growth and freedom. Already, she could see herself back in New York, taking great steps, making swift decisions, creating an empire built out of guts, out of the stuff that Hugh and her mother and her father and her brother thought had been refined out of her, out of all the Holmeses. But she would show them otherwise. She would be a whore and sensualist and a direct descendant of Samuel Holmes, and she would take in and absorb everything: friendship, enmity, success, failure, ecstasy, sorrow, love, hate.

"Hugh," she told him, "I'm not mad at you, not now." And before he could answer, before he could once again extend his aristocratic hands, embrace her with his careful phrases, she was smiling into his eager, handsome face and continuing in the same inexplicably happy tone of voice: "We still have to be friends. You still have to tell everyone about my wonderful designs, and my absolutely uncanny feeling for fashion. And you have to shake my hand and wish me luck in New York, wish me luck in the *shmate* business.

Hugh Robertson did as requested, and a week later he arranged with Milton for the use of the Mercedes 600, and

211

he escorted her from one privileged compartment to the gateway of another—the silver aircraft that would fly her to the city now magically paved, once again, with gold. On this flight there was no turbulence, no terror. Valcrie Holmes flew with an easy heart, her sample case of three dresses under an adjacent seat, her dreams of success as tangible as the food on her plate, as the strand of diamond chips about her pretty ankle.

Part Three

1407 Broadway

15

The secretary, she thought, looked very refined. A little mascara, a little blush—nothing else to accentuate fine, if rather plain, fair features. Because the secretary had been standing at a tall wood filing cabinet when she'd come in, she was able to note her dress: a sexy enough little wrap on that junior-league figure. But it was also very tasteful, very understated. The secretary turned round and fixed her with hard hazel eyes.

Then she spoke: "Yeah?"

"I—excuse me—" Well, she hadn't planned on that tone of voice. Or that accent. She drew up to her full, not very tall, height: "I'd like to see Miss Holmes."

"You got an appointment, lady?"

"No." She'd been called "lady" many times before, but never with such a successful blend of disinterest and contempt. "Actually—"

"What's your name?"

"I'm—Mrs. Holmes, actually—Actually, I'm her mother."

The secretary hardly sat up straight at this news. If her voice had any the less suggestion of contempt, it was because of the start of mild curiosity. "Valerie's mother, huh?"

"Yes." Mrs. Holmes made a noise something like a harrump, something like a sigh. "She is here, isn't she? Please just tell her that her mother would like to see her for a moment."

"Valerie," said the secretary into the phone, "you'll never guess who's come to visit." Mrs. Holmes's name was mentioned; the secretary smiled, as if just made privy to some new form of insult, and when she hung up the phone, she asked the mother if she'd mind waiting.

"She can't see me?"

"This way, Mrs. Holmes," said the secretary, getting up from behind her desk and leading her along a narrow hallway into a charming little room—a room that looked all too familiar, like a smaller version of some forgotten family parlor. The secretary left her with a nod, assigning her to a chair. "Miss Holmes will be with you as soon as possible," she said, and when she was gone, Mrs. Holmes sat down too quickly in the indicated Windsor chair, not at all used to the etiquette of waiting or waiting rooms, and rather intimidated by the four perfectly stunning young women sitting with her, companions in waiting.

Slowly, Mrs. Holmes looked about the room. The ebony coffee table, inlaid with jade figures under glass, looked remarkably like the one Valerie had inherited from her Uncle Martin— Wait. Yes. The chip in the serving woman's hand, the scratch along the warrior's blade. This *was* Uncle Martin's table. Valerie had taken it from . . . where? The California estate? No, she didn't think so. It had once served time in Beekman Place, but it had long since been banished by her decorator. She thought it might have gone to Thomas's little place on East End Avenue; but then surely he wouldn't have given it to his sister—especially not for her office.

One of the waiting beauties stood up and crossed the room, shaking her head to clear her eyes of several strands of auburn hair. Stopping in front of an antique mirror, the girl began to outline her full lips with a makeup pencil. Mrs. Holmes was too shocked by the beauty's absolute absence of self-consciousness to recognize the mirror at once; but as she wistfully began to study the lovely image in the mirror, remembering, and comparing her own youthful beauty to that in the glass, she had another shock of recognition. The gilt frame, the golden bouquet of raised flowers overpowering the mirror's backboard—the whole hideous construction had adorned her daughter's bedroom in Newport. And when that room had been dismantled, redone, the pieces had gone to her husband's brother—a fit decoration for the somber halls of the Holmes Foundation.

Now she began to look everywhere, quickly, eager to see what else was once hers. And then she saw it all: everything. The rugs under her feet, the framed lithographs, the antique sconces, the hanging tapestry, the petit-point pillowcases of the little pillows on the couch— her couch, too, once—now reupholstered in a drab brown that she supposed Valerie thought was chic. All had come from one home or another, passed on to a relation or a friend; she wondered how Valerie had been able to retrieve so much of what had once been theirs.

"Mother," she heard, and she turned briskly from a contemplation of a Greek wall hanging and saw her daughter smiling down at her from an unexpected height. Even with most of her concentration taken up by this new vision of her daughter—hair pulled back into a no-nonsense fashion; her eyes, lips, and cheekbones drawn out of her sometimes plain face into a real made-up prettiness; her shirtwaist dress smart and businesslike (and nice for lunch at La Grenouilee, she thought)—she still couldn't help but notice the sudden, eager, respectful turning of the four beauties in the room to Valerie, as if they were there for an audience with a powerful queen.

"Hello, darling," said Mrs. Holmes, but she was instantly dismayed to see Valerie raising both hands to prevent her from rising.

"Don't get up, Mother," she said, bending low to kiss her cheek with professional speed. This was the lady who'd sentenced her to Lady Oliver, and who'd been more than helpful in drying up all her sources of family aid. "I'll only be a moment, you don't mind?"

And before Mrs. Holmes could answer, she'd waved one of the beauties into the office at the end of the waiting room and shut the door. Another beauty, a redhead just released from the inner sanctum, was now trying to stuff a cardboard box she'd taken from inside into a large canvas tote bag. Mrs. Holmes noticed that this girl, like the others in the room, had a large leather portfolio with her—and she realized that they all must be fashion models come to see her daughter about a job. Without thinking, she'd ceased at once comparing her vision of herself as a young woman with these splendid creatures and begun to compare them to each other; selecting the prettiest was difficult, and enjoyable.

It was a short route from this to an instant idealization of Valerie's "job." Mrs. Holmes had, very occasionally, taken part in interviewing some new member of her household staff; usually even this was done for her. Certainly, she'd never interviewed any other seekers of jobs. And these girls were so pretty—their features so fine that they looked like they could snap in the wind. Valerie had power over these girls, she realized, and she envied that power. For the first time, the mother had a glimmering of what the daughter was up to—breaking open a new realm of responsibility—and she allowed herself a moment of pride.

"Hey, how ya doing?" said a deep masculine voice, and, as she looked up, Jonathan Singer looked down and said, "Mrs. Holmes, very nice to see you, very nice—I don't know if you remember me."

"Mr. Singer," she said.

"I'm very flattered," said Jonathan. "You look just as good in the daytime as you do at night."

Mrs. Holmes didn't know how to respond to this unconventional compliment, particularly because she was afraid that one of the beauties—the dark one slouching on a couch that had once looked out toward the garden from the enclosed patio of their Newport home—was about to laugh at her in the wake of the handsome young man's compliments.

"Be right back," said Jonathan, and he cast a summary

218

smile at the entire population of the room and walked into Valerie's office without bothering to knock. A moment later, Jonathan and the model left the office, the model carrying the same sort of cardboard box as the last girl. Jonathan put up his hands for the benefit of the remaining models.

"Five minutes, OK?" And he turned to Mrs. Holmes and asked her to go right in.

"Mother, if only you'd called first."

"Well, I wanted it to be a surprise."

"It was."

"It's lovely. More like a living room than a waiting room."

"You hate it?"

"As a living room," she said. "But you know how I feel about mixing periods."

"Well," said Valerie, "I figured it was less a question of periods and more a question of schlock."

"Of what? What did you say?"

"Schlock?" Valerie laughed. "Just a new word, Mother—my vocabulary increases every day."

"But what does it mean?"

"Schlock is junk. Everything you see out there is a hand-me-down; from us to Uncle Roger, and from Uncle Roger to me."

"But how—" Mrs. Holmes steeled herself. They hardly spoke to her husband's too-liberal brother, the director of the Holmes Foundation.

"How did I get this stuff away from him?"

"I meant to ask—How is he, how is Uncle Roger?"

"Fine."

Valerie had learned to let people ask the question they wanted answered. Jonathan had taught her that. It brought the enemy over to your camp, asking you for a favor, a request to be granted an answer.

"But," said Mrs. Holmes, "why did he let you have this stuff?" The little office was a continuation of the waiting room. Faded Persian rugs, a broken grandfather clock, several framed antique maps, a French desk, at least one hundred years old, with a wide leather top.

"I asked."

"Oh," said her mother. Valerie had called her upon her return from Paris two months before. "To check in," she'd called it. And not to forswear business and romantic connections with the garment center. Mrs. Holmes had been deliberately curt; she wanted her daughter to know how hurt "they" all were about her trip abroad, about her entire business venture. No matter what she might care to say (she didn't much care to say anything), it was obvious that she was still carrying on a "relationship" with that married man, that uneducated small-time Jew, and that her business was simply another means of prolonging what should have been ended months before.

"That was very nice of Uncle Roger."

"Yes."

"I suppose he was surprised—that you had to ask him?"

"Is that a question?"

"Darling, I didn't come to grill you."

It was a wonderful technique, she thought, thanking Jonathan inwardly, waiting for her mother's curious energy to push the question into the air. "All right, it is a question," said Mrs. Holmes.

"What's the question?"

"Was Uncle Roger surprised that you were in need of old furniture?"

"He made some sort of crack about securing a loan from the Holmes Foundation. For a needy postadolescent."

"Did you tell him we've quarreled?"

"No."

"So then he must be astounded—"

"Mother," said Valerie, tiring of dragging her mother about the Slough of Curiosity, "Roger *knows* that we've quarreled."

"He knows?"

"Of course."

"But who told him? He never told us. This is a family affair, after all—an affair of the immediate family—and I don't really think it proper of him to suddenly start mixing in, throwing about our old furniture as if they were presents from the good side of the family."

"Mother, I needed furniture. Not just for the office, but for my apartment. I thought of Uncle Roger, who was always getting donations from us over the years—to the Holmes Foundation, probably so Daddy could keep on writing everything off. He has rooms of this stuff, and no one using them, I took what I could use, and if you don't like what you see, I'll let you decorate it—and pay for the expense. As you may remember, my own access to the family treasure chest has been blocked by our darling Tommy."

"Not just Thomas—all of us."

"Well then." Her hands seemed to dismiss the whole family.

"How does Roger know?"

"That we've quarreled? For God's sake Mother, I thought you were *Vogue*'s number one subscriber."

"Yes," said her mother, remembering the oblique reference to family displeasure within the small story. "Five Hundred-Thousand-Dollar Deb Goes to Work."

"And *Nouvelles* is even more specific."

"*Nouvelles*? I didn't see anything in *Nouvelles*."

"Next month's issue. Photos, fanfare, my picture in color on a half page."

"What do they say?"

"That I paid for this myself."

"Is that all?"

"Hardly, Mother—it's a big article. They tell you how I got started, how I raised money, how I feel about the shirtwaist dress, how I react to career women now that I've joined their ranks."

"How did you raise the money?"

"I took some jewels to a pawnshop."

"A what?" Mrs. Holmes looked like she was about to

get out of her seat, but Valerie's quick jumping up prevented this.

"How do you like my dress?" she said.

"Your dress?" said her mother, still dazed about the pawnshop, wondering whether there was still time to stop *Nouvelles* from printing that terrible slander of the family name.

Valerie turned around, and her mother watched her easy movements, her amazing self-confidence, a poise that was as becoming as it was new. "Did you actually say that you went to a pawnshop?"

"Yes."

"How could you? How on earth could you have done such a thing?"

"I needed some money, Mother. I had some jewels. Ergo."

"I suppose *he* told you where to go—"

"Johnny?"

"What did you sell? I suppose you gave up everything I ever gave you—a pawnshop—I want to know where this place is—I must talk to your father—you'll have to give me your tickets, your receipts, whatever they're called—"

"How do you like my dress, Mother?" Valerie stood there, cool and elegant on Charles Jourdan pumps, her diamond ankle bracelet catching her mother's eye.

"What is that?"

"What?"

"On your foot."

"Ankle? On my ankle, you mean?"

"Valerie, that's the cheapest thing I've ever seen you wear."

"It's hardly cheap, Mother—six grand if it's a penny."

"Six 'grand'?" Mrs. Holmes sounded as if she didn't know where to begin—with a thrashing of her daughter or a gnashing of teeth. "I don't know what's happened to you, Valerie. I hardly recognize you."

"I designed this dress, Mother. I wish you'd tell me what you think of it."

"It's nice, but I didn't come here to discuss dresses."

Valerie sat down, and the features of her face set into something hard, something unfamiliar to her mother. "I've been working for months now, Mother, working harder than I've ever worked in my life. If you had the slightest interest in trying to understand your own daughter, you'd probably be aware that I'm excited, nervous, involved, a little crazy—all about these dresses. You're my mother, tell me what you think of this dress." And again she stood up.

"On you, it looks chic," Mrs. Holmes said finally. "But frankly, it's not the most exciting bit of fashion I've ever seen."

"Would you wear it?"

"Me? My dear, I don't wear little dresses."

"Why not?"

"Little dresses don't appeal to me. I mean, they don't say much. At my age, I have to help nature along a bit. My skin tone, my figure, my hair—they just don't excite people the way they used to. But with something like this"—Mrs. Holmes made a vague gesture at her wool suit (box jacket and full dirndl skirt), touching her fingertips to the collar of her cream crepe de chine shirt—"I feel more substantial."

Valerie pressed her intercom button. "Get me a nine in the shirtwaist," she said, and then she turned back to her mother.

"This is substantial, Mother."

"You asked me for my opinion. I'm being truthful. If I had a need for something that simple . . ."

"Perfect for lunch, for the museum, for shopping. Great for traveling. Feel it. Go on, feel it."

"This is silly," said Mrs. Holmes, but she touched Valerie's sleeve and nodded dutifully.

"Soft, isn't it?"

"Yes."

"Like cashmere."

"I wouldn't say like cashmere, but it is rather nice."

"If you close your eyes, it feels like cashmere. You can shove it in a suitcase and leave it there for days—then just hang it up, hang it up for an hour. Not a wrinkle."

"I prefer natural fabrics."

"You can wash it, let it hang over the bathtub—"

"I have never let anything hang over my bathtub."

The door to the little office was suddenly flung open and the secretary came in. Mrs. Holmes realized that the print of her wrap dress was similar to that of Valerie's shirtwaist.

"This for your mom?"

"Yes, Dierdre. Put it down anywhere."

"Wish my mother was a size nine. Not bad, not bad at all." And she turned and sidled out with that same overwise smile—almost as if she didn't realize who Mrs. Holmes was, as if she thought the mother had come to the office just to get a free dress.

"I can't tell you how upset your father's going to be about this pawnshop business."

"I'd like you to try this on, Mother," said Valerie, removing the size-nine shirtwaist the secretary had brought from its plastic wrapper.

"Valerie, let's not be silly. I didn't come here to try on dresses; I came here to see how you're doing, to check up on you—we're all very worried about you—"

"You could've called if you were so interested. Here." She thrust the dress at her mother. "There's a dressing room in the back."

Mrs. Holmes took the dress and put it on her lap. "If we didn't call you, it's because we felt the time wasn't right. We're not thinking of ourselves, but only of you. Naturally, if we felt you were in some kind of danger or had a real problem, we would've always been there, but we knew you weren't involved in anything more serious than a ridiculous infatuation, and Thomas and myself and your father all thought that if we just left you to your own devices—"

"I'd come crawling," interrupted Valerie. "Crawling

back home."

"I didn't say that."

"Try on the dress, Mother. Please."

"We'd like to all have dinner with you, darling. Next Thursday evening. Your father will be in town."

"Why?"

"Why? What a ridiculous question! Aren't we your family?"

"I will not give up this business, I will not retract any statements about the family or myself from *Nouvelles*, I will not refrain from using my name in advertisements, I will not allow you or Thomas or Father to dictate anything to me—particularly about who it is that I'm not supposed to be seen in public with." Valerie let a smile flicker across her face. "And I'm not going to discuss another thing until you try this on."

Mrs. Holmes went into the tiny dressing room adjoining a little bathroom at the back of the office. She felt absurd, allowing her daughter to boss her around in this way, but she let herself become absorbed in the task at hand—stripping off her suit and shirt, and wriggling into the acrylic print. The mirror in the dressing room was well lit and surprisingly flattering. Mrs. Holmes was both pleased and dismayed at the image which confronted her when she'd finished putting on her daughter's creation. She was pleased because she looked quite amazingly sexy, she thought. The fabric hugged her curves, and the print itself was both seductive and conservative—a subtly flirtatious statement, designed to inflame and tease. She was dismayed at how totally she'd misjudged the dress as being too young for her, or too ordinary. Usually, she had more sense than that. She prided herself on a fashion sense that allowed her to mix a couturier's suggestions with random selections off the rack at Bloomingdale's and Bergdorf Goodman, and that sense had failed her. She patted her hair, straightened the dress, and went out to tell her daughter that she'd been wrong.

"All you've got to do is rinse it in a little warm water and Ivory flakes," Valerie was telling one of the beautiful models, holding one of the cardboard boxes stuffed with size-seven wrap dresses.

"Can I use Woolite?"

"Sure."

"Sounds good," said the model. "I appreciate it, Miss Holmes."

"Just remember where the common folk can purchase it. And what my name is."

"Sure," said the girl, and when she'd gone, Mrs. Holmes made her entrance.

"Perfect, Mother," said Valerie.

"Yes, actually."

"I've only been giving them away to models, but for old times' sake, you can have one too."

"I can have this?"

"I'd like you to."

"What—what does it cost in the stores?"

"It's not in the stores, not yet. Just in my boutique."

"Your what?"

"Madison Avenue, between Eighty-first and Eighty-second, on the second floor. Can't miss it, if you're looking at the sky. It's small, but chic. The dress you're wearing is going for ninety-five dollars. Mine is eighty-five. Wholesale is a little less than half of that. I made them for—" Valerie smiled. "I don't want to upset the public. I figure ninety-five dollars is a good price for that nice a piece of goods."

"It's cheap," said her mother, a bit put off by the low price.

"That's right," said Valerie. "Cheap chic, that's the name of my game." And she unfolded the layout of the ad that would appear in next week's magazine section of the *New York Times*: a color photograph of Valerie Holmes, wearing the wrap dress, the diamond ankle bracelet, sitting on a flat pillow in the corner of a brick-walled room. Beautifully made up, beautifully photographed, her blond hair pulled back, a (fake) diamond necklace flashing stars across the paper, she did indeed look like a million dollars in a drab, poor world. The headline read: "RICH AS HOLMES." And under it was the copy: "Cheap Chic. The Wrap Dress from Valerie Holmes. Ninety-five Dollars."

"You look beautiful," said her mother.

"Thank you."

"But my God, Valerie—it's such an awful thing to do to Thomas."

"Mother," said Valerie. "Screw Thomas."

"I—" began her mother, not angrily, just confused and wanting so much to try to get across the message which she'd come to deliver. That all was not forgiven, but they wanted to see her anyway. That help wasn't forthcoming, nor approval, but they missed her, after their own fashion. That no matter what words had been exchanged, they would all still benefit from a shared meal around the family table. But before she could respond to Valerie, Jonathan Singer once again intruded, ready to spout compliments about how well Mrs. Holmes looked in her dress.

"Val, I've got a fabulous idea. Why not let your mother and her friends do what we're doing with the models?"

"Johnny, they can afford to buy their own."

"Yeah, but you know these society types—tight as witches."

"As witches?" said Valerie. "How're witches tight?"

"It's dirty, I'll tell you later," said Jonathan. "Jesus, you look fantastic, Mrs. Holmes. Hope she's not charging you to take it home."

"Valerie, if you're busy, we can talk later," said her mother.

"No one's pushing you out, Mother," said Valerie.

"Hey, am I busting up a family meeting?"

"Yes," said Valerie, "but I don't mind. We're getting down to dress talk anyway."

"Maybe you'd like to take a tour, Mrs. Holmes? As

long as you've come this far. Let me show you the Garment Center."

"Thank you, Mr. Singer, but I couldn't—"

"Half an hour to wisdom. Learn what makes your daughter's blood run hot and cold. Show you scenes stranger than Ripley's."

"Actually," said Mrs. Holmes, "I've got an appointment." Clumsily, she looked at her watch. "Yes, rather soon, I'm afraid. But I do thank you for asking."

A dark mood began to color Valerie's eyes; her mother could see that she hadn't acted graciously to Jonathan Singer, but, then, what was she supposed to do? Let the man squire her about this terrible building? It would be like traveling with a circus barker. And when Thomas and her husband found out . . .

"That's quite all right," said Jonathan, a trace of an English accent slipping into his speech, resorting to automatic mockery, an insult returned for an insult. "My office is just downstairs. Lorelei Paris. You ever want to buy wholesale, just tell the harpies at the desk you know Johnny Singer at Lorelei."

"You're very amusing, Mr. Singer," said Mrs. Holmes.

"Isn't he, Mother?" said Valerie, and her voice had risen half an octave since she'd last spoken.

"I still think that's a great idea," said Jonathan. "Give away a hundred dresses to skinny society ladies. You pick 'em—we tell *Women's Wear* where to snap their pictures. I mean 'Cheap Chic' needs as much 'chic' as we can get."

"I think they look better on the models, Johnny."

"Those girls look good in wet garbage bags."

"Well, most of the society ladies I know don't," said Valerie. She lapsed into a frightening silence, her eyes resting on her mother, but actually looking back into a past when her mother had been a great golden idol, warm and pretty, and impossibly kind. Jonathan worked to kill the silence by explaining to Mrs. Holmes at some length that Valerie was interviewing models for possible employment in the series of ads she planned to run in *The New*

Yorker, New York Magazine, and the *New York Times*, all featuring her boutique, and the fact that her dresses were going to be made available to a larger audience beginning with the coming fall. "That mean's we're—I mean she—is going to show to buyers in the spring, which isn't so very far away." Valerie seemed about to say something, but then shut up, her eyes as vexed as ever, so Jonathan plunged on. "May, actually, May seventh. She's gone ahead and booked the Cotillion Room at the Pierre. All we need now is five hundred buyers to show, and things'll be cool. We're saving you a seat up front."

"I do like fashion shows," said Mrs. Holmes to Valerie, but Valerie suddenly quit looking at her mother and returned to her desk. As she began to flip through pages in a large appointment calendar, Jonathan cleared his throat, forcing Mrs. Holmes's attention his way, and explained that she'd given away more than seventy dresses to models already over the last five days. "They're all here to show their portfolios, but if she likes the way they look, she asks them if they could use an extra dress. If they can, they get it. Willy—that's the guy who works with me—he saw a model get off a train in Queens the other day, wearing one of Valerie's dresses. And it looked like there were a hundred women staring at it, figuring that it was the dress that made the girl look so good."

"Thursday night seems free," said Valerie suddenly, looking up from the appointment calendar.

"That's very clever," said Mrs. Holmes. "Using those pretty girls to get you free advertisements." She was talking to Jonathan as if Valerie had said nothing.

"When the ads come out, I want people to stop and think they've been seeing that dress everywhere—all around town, on the prettiest girls in New York. I figure if Valerie starts with New York, she gets the rest of the country in her pocket a week or so later."

"Didn't you hear me, Mother?" said Valerie. "I said Thursday night seems free."

"Yes, good," said Mrs. Holmes.

"How about you, Johnny?" said Valerie, staring straight at him, not deigning to glance at her mother. "What's your Thursday night like?"

"Hang on a second," he said, and he fished a small black calendar out of the pocket of his leather jacket. "I'm through with the White House in the early afternoon," he joked, hoping that Mrs. Holmes wouldn't think him serious. "So Thursday night seems wide open."

"I *am* allowed to bring an escort?" said Valerie.

"Actually," said Mrs. Holmes, "we rather had in mind a kind of family reunion."

"Why?"

"Why?" Mrs. Holmes was crimson. "As I explained, actually, it's that we have a lot of family business to go over."

"Johnny knows perfectly well that my allowance has been cut off. I'm in debt to him for thousands of dollars, and much more than dollars besides." She stood up, tall on her high pumps, dwarfing her short mother. "There are a lot of things that I'm not crazy about, Mother. Rudeness, for example. Stupid prejudice. Stepping on other people's faces without even realizing it. Do you know that you've spent the last twenty minutes insulting Jonathan? Are you even aware of that?"

"No—I don't know what you—"

"Mother, I'm coming to dinner with Johnny. If you don't want us to come, tell me right now."

"I didn't say that I didn't want you to come—"

"Eight o'clock all right with you, Johnny?"

"Sure, Val—fine." It was incredible to Mrs. Holmes that the man had the nerve to be smiling, as if it were the most ordinary thing in the world to be invited to a dinner party at her table. And invited in this fashion.

"Thank you, Mother," Valerie said. "We'll look forward to it."

Minutes later, Mrs. Holmes found herself on the street, 1407 Broadway at her back. She looked wildly for her limousine. In a morning of crossed purposes and twisted

230

reason, it was fitting that her loyal chauffeur was nowhere to be seen, of a piece with the mad, shifting alliances of her world.

16

"Tell her, Singer," said Constantino.

"I think the man's got a point, Val," said Jonathan.

"Johnny, stop acting like we're in the middle of a bad movie," said Valerie, thrusting a hand back through her hair, crossing her legs, folding her hands neatly in her lap. "You can do what you want with Lorelei, but if you agree to this man's terms, you're either very stupid or very scared."

"Or very smart," said Constantino.

"I'm talking," said Valerie. "I'd prefer it if you didn't interrupt."

"Jesus," said Constantino. He looked for help to his associate, a very dark-haired young man whose name was supposed to be Mr. Oscar, and who said almost nothing throughout the meeting in Jonathan's office. Mr. Oscar seemed interested in Constantino's performance, as if he were rating his ability as an oral negotiator. He looked not at all at Valerie or Jonathan, and he smoked a pipe which filled the office with aromatic smoke.

"As I said," Valerie continued, "you can do what you want with Lorelei, but I decide what Valerie Holmes is going to do, and Valerie Holmes is not going to be bullied into hiring trucks and drivers we don't need."

"Look, lady," said Constantino. "I'm going to be very up front with you, because you seem like an up-front type of person. I hope you change your mind about signing for the trucks, because if you don't follow our suggestions, then it's not going to be easy for you to get hold of any trucks."

"I've already got a truck company lined up."

"No, you don't," said Mr. Oscar. "Not anymore." He sucked on his pipe, and Constantino beamed at him.

"What is that supposed to mean?"

"They got busy," said Mr. Oscar. "They can no longer handle your business."

"You know them?" said Valerie. She was very angry. If these two were simply organizational-type hoodlums, she wished they'd act in an organized fashion. But they continued to talk in vague terms, as if they were afraid of being taped. It wasn't so much the blackmail that incensed her as the nebulous quality of their threats and demands.

"We know them," said Constantino, smiling broadly, "and the thing is, they know us."

"Let me get this straight, Mr. Constantino, since you're such an up-front personality. You're telling me that you deliberately scared away my truck company so that I'd have to do business with you."

"I didn't say *that*," said Constantino, looking to Mr. Oscar.

"Jesus Christ, you guys drive me crazy," said Valerie. She stood up and walked over to Constantino, a short man with thick wrists, whose ugly tufts of hair rose out of the ends of his jacket sleeves. "Are you the Mafia or something? Is this supposed to be the Mafia holding me up for some money? Or are you just local boys out to make a fast buck? Why don't you tell me what you are and how much the hell you want and what you're going to do to me if I don't give it to you?"

"Sit down, lady," said Constantino.

"Answer me, you thick son of a bitch," she said, and Constantino was suddenly out of his chair, grabbing both her arms and beginning to push her backward. And then Valerie saw something she hadn't counted on. Jonathan had gotten out of his chair behind the desk and run over to take Constantino by the back of his shoulders and tear him away from her. Instantly, Constantino pushed Jonathan into a chair, and would have proceeded to do

233

what he did best—punch and kick—but Mr. Oscar, still seated in his chair and smoking his deliciously scented pipe, said, "No."

Jonathan was up again, much taller than Constantino, and not at all afraid at that moment. Thinking about whom he was dealing with, whom he was about to punch in the mouth—that would later make him very afraid. But now, with a furious Valerie in the room, with a cold, calm Mr. Oscar taking it all in, there was nothing to be afraid of, nothing to be afraid of at all. "You don't touch Miss Holmes," said Jonathan to Constantino. "You get it?"

"Shut the fuck up," said Constantino.

"As long as you hear me, asshole," said Jonathan. "Now you can get out of my office."

"One moment," said Mr. Oscar. "Sit down, Mr. Singer. It would be better if you calmed down and we all settled this today, rather than have to delay it to another, more unpleasant occasion."

"I'm calling the police," said Valerie, and she picked up the phone on Jonathan's desk and pressed the button for Angela.

Jonathan now spoke only to Mr. Oscar. "I'll be happy to talk to you, but I don't want to see this goon around here. We never had to deal with a goon before. I don't see why we have to start now."

"Angela," said Valerie into the phone, "I want you to call the police."

Mr. Oscar was on his feet now, but without any show of rushing. "I'm sorry we had this unpleasantness, Miss Holmes. And I'm very sorry you don't as yet see the value in shipping through Mr. Constantino's truck service. Perhaps some other time."

He was leaving, and he hadn't answered Jonathan. "You remember what I said, Mr. Oscar. Glad to see you again, to talk, but don't bring your friend."

Constantino glared at Jonathan, wondering whether he should risk a blow. But his boss beckoned, and he followed him to the door. From the threshold, Mr. Oscar turned and said to Jonathan: "Don't tell me who I bring, who you want to talk to. You don't give me conditions. You're in shit up to your ears as it is, you understand me, friend?"

And one more stupid risk: "I'm not your friend," said Jonathan.

"Very brave in front of the pretty lady," said Mr. Oscar. "I hope you know what a schmuck is."

"Yeah, it's what you don't got between your legs," said Jonathan. There was no redeeming anything now, so he might as well make the most of it. In a second he'd gone for the door and Valerie was calling his name. Jonathan took Mr. Oscar by the shoulder and pulled him effortlessly into the room and slapped the pipe out of his mouth. Before he could punch Oscar, Constantino had barreled into him, butting his chest with his head, reaching with his hands for his eyes.

"Angela, get somebody. Angela," Valerie said.

Constantino had wrestled Jonathan to the floor, and in the little space between the desk and the chairs, he'd forced Jonathan onto his back and now straddled his chest. He let a moment elapse, a moment to establish his dominion.

"I could break his nose, Miss Holmes," said Mr. Oscar, as if it were he, and not Constantino, sitting on Jonathan's chest.

Valerie said: "Make him get off." She said it softly, and then she screamed: "Get him off, make him get off or I'll kill you!"

"OK," said Mr. Oscar with a little laugh. "You'd better get off. We wouldn't want Miss Holmes to kill me."

Constantino patted Jonathan's cheeks, blowing his awful breath into his eyes. When he got off, Jonathan got to his feet in a single motion. "You're lucky," said Constantino.

"You didn't call the police, did you?" said Mr. Oscar.

"No," said Valerie. "The secretary's gone home."

"You want to talk?"

"No."

"You're sure?" said Mr. Oscar, as if both of them were perfectly aware of her childish recalcitrance. Jonathan, who'd said nothing since getting to his feet, now spoke.

"I want to talk to Constantino," he said.

"Yeah?" said Constantino.

"Shut up," said Mr. Oscar to Constantino.

"I want to talk to Constantino in the showroom," said Jonathan. "Just Constantino. You can entertain Mr. Oscar, Valerie. I'll trust the two of you alone. Come on, handsome."

"I never realized you were really that stupid, Singer," said Oscar.

"Come on," he said again to Constantino, and the short stocky man followed him into the Lorelei showroom, and Jonathan shut the door to his office, leaving Valerie and Mr. Oscar to hear the muffled sounds of a fight.

Valerie had improved the lighting months ago, and Lorelei was a place where one didn't need to squint. The cheap dresses were now arranged on little racks set in colored alcoves, and when the salesmen talked to buyers at one of the ordinary white tables, they could look up at a not-so-ordinary vista: a budget line crossed with a living room. Jonathan indicated a love seat to Constantino, and, as the goon turned, Jonathan hit him as hard as he could, swinging a blow under his chin, hoping to break each and every one of his teeth with the punch.

Unfortunately, not one broke.

Constantino was thrown a bit, but his legs seemed to be made of solid oak. A bit hazy, but acting from automatic impulse, he blocked Jonathan's second punch—he had been in more fights than Jonathan, many more.

"I'm going to kill you," he told Jonathan, and Jonathan thought it a very unlikely place to die. After all, it was his own turf. His hottest runner hung in an isolated alcove directly behind the ugly thug; white tables and mirrors and flowers in three crystal vases all gave the lie to any questions of doom. But Constantino ignored the interior

236

decoration, and didn't feint either. His left crashed into Jonathan's blocking forearm, and his right followed just above the solar plexus. Jonathan felt himself falling into a dress rack and he smelled the perfume of a buyer who'd been there that day—a redhead named Stephanie, who liked Shalimar. Constantino's next punch was a right that didn't connect, and Jonathan took hold of the shorter man's wrist with both hands, and, riding a burst of adrenaline, he ducked under the man's arm, twisting it behind his back, and drove Constantino into the dress rack, holding on to the armlock with all his strength. The short man's head hit the wall on the other side of the rack, and there was a thud, and then another, as Jonathan pulled on the armlock and beat the man back through the dresses into the wall.

Then there was no resistance, and Jonathan let go of the arm. He didn't wait for Constantino to fall and was already opening the door to his office when he heard the crash—the end of a laborious semiconscious descent.

"Are you all right?" said Valerie. She was sitting at the desk, with Oscar at the door. Apparently he'd stood guard, not wanting her to go out and see the mess made of Jonathan by his boy.

"Sure," said Jonathan.

"What the hell—?" Oscar ran into the showroom and over to Constantino. He stood frowning down at Constantino, who didn't seem too anxious to get up.

"Pick him up," said Jonathan.

"You crazy son of a bitch," said Mr. Oscar, more to Constantino than to Jonathan. Jonathan made a move to leave the office and go after Oscar.

"I said pick him up—move. I want you out of here," said Jonathan.

Mr. Oscar stared at Jonathan stupidly. He wasn't used to getting threats from his own "clients." The situation was more ludicrous than frightening. But he made the gesture of extending a hand to Constantino and helped the man to slowly get to his feet.

Mr. Oscar didn't say another word, and Constantino didn't look back. Still, their sudden absence and the sound of the slamming outer door were unsettling. The silence punctuated the entire violent gesture made by Jonathan, revealed it for what it was.

"What the hell did you do that for?" Valerie said.

"You might ask me if I'm all right."

"I did."

"Jesus."

"Now what?"

"I don't know," said Jonathan. "I guess the usual—beatings and stompings." He was laughing now, trying to prolong the moment, and Valerie tried to make up her mind whether to take him into her arms or simply walk out on him, on his useless stupidity.

"Are they really in the Mafia?"

"All I know is that Constantino's an Italian name, and he's not in the pizza business."

"If you want to keep joking around—"

"I don't know what the Mafia is exactly, but the Garment Center's got its share of something very similar to what you see on TV."

"I don't watch TV."

"If you did, maybe we wouldn't be in this mess right now."

"What mess, Johnny? I want to know what you've done, I want to know what's going to happen now."

Jonathan took her hand and walked into the showroom, leading her to a sofa, and sat her down at his side. "How much time do you need to get dressed?"

"Ten minutes."

"Because it's seven o'clock, and we shouldn't be late."

"Are you going to answer my question? I want to know what's happening. I want to know if some man is going to be waiting downstairs for us with a machete."

"Not tonight."

"Good."

"First they talk it over. This is hardly worth a killing,

unless it's not done during office hours. Constantino's time off. He's not going to be thinking kindly of me."

"Then why the hell—"

Jonathan interrupted: "Because of you." He placed an index finger across her lips. "Shut up. Listen. It's your fault, kid, but it's OK. You did a very stupid thing back there when you wouldn't listen to reason; you turned off to my signals, you started calling the shots. That wasn't smart. These guys don't follow the society pages. They don't give a shit who your great-grandfather was. The way they look at it, they're not holding us up. They're just fixing prices and providing services. If you can get along without them, that's cool, because you save money. But if they want to truck your shit, that's too bad for you—but at least you know you're getting something for your money, even if it is a little steep."

"No one's going to blackmail me into anything. Ever."

"Listen, beautiful, we've got to be in Beekman Place in an hour, so I'm not going to spend all day telling you why you're crazy. But this is like the rest of your ideas when you don't listen to me. You're trying to sell a line, and you hire me to help push it. And it's a good line, with a special promotional angle, and it's got this fantastic potential, and then—you don't let me shtick it to the buyers."

"We've already agreed not to talk about that any-more."

"Yeah, you've already decided not to talk about it, and you think that's OK with me. Let me tell you something. You blew the Seligman account."

"I didn't blow anything. No one said Seligman had to buy my line. He looked at it, he had lunch with you, you talked, he didn't buy."

"He didn't buy, because I didn't put out."

"All I know is he didn't buy. My line's going to be so hot that guys like that are going to have to stand in line just to get into the showroom."

"And in the meantime?"

"In the meantime, we're surviving."

"Seligman's buying."

"What? I thought you said—"

"I bought his wife a fox fur jacket," Jonathan said.

"Oh, Christ. I told you that I didn't want to do that, I told you that I wasn't going to allow that—"

"Here's the order," said Jonathan, and he removed the folded paper from the inside pocket of his leather jacket and placed it in her lap. She said nothing, simply stared at it. It was worth considerably more than a fox fur jacket. "I'm just bringing this up because of what's just happened. I mean, the more I think about it, the more scared shit I'm getting. You think I was a crazy hothead because I went after that hulk. But what you don't realize is that I had to do that once he started in with you. I mean who the hell is going to respect me if I let some son of a bitch punk, the lowest rung on any ladder of punks, do that to you? The point is, you let me in for it when you wouldn't go ahead with what I asked you to do. When you tried to play brave little rich girl, when all you were playing was stupid."

Valerie didn't know what to do first: tear up the Seligman order, break the dinner engagement with her parents, or explain to Jonathan why it was that her love for him was changing. The passion fired by opposite upbringings was beginning to sour into a dull awareness of irresolvable differences, differences that excited no passion other than anger. And the anger was of necessity contained in a closed box. Arguments were useless exchanges of misdirected shots. Still, with an inward sigh, Valerie tried: "I wasn't playing anything, Johnny."

"Oh, shit."

"I won't let myself be bullied into anything; that's the way I am."

"That's the way you are, because you don't know what it is to be bullied."

"And I want to show you what I think of this Seligman order," she said, and she tore the paper into long strips,

240

then crumpled these into a tight ball, which she dropped into a wastebasket.

"That's very dramatic," said Jonathan, getting out of the sofa and beginning to pace the room. "You're a very dramatic business partner. I bust my ass getting you an order and you tear it up in front of my face. Jesus, I didn't ask for you to be involved in giving Seligman's wife a fox fur jacket. I didn't want to let you get your hands dirtied with *that*. And if you hadn't had to open your mouth to these fucking hoodlums, I would've taken care of that too. I would've taken care of everything, your ladyship— because I know you hate to get your hands dirty. All I want from you is a little appreciation, and all you do is give me shit. And because I'm stuck with a partner who likes to pretend the world is just one big fairy tale, I've got to worry about getting knifed in the back by some Mafioso—"

She was dialing a number from her seat on the sofa, and when she began to speak into the phone, he shut up. "Mrs. Sharon? It's Valerie. Yes, I know. Do you think I could speak to my father for a moment? It's important. Yes, right." While she waited for Mrs. Sharon to locate Mr. Holmes, she turned her eyes to Jonathan. "I'm not your partner," she said.

"Jesus."

"I just don't want you to compound the misunderstanding."

"How can I compound it? Christ. You only tell me fifty times a day. I really think you ought to just pack it all in with me. I mean, why don't you? You don't need me to sell your line. You don't need Lorelei to make it up for you. Just sell a few more jewels. I mean, what the hell do you need me for anyway? Jesus, you don't even need me to get laid anymore."

She was furious now, but her father had picked up the phone and she stopped up his speech by starting hers into the phone. "Daddy," she said, and her rich voice was firm though tinged with a plaintive quality. "Daddy, I'm in some trouble and I need your help. Yes, of course I am.

241

Yes, we are. He's coming. No, I'd rather tell you now, not when Thomas—" She stopped talking, to allow her father to say something reassuring. Her eyes rested on Jonathan, and they were not friendly. "I had a visit from some local hoodlums. I think they're in the Mafia, or something like the Mafia—anyway, they threatened me." There was another pause here while Mr. Holmes, Jonathan imagined, was saying something like: "Mafia? My God, Valerie, don't move. I'll call out the National Guard. The President will hear about this tonight. We've always let too many Italians into the country, particularly southern Italians." But then Valerie was talking again, naming names, explaining what they wanted, painting Jonathan in a flattering light, though her eyes remained cold and condemning. "One of them, the one called Constantino, actually pushed me, and then Jonathan of course pushed him back—and it was terrible, Daddy. I don't know who these people are exactly, but if what they all say about them is true we can both be in a lot of trouble, don't you think? I'm sorry to be troubling you with all this, but I know how Mother wants a dignified dinner party, and I hardly think it proper to bring up at that time, but I didn't want any more time to go by, because actually I'm rather frightened." And again the pause, for her father's words. "Thanks, Daddy. I hope so. I don't know what you'll do, but thanks—right. In about an hour."

"Well," said Jonathan.

She'd hung up. "We'd better get dressed."

"What did he say?"

"Don't tell me I live in a fairy tale world. I know what kind of world I live in. I never had to ask for help since I started this line, and I gave up a lot, more than you realize, to work on my own terms. But if people want to play without rules well—"

"*What did he say?*"

"I'm explaining something to you, Jonathan. I'm explaining that I know exactly what kind of world I live in. I'm explaining that if I don't want to bribe buyers, I don't have to. I'm explaining that if I don't want to be forced into hiring Constantino to truck my garments, I don't have to either. Because I know who I am, even if sometimes I forget—sometimes I forget." And she was suddenly, inexplicably, crying. Jonathan stood stock still in the center of the showroom and tried to imagine what it was all for, what she had to be crying about.

There was no way for him to know that she was crying for her weakness, her ready sliding back to Daddy's help. There was no way for him to know that when she said she knew who she was, she was admitting an element of defeat in her quest for self-realization. She was Valerie Holmes, and she'd be damned before she'd allow hoodlums to tell her how to run her business. She was Valerie Holmes, and even if her family was furious with her, they were still her family, still devoted to her, still prepared to do anything to preserve her health and well-being. And if the only way to escape her name, and pander to the fiction of total independence, was to give in to hoodlums or run the risk of having them kill her lover—that was too high a price to pay for a factitious concept.

"Daddy said he'd take care of it," she said, but she was still crying, and he remained where he was, ten feet away from her. Jonathan knew from experience that she didn't like to be touched when her tears were private. He couldn't imagine how Mr. Holmes would indeed "take care of it," but something about the American character, with its singular need for mythmaking kings and queens, allowed Jonathan a momentary inward smile, and an obeisance. Yes, of course, Mr. Holmes would take care of it, he would somehow, magically, mythically, royally, somehow utter a command—and then, through the convoluted machinery of democracy-oligarchy-secret police-organized crime (or so Jonathan Singer hoped), the command would run, passed from very-high-up to very-low-down, until somewhere, maybe in Brooklyn, Constantino and Oscar would get the word: "You guys are up shit creek."

"Hey," said Jonathan. "How about if I go upstairs to Valerie Holmes and get you your dress? I'll bring it down here."

She looked up at him, no longer mad, beginning to rein in her crying. "Thanks, Johnny," she said. "But I'll go up. I'll meet you in the lobby in fifteen minutes."

"Make it twenty, and I'll have the car round in the front of the building. On Broadway."

In forty minutes, they were leaving the parked car, walking the ten yards to the Beekman Place building's entrance, waiting to be announced by a doorman. Valerie hadn't seen her brother since the Winstons' ball three months ago, and her father for many months before that. But she wasn't thinking of the family reunion so much as she was bridling at the position in which she'd placed herself. They were assuming her to be under Jonathan's thumb, madly in love with him, prepared to defend his ways and means. And she would, in face, be defending him that evening. Rudeness and snobbishness—deliberate or simply reflexive—would be noted and condemned. Anything uttered aloud as to his being an opportunist, and an exploitative ladies' man, would be seized on at once and knocked down with fury. All this, she knew, would only convince her parents the more. And Thomas. She could imagine his face, twisted into a terrible facsimile of calm. It would all be so much simpler if she could somehow bring to the fore some of her own doubts about the future of their relationship. If she could tell them some of her own maddening thoughts. Even as she watched him watch the doorman, observe the lobby, follow the elevator man with a narrow smile, she felt a cacophony of sensations, impossible to sort out for herself, more than impossible to relate to her parents.

"You look very handsome tonight, Johnny."

"It's cool, Val, I'm not nervous."

The elevator man, who knew Valerie on sight, remained silent, either servile or aloof, and Valerie, contemplating Jonathan, remained either drawn to his eager sexuality or repulsed by his too-proud mechanics. His hand reached for her knee, and he smiled straight ahead, as if playing a game with the elevator man.

"Nervous or not, you look wonderful."

But he refrained from any talk of tube steak. Be grateful for the small things, she thought. "Please don't— I mean—try to behave with Thomas."

"I'm looking forward to this, kid. And I'm very glad that we've started over again." He was referring to the kiss in the car, her hand on his forearm as he muscled the stick shift. If they'd had a fight, it was over, or at least held in abeyance until this evening was through. She didn't know, she couldn't know, that through all her own growing doubts about their relationship, his own flippancy concealed a growth in another direction. He was certain that he was falling in love with her. Because Valerie had herself never experienced such a chaotic period of living, turning from dependence to strength, from a frigid isolation within her family circle to a passionate involvement in the world, she couldn't respond to the hints of change in Jonathan. She was changing, he was a rock: That was her view. He had always wanted to go to bed with her. He had always wanted to go into business with her. He had always enjoyed talking tough with her, driving her fast around the city, putting his arm around her in public.

As they emerged from the elevator, he took hold of her hand and slowed her walk to the door.

"Val?"

She looked at him quizzically, not used to the thread of weakness in his voice. The elevator door closed silently behind them, and they stood not three steps from the entrance to the Holmeses' apartment. She was struck by the change in his face, seeing not fear but an extraordinary tension—the tension of knowing that she was not prepared to hear what he had to say.

"I couldn't tell you earlier," he said. "It wasn't right, not after we got through with those hoods." She waited for it, standing very still. "I've spoken to Eddy," he said.

"You've what?" she said, afraid of some new wave of circumstances, a new twisting of fate that would once again take her life out of her own hands. She had never seen Jonathan so handsome, so open to hurt. A split second passed, and in that time she knew what he was about to say, understood it at once, had the common experience of being able to expand the moment and fill it with horror. He answered her before she'd even finished questioning him.

"I've spoken to Eddy," he said, pressing her hands. "And I've told her that I want a divorce."

There it was, and again she felt the fragment of time expand to encompass her fear, to allow her guilt room to grow. "My God, Johnny," she said, but he was still talking, and, in the same split second, the door to the apartment was being opened.

He was saying, "I love you," and what she said made no difference, obscured for him by the speed of the moment, by the necessity to screw his face back into the same handsome uncaring mask. The mask that had fooled her too. Mrs. Sharon was saying hello with an uncharacteristic formality and behind her were voices, familiar voices, and Valerie couldn't keep up with the surprises, the flood of new thoughts and associations, the questions of how to behave, how to perform. Jonathan Singer pressed her hand, and, as they entered the apartment, Mrs. Holmes and Hugh Robertson turned their handsome heads and began to utter polished phrases of greeting.

17

"Darling? Darling, it's for you. Hello? Do you hear me? Johnny? He said it was important. Should I tell him you'll call back?"

He opened his left eye and squinted at his wife's paint-smeared work shirt. It was light in the bedroom, light enough to be quite late, and he shook his head at Eddy and got to a sitting position on the bed. "Good morning," he said to her, mostly to try out his voice. He cleared his throat. "Who?"

She picked up the extension on the night table. "A Mr. Moscar—Oscar?"

"Oh," said Jonathan, and he cleared his throat again and tried to smile at his wife. She smiled back at him a shade too quickly, and already, with only one eye open, he was being exposed to the day's first helping of Guilt. "Thanks," he said.

"Here he is," she said into the phone.

He took the receiver from her. "Yeah?" he said, trying to make it as gruff as possible. Eddy smiled again and left the bedroom. She'd been smiling ever since he'd told her that he'd fallen in love with Valerie Holmes and wanted to live with Valerie instead of her. "I'm surprised," she'd said. "But then I never really understood you completely, Jonathan. Maybe she will. I hope so. I love you. I know you love me. I won't do anything to spoil what we have, you know that. Whatever you want to do is cool with me. As long as you're happy. Just think about it, and tell me what and where. Just be true to yourself." And she'd smiled, and told him that she was happy, and was glad that he was honest with her, and for a day there'd been nothing but quiet looks, shy glances—almost as if she were falling in love with him all over again. And then Thursday morning, the morning of the day of the Holmeses' dinner party, he'd woken up to find her crying, sitting at a table in her studio, her chin propped on the palms of her hands, very quiet, very terrible. He'd put his arms around her, and she'd kissed him immediately, her face wet with tears, and once again she'd told him that he must do what was right for him, and not for her, that he must remember their agreement—that each one's individuality was sacred, that his guiding principle must always be his own desire.

It was no wonder that he'd been so quick to attack Constantino, so clumsy with Valerie afterward. Some of his anger at his situation—in love with his wife, in love with Valerie, frustrated by the lack of forward motion, the lack of a sweeping mutual declaration of intent with the girl for whom he'd break up his marriage—primed him for the call at hand.

But Mr. Oscar's voice didn't seem to suggest the need for any angry histrionics. He said, "Mr. Singer?"

"That's right."

"I'm very sorry to disturb you at home, Mr. Singer, but I've been phoning your office since nine o'clock this morning, and I really wanted to get this done before noon, and your girl was nice enough—"

"*Who is this?*" Jonathan knew the name, but the voice, the tone, none of it made any sense. But he heard a gulp of air, and then of course he realized, he realized at once what had happened. Again he remembered how close he'd stood to the raw mouth of power, drinking Scotch with the current Mr. Holmes.

"I'm sorry," Mr. Oscar was saying. "This is Robert Oscar. We've always gotten along pretty well, but yesterday things got a little out of hand, and, well—that's what I'm calling about."

Jonathan opened his right eye too and got out of bed. He walked with the phone body cradled in his hand and looked out first the east, and then the south windows of the bedroom, at the brilliantly sunny day. Though it was not his victory, he reveled in it, in its perfection. It reinforced the fantasy he'd had yesterday; and the sense of the power that he was privy to, that had been wielded (if only incidentally) on his behalf, made him heady with delight. "You're calling about yesterday, Oscar. You mean the little number you tried to pull on us with fat boy? What're you calling for? I mean what're you calling for exactly? You're not exactly one of my favorite people right now, so why don't you just come right to the point?"

"To apologize."

"What?"

"I'm calling to apologize, Mr. Singer."

"Have you spoken to Miss Holmes?"

"Yes, Mr. Singer, and I apologized to her too." Oscar cleared his throat and returned to his prepared speech. "I just want you to know that I'm very sorry for what happened in your office yesterday, that you can be sure that nothing like that will happen again, and if you want to use your own trucker, that's fine with us—and I think he'll be available."

"My trucker?"

"Yes, sir."

"And Constantino?"

"What about him, Mr. Singer? He won't give you any trouble. Believe me. He's sorry, too. We're all sorry."

"So no one's going to kill me, that it?"

"Of course not."

"All right, Oscar. You've made your call. You can tell your boss that it's OK now."

"Thanks, Mr. Singer. And, Mr. Singer. I'm sorry, *we had no idea*."

No idea that the little blond was so *connected*, Jonathan thought, having hung up. The idiotic grin on his face began to dissipate as the fact of his hangover hit home and he remembered the shambles he'd made of the previous evening. And not because of brother Thomas, or the snooty mother, or the surprisingly offhand Mr. Holmes. But Robertson, Hugh Robertson.

Jealous of a fag, he thought. Of all things.

Jonathan hadn't liked him when he'd met him in Paris. It was too obviously a case of one of those midwestern queens who make it in New York and develop a British accent to go with their new wardrobes. And, besides, it was clear that Hugh hadn't approved of *him*.

"Oh, my God, Hugh, what on earth are *you* doing here?" Valerie had said when she'd caught sight of him, forgetting at once what Jonathan had just told her, what Jonathan wanted to let out into the air with a flourish that would send her wildly into his arms. And Hugh Robertson's explanation: Mrs. Holmes was visiting his "house," selecting some new overyouthful outfit, and they'd gotten to talking about Valerie's trip to Paris, about her exciting new adventure in the garment business, and about what good friends they'd become on the other side of the Atlantic. And so of course Mrs. Holmes had extended an instant invitation to their little dinner party. And so of course two "old friends" were hugging each other with happy abandon.

Until: "Oh, Jonathan, you remember Hugh, of course?"

"Of course," said Jonathan, and the fag's grip was surprisingly strong, nearly equal to his own. Mr. Holmes appeared, and several silent servants, and before he quite knew what was happening, Valerie had gone off with Hugh and her mother for a tour of the apartment, and he had found himself sitting on an uncomfortable eighteenth-century Windsor chair, trying to balance his second Scotch about his crossed knees and not break any of the delicate spindles against which he was leaning. Mr. Holmes had taken a seat perhaps five yards away, directly across the room from Jonathan, in an identical Windsor chair. Each man had his back to an expanse of glass-windowed bookshelves, and each sipped his drink and tried to smile.

"I have to thank you, Mr. Singer."

Jonathan was thinking: Rich as Holmes. This weakling golfer, his tan face mismatched with the unhealthy dandruff on the collar of his badly cut tux. And his face, hating me, hating me with every pore. "Thank me, Mr. Holmes?"

"For Valerie." He paused now, letting the statement gather a cloud of ambiguity. "She's happy. I can see it in her face. The whole thing you've done for her, giving her a start. Naturally we had no idea she was this serious. Or had this kind of inclination. We could've helped her too, as you can imagine. If it's business she wants, well—" Mr. Holmes opened his hands and smiled.

All right, fucker, come to the point. If it's business she wants, it's business she gets. She doesn't need a little kike like me to get her into the nickel-dime dress business. Where the hell is she anyway? Tell her I'm divorcing my wife, tell her that I love her, and she splits to show super-queer how her mother's fag spent a zillion bucks decorating her tomb.

"But you see," Mr. Holmes continued, "we had no idea she'd stick it out this long. Sometimes young women get ideas in their head—they want to be painters, actresses, fashion models—and then they drop those ideas. They drop them completely, Mr. Singer."

"So you thought her business trip might just be a kick—temporary?"

"Yes. But, I was wrong. She'll probably stick with it another month or so."

"Oh, no."

"Well, we have a difference of opinion, Mr. Singer." Mr. Holmes opened his hand again (and Jonathan wondered if this was some sort of code gesture—if it meant, Jesus, you're a dumb asshole, for example), and then he placed them on his lap. "But in any case, I still have to thank you. She's happy, she's suffering under the not-uncommon illusion that she's doing something productive, useful. She's gotten to the point where she's convinced herself that she's found her true vocation, and that she's not simply doing this as a hobby to stick around her handsome young boyfriend. Her handsome young married boyfriend."

"Whether or not you know it, Mr. Holmes, your daughter is running her own business. I work for her, part time, as a salesman and consultant, and she very often doesn't take my advice—not about selling, not about anything."

"Ah, here comes Thomas," said Mr. Holmes, and Jonathan turned to watch the heir apparent's entrance. Mr. Holmes remained seated, but Jonathan got to his feet.

"Hi, Thomas," said Jonathan, but didn't extend his hand. Thomas turned away from Jonathan and looked at his father.

"Did you offer him money?" said Thomas, his eyes radiating hate.

"No."

"How much do you want?" said Thomas, turning to Jonathan.

"Not a thing. This Scotch is fine."

"I told you," said Mr. Holmes to Thomas. "This has got nothing to do with money. And you'll please remember that this man is a guest in our home."

"Oh, please, Father. A guest in our home. He's waiting for a specific figure. You'll see." He addressed Jonathan again. "You're a businessman. You know what you want. You have specific goals and requirements. Think about it. Think what you invested, think what you anticipated in the way of return, and then come out with a figure. Obviously, you're not going to marry my sister, even if you weren't already married yourself. Look at it this way: If you'd been planning on a long, slow, .ingratiating process, forget it. The family gives in. We want to give you your reward. Name your figure."

"Here's my figure," said Jonathan, raising the middle finger of his right hand.

Thomas remained standing, momentarily at a loss for words.

"I hope you won't think that you were invited here tonight just for this, Mr. Singer," said Mr. Holmes.

"No, I know why I was invited. Valerie insisted. This was just a sudden inspiration on your son's part. He was always the smart one in the family, I can see that right away."

"Am I supposed to just listen to this, Father?"

"Go ahead and swing," said Jonathan.

Thomas looked at him, feigning fearlessness, waiting for his father to interfere.

"He's bigger than you, Thomas," said his father. "And I never cared much for your boxing teacher. He was too soft with you."

Thomas took a step back from Jonathan and said to his father: "You're making a big mistake. You can break this in a few hours. But you'd rather let this go on, you'd rather see the whole family humiliated." And he walked off at once, his leather heels clicking on the bits of polished parquet not covered by Persian rugs. Mr. Holmes asked Jonathan to sit down, and Jonathan did, and then both men finished their drinks. Because it hadn't been worse, and because Mr. Holmes hadn't seemed supportive of Thomas, Jonathan felt that he'd had a little victory, and the neat Scotch sent a glow through his body.

"Now, Mr. Singer, perhaps you'd be good enough to tell me a little bit about your problem with the men Valerie mentioned to me over the phone."

And then there was dinner, at the absurdly long dining table in the largest dining room he'd ever seen—either in a house, an apartment, or a museum. There was a butler with white gloves, and he whispered the names of the wines he was pouring into Jonathan's quickly drained glasses. There was a dish with asparagus, and something with a taste of chicken to it; but it was otherwise all unknown, all mashed up, puréed, rich food for toothless people. It was all very gourmet, he knew, but, still, he was starving for a hunk of steak, and all the wine, on top of the big Scotches, had made him light-headed. Thomas wasn't

253

at dinner. Jonathan sat next to Hugh Robertson, and both faced Valerie across the table. Mr. Holmes faced Mrs. Holmes across its enormous length. Talk was general. How did Paris compare to New York? Was Europe going to go Communist? Why were the Parisians able to put so many poor people to work sweeping the streets while in New York the poor all went on welfare?

He could see Valerie looking from Hugh to him and back again as the conversation filtered about the table and echoed throughout the great hall. Jonathan noticed that he'd eaten his main course—a whitish purée surrounded by bits of mashed-up vegetables in various colors—almost instantly and looked guiltily at Hugh's plate: Hugh had lifted only one forkful of the mush. No one asked him if he wanted more to eat—maybe he was supposed to ask—but the butler kept pouring the rich wine, asking nothing, not even meeting Jonathan's eyes.

"Valerie tells me that you had a colorful start in the dress business," said Hugh Robertson at one point in the meal. Jonathan looked up from his empty plate and put down his crystal wineglass.

"Not really."

"Johnny bankrolled a one-shot proposition with all his money," said Valerie.

"Do you hear how she's talking?" said her mother to Mr. Holmes. "Like a man with a cigar in his mouth."

Hugh laughed. "That's the garment business. A man with a cigar in his mouth." He turned to Jonathan. "What was your one-shot proposition?" He made the words sound as if they were impregnated with dirt.

"I pirated something from Saks, some number their buyer'd ripped off from someone's Paris collection, and I did a change from silk to acrylic, and I made up as many as I could—and then I sold it, and it was a runner. So I made a bundle and moved into a real place in 1407. Not colorful, just typical."

Mother and father were looking at him as if he were some low species of toad. The butler poured more wine.

Hugh's smile seemed to suggest to Jonathan that even though he was making an ass of himself, it was all right, he had nothing to fear.

"This pirating isn't as bad as it sounds," Hugh said to Valerie's parents. "It goes on all the time, and it's quite respectable, almost."

"Oh, very respectable," said Jonathan.

"Just don't steal any of my new line," laughed Hugh. But no one else laughed, and Jonathan, eager to show off his good spirits, finally let out a little too-late chuckle.

Then he said: "You know what they say in 1407? There are three seasons, Fall, winter, and off." Only Jonathan laughed, and Valerie's face grew a bit whiter.

"Yes, I've heard that," said Hugh, smiling broadly, less at the joke than at Jonathan's slowly disintegrating delivery. "But I must say," he continued, "that I'm glad Valerie's line is going to be her own, and not just a copy. Even if copies are what the industry runs on, I think it's nice that her name is going to be on something that's really all her own."

This was such a rebuke to Jonathan that Valerie had to speak.

"I'm not really designing so much as I'm adapting."

"I'd call it a design," said Hugh. "You may have gotten the idea from some basic dress styles, but those styles have been around for years. You've changed them to suit your fabric, the kind of market you're looking for, and you've orchestrated the whole thing. That's hardly the same thing as an out-and-out pirate job."

"Coming from Hugh," said Mrs. Holmes, "Hugh Robertson, I think it best to agree with him at once and thank him for the compliment."

"Are you all right, Johnny?" said Valerie, speaking loudly enough for everyone to hear, though her words were directed at him. At that point, she was more worried about a delayed reaction to his fight with Constantino that day than the chance that he might have had too much to drink.

255

"I've just been trying to decide if I've been insulted."

"Well, if you're worrying about me, my good man," said Hugh, "you needn't wonder. You people who pirate us do us a world of good. I have nothing bad to say about you at all."

"Sounds like a left-handed compliment to me."

And again the white-gloved hand swam into view. Jonathan had a flash: If he didn't drink from the glass, and it didn't become nearly empty, then the hand wouldn't appear. So the question was, Why was he drinking so much? What the hell was he afraid of anyway? This big room? This nouveau-riche fag with pretty manners? The parents whose son he'd once walloped and now sent to bed without dinner? Or was it, more than anything, the simple disappointment of having cast his words of love, his words of sacrifice, to the wind?

"I surely didn't mean it as a left-handed compliment," said Hugh. "And I'm very glad that Valerie is going to have a chance to see some of the benefits we get from being copied so much.

"I didn't say definitely, Hugh."

"Oh, Valerie," said Mrs. Holmes. "How can you turn down such a delightful opportunity?"

"I haven't turned it down yet either," said Valerie. She was looking at Jonathan to see if he had caught on yet to the fact that she was taking a two-week trip out of the city. "I just wanted a little more time to think about it, talk it over."

This last phrase was directed so obviously at Jonathan that he paused, lowered his half-empty wineglass, and said, "Talk what over?"

"I'm thinking about maybe—"

"Actually, it's all my idea," Hugh broke in. "I'm going on a ten-city promotional tour. Two weeks. We'll visit major department stores, meet with the customers, explain our fashion philosophy, give some local press conferences—"

"What do you mean by 'we'?"

256

"I'm referring to my organization. The Robertson Group."

But Valerıe was obviously embarrassed, and Jonathan didn't give Hugh a chance to finish his explanation. "You're going?"

"I've been invited."

"Have you?"

"By Hugh, I mean. Just now. Tonight."

"Spur of the moment," said Hugh, smiling.

Jonathan noticed that the butler was busy pouring wine into Mr. Holmes's glass. It was possible that that's where the white-gloved hand had been during its absence from under his nose. The world's richest golfer seemed rather flushed, and jokingly disinterested in the company and conversation. "Invited as what?" said Jonathan. "A warm-up act?"

Drunk as he was, Jonathan felt the sudden rise of anger in the man at his side, and he was surprised at its intensity. "Hardly—" said Hugh, but Valerie interrupted him.

"Johnny, it's a chance for me to get into the stores. Hugh's going to introduce me, and we're going to be traveling with a small group of models for informal modeling. If there's interest from the customers who see the line, they'll be able to order right then and there, directly through the store. And that means I'll be in the store. And because Hugh is showing his own ready-to-wear, we're guaranteed entry, crowds, press—I mean I can be his warm-up act, if that's what you want to call it, but *he* doesn't *need* any warm-up—I *need* the chance to show my dresses."

"Beats bribery and blackmail, doesn't it?" said Jonathan.

"I beg your pardon?" said Hugh.

"Doesn't it?" said Jonathan.

"Mr. Singer," said Mr. Holmes, "do you, by any chance, know how to play pocket billiards?"

Jonathan did, of course, and before dessert had been served, the two of them had gone off to shoot pool, smoke cigars, and drink brandy. Mr. Holmes told Jonathan that he didn't seem "Jewish." And Jonathan nodded at this and kept drinking. Downstairs, Hugh was continuing his talk about the classy dress business, and Jonathan much preferred this excellent pool shooter's company, even if it necessitated fielding compliments and questions that would ordinarily have led to blows. Below the framed paintings of famous forebears, Jonathan explained why it was that so many Jewish people were involved in the garment business (they were often tailors in the "old country," so when they came to New York, looking for sidewalks paved with gold, they found a new industry—new, because poor people used to make their own clothes, and had then just begun to buy ready-made—and jobs for men and women who could sew), and why it was that so many designers were fags (they were sweet and neat and had grown up loving their mother's dresses), and whether or not he was screwing his daughter ("Your shot, Mr. Holmes").

The brandy got them both drunker, much drunker—but in a very easy, civilized way. For one thing, it was obvious to each of them that they had never played such good pool. The liquor calmed their hands, muffled the crash of the balls, helped them discover new angles, and allowed them to forget about keeping score. Mr. Holmes began to list some of his accomplishments as a golfer, tennis player, sailor, and ladies' man. Jonathan said that with his money it wasn't such a big deal being a ladies' man; and then he told Mr. Holmes about some of his own accomplishments. Mr. Holmes pointed out that he spent most of his time in California, and it was obvious to both of them that there was more opportunity for depravity in New York than anywhere else in the country. Jonathan showed Mr. Holmes a picture of Eddy. Mr. Holmes said that it was a beautiful picture, that that was just the sort of girl he'd like to fuck. Jonathan said that he couldn't fuck her, not in a million years. She was one broad who didn't care about money. Mr. Holmes said that he didn't care about money, not really. He had anything he wanted. Family, place to sleep at night, a pool table, a swimming pool. He invited Jonathan to come out to California to swim in his pool, and Jonathan said that he was a much nicer guy than his son. Mr. Holmes said that Thomas's problem was that he walked around with a broomstick up his ass. Too much training, that was his problem. Jonathan said that he'd take Thomas to a good place to get laid, if Mr. Holmes thought that would help. Mr. Holmes laughed at this. He put down his cue stick and laughed and laughed, and he poured Jonathan a sloppy snifter of brandy, and both men were leaning against the antique billiard table, their cue sticks on the floor, when Valerie, her mother, and Hugh Robertson entered.

"Oh, no," said Mrs. Holmes.

"Your father's invited me to his house, Val," said Jonathan, smiling proudly. "To the other one, the one in California. With the swimming pool!"

"How in the world are you going to go home like that, Johnny?" said Valerie.

"Are you going?" Johnny smiled at Hugh Robertson's beautiful face. "Are you going with him?"

"I don't want to talk about that now. All I want to talk about now is how to get you home."

Mrs. Holmes steered them all into the library, refusing to take her husband's arm. Mr. Holmes had a bit of trouble negotiating the steps, and he was making loud talk, telling Mrs. Holmes that Johnny was a nice "feller," that he didn't want any coffee, that he wasn't going anywhere except to bed.

"One of the servants," said Mrs. Holmes, "could drive his car and leave him with his doorman."

"It's a sportscar, Mother. It's got a stick shift and lots of funny gadgets."

"I'm sure we've got a servant who can drive a stick shift."

"I can," said Hugh.

"What?"

"I'll drive him home, Valerie. I came by cab."

Jonathan heard all this and was trying to squeeze some of the fog out of his head, so he could properly respond to it. Apparently, this fag whom Valerie seemed so wild about was now offering to drive him home. Not only that, he was looking at Jonathan with what most people would consider a "grave expression." But, miserably, the fog wouldn't lift. When Jonathan told them that he was OK, he could drive back, no problem, the words were a slur, and the eyes that were looking at his condition with disapproval did a bit of blinking.

"I was just trying to be friendly with your father," said Jonathan, when Valerie came up a little closer to him.

"Good," said Valerie. "You did a good job of that."

"And you didn't care. What I said. When I told you."

"Johnny, all I care about now is that you get home without getting killed." And that was the end of their love talk. He sat down heavily in a stuffed chair, and he drank too fast from a coffee cup and nearly scalded his throat. Mr. Holmes had gone off, and Mrs. Holmes too—perhaps he was sleeping, and she was with her butler, peeling off those clean white gloves. Hugh Robertson was sitting where he'd distinguished himself before, in the Windsor chair, against a wall of books; and in the opposite chair, where Mr. Holmes had faced him, Valerie now sat, leaning forward, with a concerned, conspiring look about her. And then someone, a servant perhaps, had taken the coffee cup from his hands, and he'd slept for maybe ten seconds, maybe ten minutes, and he remembered Valerie's face, shaking from side to side. How could you? it seemed to say. And then the shock of the air—the very cold, very lovely air on the most beautiful block in the city, in the world, perhaps. Jonathan was suddenly ecstatic about the block's prettiness, its quietness, the quality of its air. But when he turned to make a remark about this to Valerie, she was standing with Hugh in front of his Porsche, and Hugh was opening the door.

She must have said goodbye, but he didn't remember

the words she used. It was his fault, Hugh Robertson's, that he'd gone upstairs with the bored host and allowed himself to get drunk. His fault. One insult after another. Next to him, Jonathan felt like a flat-out underachiever, a no-talent thief without a penny to his name. With Robertson, you couldn't very well use the excuse that the son of a bitch was born with the stuff, like Valerie's father and grandfather; Hugh Robertson had made it himself. With his designs, his manners, his party-pretty looks.

And now the son of a bitch was sitting in the driver's seat of his Porsche. Turning over the engine. "Needs tuning," he said.

"Why are you driving?"

"Because you're drunk, my dear fellow."

"I'm not your dear fellow, let's get that straight right from the start."

"Sixty-fifth?" Hugh said, but didn't wait for an answer, simply shoved in first, stepped on the accelerator pedal, and popped the clutch. Jonathan's grunt brought Hugh a great deal of satisfaction, and the designer hit fifty miles an hour on Sutton Place South and took a left-hand turn without hitting the brake, letting the clutch grab second gear as the screaming rear tires tried to keep on the asphalt.

Jonathan mumbled something, and Hugh, not hearing, slammed to a halt at the traffic light on First and Fifty-seventh. "Stop the car," said Jonathan again.

"I am stopped."

"No, man," said Jonathan, and he indicated the deserted sidewalk with a plaintive expression. Hugh shoved in first, drove through the red light on the empty street, and pulled over in front of a minor-league boutique, in the shadow of an expensive co-operative apartment building. Jonathan pulled open the car door and hung his head over the sidewalk, puking. Hugh Robertson turned on the radio and was treated to a loud burst of unfamiliar, unpleasant rock-and-roll. Watching Jonathan's shoulders shake, he fiddled with the dial until he found WNCN and a Beethoven concerto. He closed his eyes and imagined Rubenstein at the piano, the concert hall filled with a delicious anticipation—waiting to be raised from adulation to climax. Jonathan pulled himself back into the car.

"OK, man," he said.

"Shut the door," said Hugh. Jonathan did. Hugh pushed in first, and they were off heading west on Fifty-seventh, getting up to sixty miles an hour in third gear, but easily, without offense to Jonathan's empty stomach. Slowly, Jonathan became aware of the music on the radio, and, without meaning to be nasty, he reached forward and pressed one of the tuning buttons, automatically—as if the radio had inadvertently drifted to the wrong station—and loud rock music ran once again through the car.

"You son of a bitch," said Hugh.

"What?"

Hugh shut off the radio, stopped at a light, and looked at the man with whom Valerie had fancied herself in love. "You drunk son of a bitch," he said.

"You watch who you call a son of a bitch," said Jonathan, but he smiled suddenly, stupidly—realizing that he had changed the radio station and that Hugh had been listening to the first station. "Hey. I didn't know you were listening to that shit, man."

"It's not shit."

"Why don't you wash my mouth out with soap?"

"Just lean back and shut up," said Hugh. "We're almost there." And then, a further ignominy: being driven into his own garage and left alone in the car, in the passenger seat. Hugh hadn't said anything in parting, except to mention that he was leaving the keys in the car, and it was several minutes before one of the garage workers found Jonathan slumped in his seat, not very anxious to face the elevator to his own apartment.

He didn't know if he'd woken Eddy, though he had to assume that he had. And now, stepping into the shower to try to combat the throbbing in his head, he wondered if it would make a difference to her to know that his evening had been miserable, that he'd made a fool out of himself, getting drunk rather than face the fact that he was out of Hugh Robertson's league. But then, in the midst of lathering his body, shampooing his hair, letting the steamy water massage his nervous, tight back, he thought of other things—the buyer from Los Angeles he was taking to dinner, the fabric salesman he'd missed a meeting with that morning, the trimming that was two weeks late and holding up orders. Stepping out of the shower to shave, he had stopped thinking about Valerie and Hugh and had begun computing the advantages of expanding Lorelei's floor space and hiring four or five more workers for the factory. If Valerie Holmes was too good for the Seligman account, then the hell with her; he'd snag it. If she was going to go off with Hugh Robertson, he'd show her what a pirate meant. He'd be turning out wrap dresses faster than she could put one on. If she was going to use him to show her the rag business, only to turn round and hold Hugh Robertson's hand for a tour of tony America, he'd show her how he'd get along without her. As the razor tore through stubble and lather, he felt the fog lifting from his head, the hangover being replaced by a new vision of success. She was blond, she was pretty, she was the richest girl in the world. And he'd been sleeping with her for months. Jonathan Singer from Union Turnpike in Queens—getting drunk with Mr. Holmes on Beekman Place, screwing his famous deb daughter in Paris and in his office at 1407.

"Eddy!" he called out, wiping his face with a towel. "Eddy, where are you?"

They met in the hall, his beautiful wife's ethereal face open for a slap, a rebuke, for any further revelations of love for another. But there was no need for that. Eternally optimistic, eager only to be in the best of all possible worlds, Jonathan had stumbled on the self-created notion that his love for Valerie was not love, that his declaration to her last night was invalid, that his entire emotional

263

episode with her had been a chimera, an absurd fantasy fueled by the famous name. He took Eddy in his arms and spun her around, letting her see the ecstatic grin on his handsome face and know that it encompassed the two of them, together. Two hours later, when he finally made it to 1407, he read the message from Valerie without a tinge of regret:

Darling, have decided to go with Hugh on the two-week promo. Hope you won't be mad, but will see that it's all for the good of the line. Have long since forgiven you for last night's mess. Daddy looked bad this morning, and Mrs. Sharon thought you looked like Tyrone Power. (She liked Tyrone Power.) If you try and divorce your wife, I will never talk to you again, never. I'll miss you this trip. Sell a lot of dresses. Love, Valerie.

18

The store had set up a little display of Valerie's dresses in the back of their Hugh Robertson boutique, and the two dozen women who'd been curious enough to stand around while the four pretty models Hugh had imported from New York walked around in Valerie Holmes numbers uttered polite little sighs of approval.

"I wish I was a couple of sizes thinner," said one size-sixteen, looking from the razor-thin models to the dresses on the rack.

"Try it on."

"I beg your pardon?"

"Try it on," said Valerie Holmes, smiling like a novitiate salesgirl, and the department manager made a point of swooping down on the fat customer and explaining who it was the hard push was coming from.

"This isn't one of our salesgirls, madam," he said. "This is the designer. This is Miss Holmes, herself."

"You're Valerie Holmes?"

"Yes. And I couldn't help but overhear what you said. I wish you'd try one on. I know it'd look wonderful on you."

"You're really Valerie Holmes?" said the woman. They were in a fashionable suburb of Chicago, but not nearly fashionable enough to contain any gossip-column names. And the notion of the richest girl in the world telling her to try on a dress . . . Well.

"Please," said Valerie. "I'd like to know how you feel in it. I'm trying very much to learn what I can about what my customers want." And she extended the dress—the

265

biggest size, the sixteen—and gave it to the woman. When she'd gone off to the dressing room, Hugh appeared at her side.

"That's the hardest sell I've ever seen in one of my boutiques," he said.

"I've only just started," said Valerie. When the woman came out of the dressing room, her face a mask of doubt, Valerie stood behind her facing the mirror. "Oh, it's wonderful on you!"

"It's too young. I really think—"

"Young?!" Valerie shook her head violently in the mirror. She was wearing almost the identical dress to that of the woman in the glass, and she shook a bit of fabric from above her thigh. "Is this young? This isn't young. This doesn't have a thing to do with chronological age. It's purely an attitude. I'm selling to women in their eighties, I'm selling to college girls, I'm selling to anyone who feels right in this dress. The question is, the only question is—do you feel strong enough to feel right in this dress? Do you feel yourself to be an independent woman, do you think of yourself as someone assertive enough to wear something that's simple, attractive, and practical, but not part of some new fad?"

The woman looked up at Valerie's image in the mirror. "It's pretty," she admitted. "You really think it looks well on me?"

Valerie turned the woman away from the glass and faced her squarely. She looked at the woman's face, at the woman's figure, at the way the cloth draped her heavy frame. "Yes," she said, simply. "Yes."

The woman smiled slightly, then turned back to the mirror and grinned. "Actually," she said, "it is very pretty, isn't it? Sometimes you can't tell from the rack. And everything looks pretty on those skinny models. Thank you so much, Miss Holmes."

"Thank *you*," said Valerie. "You're the one buying the dress."

And then Hugh finally, and firmly, took Valerie by the

arm and led her away from the boutique. He had the uncomfortable feeling that she'd prefer to hang around till the woman had made the purchase and left the store, dress safe in a box, sitting in a shopping bag.

"Anyone watching would think you were hard up."

"Please, Hugh."

"I want to talk about it. You said you wanted to learn, let me teach you a few things." He was wearing a camel's hair blazer, an open-necked silk shirt, dark glasses; matrons patrolling the store for bargains stared at him, not in recognition, but in surprise at his theatrical elegance in this very mundane environment. She didn't want to leave the store, not yet, but she allowed him to steer her outside, to where the rented Cadillac limousine sat under the gaze of a hundred curious passersby in the quiet suburban mall. Their driver didn't see them approach, and Hugh pulled open the door for her and followed her inside.

"Is there any pretty country around here?"

"No, sir, just houses."

"Drive anywhere, then," said Hugh. He leaned back, very upset, and Valerie again had the notion that her traveling companion, mentor, and dear friend harbored a resentment against her that he was forever trying to keep below the surface. Their two-week trip had expanded into five weeks, with a short hiatus in New York to make apologies, delay other commitments, and allow Valerie a chance to hire additional staff, most of them carrying references from the Robertson Group. Hugh had been better than his word. The world of department stores located beyond the pale of New York and Los Angeles had been largely unknown to her. And she'd learned who her audience was, learned the voices and the faces of those women who would largely make up her growing business. Most stores had given her small orders, to see how her dresses would fare; a few, impressed by her presence, and by the enthusiasm of shoppers happening upon the informal modeling, gave her large orders—

orders that had become increasingly difficult to fill.
Jonathan had complained of Lorelei being overburdened
with her orders and had continued to ask her for more and
more time. Hugh had contributed to her little success by
dropping her name in all his press conferences, bringing
her forward to meet the local press, making a public
differentiation between young dilettantes and young
workers, and talking up the essential need that her line
was filling. Privately, she sometimes doubted his enthusiasm, thought it put on for her benefit, out of his
patronizing notion of friendship. Surely, her dresses were
of a totally different conception than those in his new line.
And his own elitism was largely aesthetic; he was more
interested in dressing a few beauties in extravagant silks
and taffetas than a hundred career women in acrylic
jersey. If friendship explained the tour, and the promo-
tion, it was simply because friendship was a better explanation than imagining him really interested in her
talent as a designer. But it wasn't an adequate explanation. And there was, too, the nagging question of this
unconscious resentment, his very infrequent sudden rising
to anger, anger out of all proportion to the misdeed of the
moment.

"There was no reason in the world for you to behave in
that fashion," he said, breaking the little silence. He
spoke quietly, attempting a monotone, taking off his dark
glasses to fix her with his eyes. "If a designer isn't
dignified, he's nothing. If a designer isn't head and
shoulders above the paltry business of selling, he's nothing
better than a merchant."

"OK, Hugh, so I'm a merchant," she said. She hadn't
meant it to sound flippant, but there it was—light and
empty-headed, rubbing against the rawest part of his
anger.

"You're not a merchant, goddam it," he said. "And I'm
beginning to think that you don't know what you are."

"I know what I am."

"You're not a Seventh Avenue rag lady; you're a

million times better than that. You're not another kiss-ass phony trying to go for broke in ten minutes, you're not another 1407 hooker, you're not another up-from-the-gutter girl trying to stay on top of the pile. For Chrissake, you don't have to sell a single dress in the next twenty years and you'll be just as fine as you are this minute."

"That's not true," she said, but his words were rushing past her, and he had no understanding of what anger was rising up in her to meet his own.

"Jonathan Singer, there's a guy who has to sell dresses. He's got to sell them, and sell them, and it doesn't really matter to him how he does it, or what he sells, just as long as the money comes in and he can hide most of it from the government. I can see him pushing the dress on that fat lady today, smiling at her like he'd love to crawl into bed with her the second after she'd bought his dress. I can see him punching her head in if she *didn't* buy it. I can see him bribing the store, bullying the department manager to give it a good display, I can see him pushing and pushing and pushing, because that's all he's ever known, and that's all he'll ever do. And I always thought you were different. I knew you were different. You're not meant to be a pusher, because there's no reason for you to push. You've got a good garment to show, and you're not going to keel over and die of malnutrition if some two-bit store in Chicago doesn't go for your line. Goddamn it, you could buy this store and use it as a garbage dump if you felt like it."

"Are you through?"

"Yes."

"I heard from Johnny this morning. He's not cutting any more of my goods. There was no point to it, he said. I was just doing him a favor, that's how he felt—that's why he wanted to be the one to end the business relationship. He was trying to reverse the favor. Make it easy for me to break it off, you understand. I said OK. And I'd like it if you'd try and stop using him as an example of everything that's cheap and rotten." Hugh said nothing, merely allowed the shock to register pleasantly in his face. "So now I've got people looking for a good cutting shop, I've got people looking for new sewing contractors, I've got people trying to find out what orders Jonathan's filled and what orders he hasn't."

"Well?" said Hugh. "So what? If you need some cutting work done, you can just ask me. I can get you anything you need, I've told you that a hundred times, and I'm sure I can do a lot better, in price and quality, than Lorelei Paris, for God's sake."

"You don't understand, Hugh. Jonathan might be screwing me. I mean right this second."

"How?"

"Pirating my line. He's been late with my orders for weeks. Maybe he's cutting up his own stuff, his own copies, and rushing them off to the buyers of all the stores that're waiting for my stuff. He can underprice me, he can bribe the buyers, he can set them up with whores—he can push everything I've started to do out the window."

"I don't think he could," said Hugh. "But even if it were possible—do you think he would?"

"Yes," said Valerie, without flinching, and without malice. Better than anyone, she understood the erratic flight taken by her fancy in pursuit of and in flight from the love of Jonathan Singer. Better than anyone, she could understand what right he'd have to hate her at that moment. He had called her out of the blue, wooed her first with his voice, then with the sheer exuberance of his presence, turned her from useless boredom to a vision of empire. If Hugh Robertson could do more for her than Jonathan, she would still not forget that it was Jonathan's prodding that led her to have any interest in Hugh at all. Over the phone from New York that morning, his voice had been bruised; there was a catch in the rhythm of his phrases that belied all his bravado. She'd seen him after the first two-week tour with Hugh, and, at that time, in his office, she'd explained to him that her love for him had been confused with her love for what he'd given her—a sense of purpose, a sense of ambition.

"You don't have to explain a thing to me," he'd said at that time. "I know it's over. I knew it was over on Beekman Place." And then he'd made the extraordinary statement that his relationship with Eddy had improved, vastly improved, since he'd told her that he wanted a divorce and then retreated from his request two days later, explaining that it had all been a mistake—a mutual, stupid infatuation. "Let's face it, kid," he'd said. "You fell in love with me because I'm practically a hoodlum. And I fell in love with you because you're practically a virgin. And a famous one, Miss Holmes." And his smile had been sincere, ineffably sad and final. It was as if he'd just acknowledged having been run over by a truck, but harbored no ill feelings for the driver—a driver he'd recruited, trained, and inspired. If he did hate her, she accepted the hate, took it as her due. But should he use this hate to attack her line, then she must do more than understand it; she must fight it. No broken love affair could justify the surrender of her business.

"I didn't realize he would go so low," said Hugh.

"I told you, I don't want you to talk about Johnny like that."

"But if he thinks he can pirate your line, after agreeing to contract it, he's crazy. I'll put my lawyers on to him; I'll have him out of 1407 and into the street if he—"

"No," she broke in.

"I don't understand you, Valerie. You're ready to do everything but lie down and die to sell one woman a dress, but you won't take a few painless legal steps to protect yourself from an illegal action."

"Listen," she said. "If I want to take legal action, I'll take it. If I want to fight Johnny, I'll fight him. If I want to sell a woman a goddamn dress, I'll sell a woman a goddamn dress. People don't have to always take me by the hand and do everything for me. Everything. Jesus, you act like you don't think I'm capable of a goddamn thing. Just like everyone else. You've helped me,

271

Johnny's helped me, Daddy's helped me—but for Chris-sake, Valerie Holmes is still more me, and is going to be more me, than anyone else. It's my company, it's my idea, and no one is going to take that away from me."

"You still don't understand a goddamn thing," he said, his voice again at its angriest, a quiet monotone that tore through her inflamed speech, and made her question everything she'd just said, made her wonder about the reason for the strength of her fury. "You don't even listen to what I'm saying. I might as well just be the palace eunuch, for all the attention you pay me."

He told the driver to take them back to Chicago, to their hotel, and then he slammed the glass partition shut and turned to face her.

"But I thought we'd be going back to the store," Valerie said.

"Oh, Christ."

"If I've said something to make you think that I'm not grateful, or not listening, or—"

"Please stop, please stop *looking* at me like that," he said.

"Like *what*? I don't know—"

He had taken hold of her right hand, and he was squeezing it now in his. "First of all, I don't want to take away your business, or what you've done, or what you're trying to do," he said.

"I know."

The anger hadn't dissipated, and the hold on her hand seemed a direct link to its secret. He didn't want her to talk. He wanted to tell her something that he didn't know how to say, that he wasn't sure of himself, except in the vaguest, most metaphysical terms.

"I want you to be wonderful," he said. "I want you to be happy. I want you to be fulfilled. That's what I want for you. That's what I want for you, because I'm in love with you. That's why I don't want you to lower yourself, I don't want you to associate with low people, I don't want you to do anything except those things that will make you happy.

272

Do you understand what I'm saying? Do you understand that I'm in love with you? Do you understand what I'm talking about at all?"

The pressure on her hand was frightening, but she made no comment about this; she was too busy wondering what to say, how to answer this impossible question. It was not as if she knew the answer he was waiting for. It was not as if she were certain, horribly certain, that his anger was sexual in nature, that his love for her was a passion that made no sense, that what he wanted from her was what other men had always seemed to want—nothing less than total surrender. What her husband had loved in her was something that Jonathan had still found in her after the divorce; and that was the potential to yield, to fall prey to someone else's vision. She didn't understand Hugh's vision, didn't know in what way he wanted her, but in the grip of his hand, in the anger of his face, she could see that his love was something possessive, something from which she must recoil.

"I love you too, Hugh," she said, smiling as mildly as possible, taking every bit of importance out of the empty words. She would've gone further, far enough to explain the love as friendship, but in an instant he was done with talking, and, disregarding the chauffeur, disregarding the terrible look on her face, he plunged, pulling her toward him, placing his handsome lips over hers and attempting a passionate, bruising kiss.

But the potential to yield was no longer there. It wasn't simple rebellion that fueled her anger now; it was a definition of self. She wouldn't allow him to see something in her that was his own fabrication. She wouldn't allow him—or any man, or any one—to define her in terms of his own needs and demands. She was strong, she was sure, and she was as angry as if his act of love had been an act of aggression, an act intended to take from her a birthright, an absolute, essential freedom.

She pushed him, she hit at him with her one free hand, she shut her lips, she opened her eyes, she tried to breathe through furious nostrils. When he finally let go the hold on her neck, she shrank back from him and looked at him as if he were mad. She didn't have to wait for an explanation. "That's how I want to love you," he said.

"No you don't," she said, and she believed this, and understood that her greatest anger came not from the attack on her virtue, the absurb seduction scene in the back of the Cadillac, but from feeling the whole episode wrong, made up by him on her behalf. "You don't love me that way, that's not what you want."

"Let me show you," he said.

"No."

"I'm not what you think I am."

"I don't think you're gay, Hugh. But I don't think you're in love with my body either. And I don't want you jumping on me to try to prove a point that's not true."

Again that mad stare, anger, frustration, not knowing where to go. Suddenly he acted. He threw open the glass partition and ordered the confused driver back to the shopping mall from which he'd just taken them. For the first time, Valerie realized that Hugh had planned to take her to the hotel, lay her out on the bed in her suite, obtain an erection from some fantasy outside her ken, and slowly, practically, professionally, penetrate her body and drive her to a fabricated ecstasy that would establish once and for all what their relationship meant to him.

Leave me alone, she thought. Everybody just leave me alone.

The following morning she flew back to New York, leaving Hugh to complete his unnecessary promotional tour of the Midwest alone. She kissed his handsome expressionless face on the cheek and promised that there were no ill feelings for what had happened the day before. The flight was uneventful, and when the cabdriver at La Guardia tried to get on the Grand Central Parkway going in the opposite direction from the city, she barked at him like a sergeant major and set him straight at once.

No one, she told him, no one was about to lead her or

mislead her. Not now, not ever again. With her directions clear, Valerie Holmes sank back in her seat and contemplated a future of her own.

19

"What's the first thing you do in the morning?"

"Exercise. Specifically. I lie down on the rug and do fifty sit-ups. I also do several kinds of stretches, lots of leg raises—just things in general to wake up my muscles."

"So you think morning exercise is important for a day of mental stress?"

"You can quote me, kid."

"I will," said the young man. The photographer asked her if she'd mind stepping over to the large windows overlooking the city, and Valerie did so at once, moving with grace in one of her own jump suits. "It seems to agree with you," he said. "The exercise."

"Only the photographer's allowed to look at my ass," she said.

"What do you have for breakfast, Miss Holmes?"

"Orange juice, Granola, and about a quart of coffee."

"Every day?"

"No, sometimes I have buttermilk pancakes, *Jesus*, does anyone really care what the hell I have for breakfast?"

"Well, yes," said the young man. He watched her move lithely from the window, smiling professionally at the photographer, who continued to shoot her as she walked over to the couch under the huge impressionist painting, a contribution from Hugh, and one of which she approved highly. "I like to be able to put it down. How you get up, what you eat. It makes people identify with you. I learned it in journalism school." He smiled at her to let her know that this was partly a jest. "It's good to give the reader something he can identify with in your life—like eating Granola—just because so many of them can't identify with you in other areas."

"There's lots of that in the press kit. I read the *Daily News*, the *New York Times*, and the *Wall Street Journal* with breakfast. A chauffeur takes me to work. In a Lincoln limousine. Blah, blah, blah, et cetera. You look like a smart young man—why not grill me on the new cosmetics line?"

"I will," he said. But he had his own list of questions first. If she wanted the free publicity, the very good publicity of this young man's magazine, she'd have to continue to behave. She missed his next question, becoming momentarily distracted by a mental list of tasks to complete that morning. She was waiting for Weintrob to call back from Paris—it was late afternoon there, and she hoped he'd gotten her message before the trip to Italy. There was a meeting about the new fragrance display at Bloomingdale's, and even at this moment she was far from satisfied with the display material and the chintzy "free gift" cosmetic case being offered with the minimum ten-dollar purchase.

"Miss Holmes, do you think of yourself as a model of a liberated woman?" the young man was saying, perhaps amplifying his earlier unanswered question.

"Less a model, more a bad example."

"Do you mean that seriously?" said the young man. He had a pencil and a brown note pad, and a tape recorder was running all the while. He was obviously a competent sort, one of whom to be wary.

"No, not seriously," said Valerie. "I can't really take myself as an example of anything. My case was very special. I've had more advantages than most people can imagine. If I've had to struggle, it's to a large extent been a struggle away from those advantages."

"But there's the question of your marriage," he said. She could see the young man's ears grow red. Competent, but nervous—and she knew where he wanted to lead her

277

all along.

"My marriage is not to be part of this interview," she said.

"I'm not referring to your first marriage, of course, but to—"

"Next question," said Valerie. And she was not smiling now. This was not a joking matter, and if he needed to see that, let him look at her face.

"Of course, if you prefer—" The young man made a furious underlining motion in his pad with his number-two Mongol pencil, and the photographer, noting Valerie's assertive mood, took the opportunity to snap half a dozen photographs. "Let's see. I did want to ask if there's some rationale behind your using your face in most of your ads instead of a series of fashion models."

"That question's been asked a hundred times," said Valerie. "You can find the answer in my press kit." ("Miss Holmes believes in presenting herself not only as the woman behind the dress she sells, but as the woman who wears those same dresses. Not a great beauty or a famous film star, she is rather a woman who has many of your needs as well—a practical garment that can be worn to the office and still look right for a cocktail party or a dinner engagement. Like you, she travels as lightly as possible, and it's to her advantage to pack her own dresses—dresses that won't wrinkle in a shut-up case, dresses that can be washed and left out to dry overnight. No flawlessly beautiful model has to wear her dress to make it look good, though it's a well-known fact that half the models in New York thrive on the Holmes dresses.")

"Yes," said the young man. "Could I ask you about some of the nasty things said about you by other designers, like Milton Brommel? Specifically, his comment that you're not a designer at all, just a copyist who's inherited your family's business sense."

"I'm tired of talking about that flea," said Valerie. "And that's also in the press kit." ("Miss Holmes doesn't

278

bother with distinguishing terms like 'designer' and 'dress-maker.' She's satisfied that she's developed a new style of wearing dresses over the past two years that has been widely acclaimed and copied, whether or not it's won any fashion awards. The facts of market approval speak for themselves. She's selling close to thirteen thousand dresses a week around the country, and it's to the women who buy her dresses that she wishes to speak, not to snob-appeal designers who look down their noses at her success.")

"Yes, of course," said the young man. "I thought you might have something more to add, or perhaps comment about the notion that some fashion writers have that you've reinvented the dress."

"I didn't reinvent anything. And I'm beginning to think you didn't read the bloody press kit. I jumped in with the dress when lots of women were still wearing pants, so I made it big. I was lucky, but I was also smart, because I played my headstart advantage for all it was worth. While they were copying my shirtwaist, I pushed my wrap dress, and I always kept my prices competitive, and I always used the best fabrics available in my price range. And I tried to use one success to foster another. Not just to give me the money to go ahead into cosmetics and perfumes for example, but to add to the whole aura of the line. I want my cosmetics to increase my dress sales and vice versa."

"May I ask you how old you are, Miss Holmes?"

"It's in the press kit." (Twenty-five, pushing twenty-six fast.)

"Do you plan to keep most of your operations head-quartered in the same place?" He was looking at a sheet for the address and picked it up and said, "1407 Broadway?"

"Because," he continued. "A lot of people wonder about that, because it's really mostly a sportswear house."

"It's in the press kit, but I'll tell you anyway. Sentimental reasons."

279

"Yes, I saw that, but I didn't understand what you meant by that."

"Look, am I asking you to tell me personal details of your latest affair?"

"No, but—well, I see what you mean," he said. Struggling with his sense of purpose, the young man found what he was looking for somewhere in his pad and said very quickly, all at once: "You see, I don't want to disturb you or upset you or anything like that, Miss Holmes, especially since I'm an admirer of what you've done and what you stand for for a lot of people. And I hate like hell to have to ask you stupid questions, especially if you're even more bored with them than I am. And I've read the press kit, of course I have. And I know it's not right for me to be prying and asking questions about very personal things. But the point is, I want to, I feel I have to, get back to your husband."

"Hugh," she said. "After all, we're not afraid to say his name."

"Hugh. Yes." The young man gulped. A press blurb with Miss Holmes's daily exercise schedule was hardly going to be a scoop. Nor would more inane comments about her dresses. But *this*. He dashed ahead, not daring to look at her, while the photographer sat down, his camera in his lap, and listened.

"People were very surprised when you married Hugh Robertson," he said, reading it from his pad in a careful monotone. This was either a very brave or a very gauche reporter, probably a bit of both. She was waiting for oblique references to homosexuality, to sensationalized hints of previous lovers, to the notable absence of her parents at the wedding more than a year ago. But in the tiny pause while the reporter glanced at his notes and gathered his courage, she had a sudden flash of weariness. She was tired of dodging with bravado what were nothing but barbs aimed at something beyond her attackers' understanding. The man she'd married was elegant, aggressive, cultured, powerful. His empire was self-wrought, and his horizons were self-created. But when he had first fancied himself falling in love with her, he'd resorted to chicanery, to a delusion of self that would lead to her becoming "his." This was what she'd rebelled against, and rebuffed. This was what the women's movement should congratulate her for—and not for the fact that her name had (through two marriages) remained Holmes, or that her business had not been absorbed by her husband's. She would have liked to hear the young man ask something sensible: whether she was happy, whether she was fulfilled, whether Hugh Robertson and Valerie Holmes viewed their love as self-enclosed, perfect, the end product of equality. But he was only interested in stale words, sensational press notions. She heard the words "marriage of convenience," then, "Isn't it true that your home in Connecticut has two bedrooms," and then, "Bisexual chic is really becoming—"

"What?" said Valerie.

His face was crimson. "I'm sorry if I've said anything—I mean if I've embarrassed you . . ." he said.

She didn't answer him at once. Her mind was still drifting, remembering a courtship that was asexual, passionate only with a lust for a union of goals. Perhaps he did simply want to resurrect his sister, perhaps his desire for things beautiful was derived from a different place in the heart than her own, perhaps—as Milton Brommel had told her, with hate—their union was a symptom of disease, the end product of the American dream, an instant bit of sculpture for our most modern wax museum. But she had viewed Hugh and his courtship in an entirely different light once her own business had begun its great growth, once success had been allowed her in her own right, and not as a family subsidiary or a wing of the Robertson Group. Once he had come back to her not to lead, not to instruct, but to share. Once his love was offered as to an equal, to a woman whose qualities were commensurate with his own. If he didn't have a sexual desire for her, that didn't have to be the canker, the slow destroyer of their relationship. It was simply a fact to be understood and dealt with, a given. She understood. Still, their union wasn't a lie. And it wasn't a convenience either. It was a joining of lives, of destinies, of homes. And Valerie didn't need to deny her sexuality, though her desire no longer burned with a constant flame. She'd had lovers, and she'd have them again, much as a man in love with his wife, but unhappy with her lovemaking, might take a lover. But the union, the emotional union, the irreplaceable union of husband and wife, was there with Hugh. This Valerie knew when he entered a room in which she sat with others and she felt herself bolstered, strengthened, doubled in intensity.

But she could tell none of this to the young man from the magazine, younger even than she. She could see the unbridled passion in his face: passion for life, for success, for blinding romance. She wished she could tell him to calm down. To use his passion to spark his vision, his strength—and not to obscure it with categories.

"I'm sorry," he was saying. "I don't really deserve an answer. Especially since you were so kind to give me an interview in the first place. I appreciate that, I hope you know I do. In fact though you may not believe this, I really thought that if I wrote something about Mr. Robertson and you, something with your seal of approval, as it were, that it might help stop some of the rumors and unpleasant little stories that crop up every now and then in the pulp magazines . . ." Again he let his sentence drift, catching his breath, trying to look innocent.

"All right," said Valerie. "You can say this, you can print this. My marriage is not a marriage of convenience. It's a beautiful marriage, a marriage of love, and Hugh and I are happy, perfectly happy, together."

When she read it weeks later, it was trite but it was true. And it was one of those rare, exceedingly rare, interviews in which she was simply called Valerie Holmes, the fashion queen—not Valerie Holmes, heiress to the Holmes fortune. In a world of disharmony and chaos, she

ad created something harmonious and strong: a charac-
r, a personality, transcending the limited horizons of
nvironment; a self that was less influenced by family than
was forged out of the hardier strain of the family's
enes. And because the creation was all her own, Valerie
olmes had no one but herself to blame for the shape of
er life, no one but herself to blame for her happiness.

1407 BROADWAY is a sizzling passionate story of two unusual people. Joel Gross captures with astonishing accuracy the frenzy and incandescent sexuality of his characters: Jonathan, a good-looking, hard-driving sportswear manufacturer and Valerie, a beautiful shimmering blonde and heiress to one of America's largest industrial fortunes.

Valerie is 'on the market' again, having divorced her husband, but nonetheless she is totally unprepared for the effect Jonathan has on her. Jonathan is also knocked out by Valerie. He has never met anyone like her before. And he also realises that using her name on a new line of clothes could mean the survival of his ailing company. Valerie is also determined that she must leave her own mark on any business venture – much to the horror and disgust of her parents who are singularly unimpressed by Jonathan.

JOEL GROSS

THE BOOKS OF RACHEL

The diamond blazed and spat iced fire. A sixty carat symbol.

For five hundred years, in five continents the family had worked and traded in diamonds. A network bound by ties of blood, business and a name. Rachel.

In every generation there was a Rachel and her legacy was the diamond. Symbol of the scattered family, it linked the first Rachel who faced the Spanish Inquisition, with the Baroque splendour of Venice, the pomp of the Prussian Court, the squalour of nineteenth century Jerusalem, down to the safe haven of England in the 1930s when another Rachel was to discover that even there she could be touched by the horror of Nazi Germany and the Holocaust.

In love and death, passion and despair, settled state and hunted wretchedness, the name Rachel and the diamond testified to the will to survive and fight.

History, Romance, Danger and Courage. . .'
Publishers Weekly

JOEL GROSS

HOME OF THE BRAVE

Safe Haven the house was called.

It was to *Safe Haven*, built in the 1630s on the Connecticut shore surrounded by the game-teeming New England woods, that the trapper John Collins brought young Virginia Taylor, rescued from virtual slavery with a Puritan settler family.

And it was *Safe Haven*, extended, rebuilt, threatened and restored over the full sweep of 300 years, that sheltered their descendants: men and women whose ideals, ambitions and loves would interweave with the great movements and events of their country's history.

The Revolution, the bitter and bloody time of the emancipation of the slaves, the war against Hitler's Germany: through all the generations the old house endured, a place of serenity and high adventure, of sorrow and joy, of anguish and passion.

Safe Haven, Home of the Brave

NEW ENGLISH LIBRARY

JOEL GROSS

THIS YEAR IN JERUSALEM

They were three very different people.

Diana, the beautiful pampered Jewish princess from
Beverly Hills, ambitious for herself alone.

Joey, the young street-wise New York mobster, greedy
for money and savouring violence for its own sake.

David, the Holocaust-hardened resistance leader who
would make any personal sacrifice in his fierce
uncompromising determination to see the creation of a
homeland for his people.

In any other time, in any other place, they could never
have come together. But Jerusalem in 1947 was a white-
hot crucible of seething hatreds, torn between Jew and
Arab, waiting only for the British withdrawal before
bursting into all-out war.

Flung together and driven forward by an ideal, a dream
and the fearful needs of a people, they played out their
passionate love story and explosive adventure amongst
events and scenes the world can never forget.

NEW ENGLISH LIBRARY

ALSO AVAILABLE FROM NEL

JOEL GROSS

☐	05266 4	The Books of Rachel	£1.7!
☐	05657 0	Home of The Brave	£2.5(
☐	05774 7	This Year In Jerusalem	£1.9!

HELEN VAN SLYKE

☐	05309 1	Always Is Not Forever	£2.5(
☐	03351 1	The Best People	£2.5(
☐	03702 9	The Best Place To Be	£3.5(
☐	05032 7	The Heart Listens	£2.9!
☐	03055 5	The Mixed Blessing	£1.9!
☐	02552 7	The Rich and the Righteous	£2.2!
☐	05283 4	The Santa Ana Wind	£1.9!

All these books are available at your local bookshop or newsagent, or can be ordered direct from the publisher. Just tick the titles you want and fill in the form below.

Prices and availability subject to change without notice.

Hodder & Stoughton Paperbacks, P.O. Box 11, Falmouth, Cornwall.

Please send cheque or postal order, and allow the following for postage and packing:

UK – 55p for one book, plus 22p for the second book, and 14p for each additional book ordered up to a £1.75 maximum.

B.F.P.O. and EIRE – 55p for the first book, plus 22p for the second book, and 14p per copy for the next 7 books, 8p per book thereafter.

OTHER OVERSEAS CUSTOMERS – £1.00 for the first book, plus 25p per copy for each additional book.

Name ....

Address..

....